WAITING
FOR THE
SNOW

WAITING FOR THE SNOW

The Peace Corps Papers of a Charter Volunteer

Thomas J. Scanlon

Thomas J. Scanlon (signature)

Posterity Press

© 1997 Thomas J. Scanlon. All rights reserved
Printed in the United States of America

Published 1997

Posterity Press, Inc.
PO Box 71081
Chevy Chase, MD 20813

http://www.posteritypress.com

202/342-5591

Second Printing

Library of Congress Cataloguing in Publication Data

ISBN 1-889274-03-8

This account
of the second greatest adventure of my life
is dedicated with love
to Faith, Cashel and Garrett
—for the greatest adventure of all
has been my life with them.

Recently I heard a story of a young Peace Corpsman named Tom Scanlon, who is working in Chile. He works in a village about forty miles from an Indian village which prides itself on being Communist. The village is up a long, winding road which Scanlon has taken on many occasions to see the chief. Each time the chief avoided seeing him. Finally he saw him and said, "You are not going to talk us out of being Communists." Scanlon said, "I am not trying to do that, only to talk to you about how I can help." The chief looked at him and replied, "In a few weeks the snow will come. Then you will have to park your jeep twenty miles from here and come through five feet of snow on foot. The Communists are willing to do that. Are you?" When a friend [Father Theodore Hesburgh] saw Scanlon recently and asked him what he was doing, he said, "I am waiting for the snow."

President John F. Kennedy
Welcoming summer interns to Washington
June 20, 1962

CONTENTS

Portfolio of photographs follows page 108.

FOREWORD

The Need—Now More than Ever

Sargent Shriver
Founding Director of the Peace Corps

Times change, and the more times change the more the challenges remain the same. Tom Scanlon's motivation in 1961, his readiness to volunteer to go anywhere, and his success now as well as then all help to explain the success of the Peace Corps. The need for such initiative exists today more than ever.

In the days of Tom's youth, some Peace Corps volunteers were motivated by the threat of communism, or the glamour of travel, or the challenge of life overseas among the have-nots. Almost without exception, however, they were also inspired by the unselfish desire to serve the most needy, or forgotten, or rejected on earth. Today the world has grown smaller, but the mission of the Peace Corps is more important than ever. Why? Because today nothing unites all the countries of present-day Europe (all 52 of them), or the nations of Asia, or the Middle East, or Africa, or Latin America. Nothing unites them today, except their common humanity.

Yet too many politicians are driven by their lust for power, too many business magnates by their greed for profits, too many religious elders by their belief that only Christianity (or Judaism, or Hinduism or Islam) can save humanity, too many scientists by their conviction that human beings can know and control everything. In fact, all of these must accept our common fragility, our universal dependence on one another, and (as many have come to believe) our reliance on God who made and makes us all and without whom nothing and no one would even exist.

Once in a while a book comes along that strikes a special note, charts a course, and nourishes our souls. Tom Scanlon's memoir does all that. His Peace Corps papers let us imagine what America's role should be in a new world without order, without a cold war, without strong ties that bind. In a world now filled with ethnic strife, *Waiting for the Snow* reminds us of the enormous greatness that can happen when ordinary people do what is right and good. This is a great read, for the serious student of international affairs and for the dreamer, the lover of a gentle story about the humanity of humankind.

Tom Scanlon was a creator of the Peace Corps, the real Peace Corps. While his book mentions other founders—President Kennedy, Father Hesburgh, myself and all the usual suspects—it was Tom and a few hundred others who actually created the Peace Corps. He was among the first volunteers to go into the field in 1961. These early groups made the Peace Corps in villages and towns. They defined the programs and projects in the real developing world. They identified the people to be served and the issues to be faced. In the invisible ink of their boundless energy, they wrote the living philosophy of the Peace Corps, and with their sweat they conceived the can-do tradition that made the Peace Corps unprecedented and inspiring.

In his inaugural address President Kennedy said, "Now the trumpet summons us again; not as a call to bear arms, though arms we need; not as a call to battle, though embattled we are; but as a call to bear the burden of a long twilight struggle, year in and year out...a struggle against the common enemies of man: tyranny, poverty, disease and war itself." For the first time Americans were called to volunteer in peacetime to serve their country and the world. And volunteer they did, in numbers unmatched since the days following Pearl Harbor. Tom Scanlon's generation was called to enlist in the battle against "the common enemies of man," and Tom was one of the first in line.

His willingness to give two years of his life to people in the mountains of Chile sent a powerful message, then and now. He chose to face down communist leaders—not by anger or words or public relations or diatribes on behalf of a free market, but by his deeds. By being there, and staying there, and bringing hope to people who thought no one cared for them,

Tom served his adopted land of Chile, just as he served his own country and his own soul.

Today when much of America and its leaders want to withdraw from leadership in the world, the letters of a Peace Corps volunteer explain why we cannot drop the mantle nor eschew the glories and the challenges of leadership. In a letter to President Kennedy—which could reach the White House only after passing through channels—Tom singed our souls by saying in essence, "It is the responsibility of every Peace Corps volunteer to educate the American people in their enormous possibilities for doing great things in the world."

We had already taken Tom's message to heart. In a historic first we had previously sent one of his earlier letters to Congress, when we made it the preface to the Peace Corps budget presentation asking for Congressional support. We carried Tom's message, and our own, like a banner throughout the early years of the Peace Corps.

Now, more than 140,000 men and women have served under that banner in 130 countries, carrying the message that Americans believe in the "the enormous possibilities for doing great things in the world." Today, 7,000 Peace Corps men and women are serving in 90 countries including Russia and seven other nations once ruled by Communist regimes. But given the enormous challenges and the huge numbers suffering from the common enemies of mankind, an American Peace Corps of 7,000 is not enough. Mankind needs a worldwide Peace Corps, a universal Peace Corps. It should have 70,000 volunteers or even 7,000,000 volunteers, God willing. It should be the greatest army for peace in the history of the world, and it can be created if only we Americans follow the vision. All of us should commit ourselves to the service of all human beings through cooperative help and non-nationalistic efforts—to the work that must be done everywhere, by everyone, for everyone, and for peace.

How can our common humanity be effectively made the centerpiece of all our works? By agreeing—all nations and all peoples—that we must all unite as volunteers to help the world. Who will pay for all these volunteers? Each and every country or its citizens, acting with or without the help of their political leaders (who are too often brain-bound and ego-bound by their lust for power). If the people don't have the money, the United Nations and worldwide foundations could come forward and help in a multitude of ways. Let "Volunteers to and for the World," inspired by the cry of 140,000 Peace Corps alumni, call us all to volunteer to save the world from our baser selves.

Read Tom's wonderful story. Be inspired by the history, the truth and the timeless challenge. Draw from it the spiritual energy to believe again that human beings can be good to one another. Read and become a creator of the next great generation in the history of the world, the first generation to defeat those enemies of mankind. In the next millennium let us resolve that there will be no more Kaisers, no more Lenins, no more Mussolinis, Hitlers, Stalins or Mao Tse-tungs. Read Tom's letter to President Kennedy, which is as timely in its essence as it was thirty-five years ago. See Chile through his eyes and glimpse the challenges that await us now, everywhere.

FOREWORD

Present at the Creation—
A Perspective on the Peace Corps

Theodore M. Hesburgh, C.S.C.
President Emeritus, University of Notre Dame

E verybody knows about the Peace Corps today. Let us
remember when it was a brilliant new idea, exactly what this
country needed at a period when America's reputation as
leader of the free world was declining and many of our own
young people needed a constructive outlet for their own pent-up
idealism. John F. Kennedy made the Peace Corps a campaign
promise in 1960, and when he was elected it became a priority
item on his agenda.

My university played a role in the earliest beginnings of the
program and Notre Dame trained the first group to go abroad with
Congressional approval. Those original forty-five volunteers who
went to Chile were some of the greatest youngsters I have ever
known, and one I'll never forget was Tom Scanlon, who had grad-
uated magna cum laude the year before and gone on to Toronto to
pursue a master's degree in philosophy. Then instead of more
schooling, he decided to get out in the world and do something
for his fellow human beings. He returned to Notre Dame as a
Peace Corps trainee in that first program. At that time he did not
know a word of Spanish, but he mastered the language quickly.
When he arrived in Chile, Tom hardly knew a horse from a cow,
but he organized farm cooperatives that are still in existence.

A year later, I visited all those volunteers in Chile in order
to report back to Notre Dame and to the Peace Corps. (This
essay draws on notes I took during that trip, and on writings published later.) I arrived unannounced in Río Negro and found the
house in the slum that Tom was sharing with a volunteer named
Janet Boegli and four Chilean colleagues—*delegados* or local community development workers. I had had a letter from Tom just
before leaving the States in which he informed me that they had

divided the house between them, the girls on one side and men on the other, and all were sleeping on the floor. They had been so glad to get a roof over their heads that they hadn't complained too much about the fact that there was then no stove, no water, no gas, and not even beds or chairs. Some nearby American missionaries had then come to the rescue with simple furniture and mattresses.

I happened to arrive at the end of a long day that Tom had spent high in the mountains launching what was to become one of his most famous exploits—in a community that was decidedly pro-Communist. When Tom heard these poor Indians lived in remote villages up there on the top of a mountain, he drove up in his jeep and approached the Communist leader saying, "I'm Tom Scanlon with the Peace Corps. I'd like to help you form a food cooperative." The Communist fellow, who probably had never seen an American in his life, scoffed at Tom, complaining that he was like other Americans—all talk and no action. "If you want to visit my villages," he said, "come in July," the middle of the southern winter. Tom promised he would, and that was just the beginning, of course.

For the moment we had a great reunion in this small room which was warm for the first time, because the stove had just arrived! Since the volunteers were low on food that night, we imposed on the American padres nearby. In very good humor, they cleaned out their own kitchen and icebox and whipped up a very enjoyable meal on short notice, as we all sat around talking excitedly about the news from home and answering questions about volunteers posted farther north. Tom and Janet seemed to be doing an unusually good job, although as I continued my tour of Peace Corps outposts each one seemed unusual because of the quality of people and their generosity in digging in to do a job that had never been done before. They made a great set of pioneers.

Tom stood excitedly before a large map of the area around Río Negro pointing out the places that they were covering. Here was the Indian village high in the mountains soon to be cut off by the winter snows. There was a large agricultural area where the *patrón* was paying his workers very well. In another part to the west were beautiful lakes and mountains and a series of farms where the workers were not being treated very well and there was much more to be done in the way of community development because of the backwardness of the *patrones*. In another area Tom was trying to get a marketing cooperative set up, so that the farmers and small property owners could market their vegetables collectively.

I thought I should have a taste of the volunteers' life so I spent the night with Tom and the male *delegados* in their part of the house. Because the water system had been ruined in an earthquake, they only had water for an hour or two a day, and in this small house they had only cold water at that. My bed was a bunk with boards put across for slats and a thin mattress. The night was very cold, and we were all glad when morning came.

Instead of taking the train the next day, we drove to Osorno. The road was just about as bad as any I've ever seen, and the jeep bounced all around on gravel as big as goose eggs as we plowed through clouds of dust. Tom looked at me with a grin and said, "This is one of our better roads. The ones over the mountains are just barely passable in a jeep, and once the winter comes we can only go so far and then we walk. But at least the people are letting us in and that's quite a feat because, up to this point, they thought that only the Communists were interested in them."

When I think of Americans abroad, I still think of Tom Scanlon as a true representative of what is best about our country. And he was not different from so many of the other idealistic young men and women I knew in the Peace Corps. I told Tom's story, among others, to Sargent Shriver, the Peace Corps' founding director who related it to Kennedy, and the President used it in a widely quoted speech. That made Tom Scanlon famous for a while. (Among his fellow volunteers in Chile, though, he was best known for his humorous imitations of me.)

The Notre Dame volunteers did a great job in Chile during those first five years, and afterward too. Some of the agricultural cooperatives they founded are still operating. Most of the volunteers are still using their Spanish in one way or another. About a third of them came back and went to graduate school. About a third worked on other projects connected with Latin America, like Tom, who has had a very productive career in international development. Several of them married Chileans, some still live there; and now as some of those young people of the '60s approach retirement age, I hear that a few couples are returning to Chile.

Over and beyond the immediate good that volunteers did in far-off places of the world, the Peace Corps has continued to influence the global and environmental awareness and attitudes of many Americans to this day. To my mind, the Peace Corps is one of the most significant legacies of the Kennedy administration. President Kennedy brought the glow of youthful enthusiasm to the country, and the thousands of volunteers in the Peace Corps came away with the experience and knowledge that people can do good for others less fortunate, and in so doing reap the personal gratification and satisfaction of knowing they have helped their fellow men.

I take pride in the fact that Notre Dame has sent more volunteers to the Peace Corps than any other Catholic university. When I hear the stories these youngsters bring back, I think back fondly to Tom and that group of eager pioneers who comprised that very first contingent of Peace Corps volunteers a generation ago. It was, and still is, a beautiful concept, a fitting legacy: Wage peace, not war.

Introduction

THE ROADS I'VE TAKEN

Sometimes it seems that John Kennedy created the Peace Corps for me. I was ready to join before it even existed, so ready that I decided to volunteer the day the organization was announced. That decision—made thirty-five years ago—changed the direction of my life.

The fact that the Peace Corps was such a critical and formative experience in my life was reason enough, I guess, to open the drawer that contained these letters and papers last winter and decide to publish them. I am doing this for my family, especially for my children who love to hear "Peace Corps stories" at bedtime. Also, I am publishing these papers for my friends and professional associates to give them an idea of how I became involved in international development work in the first place. In addition, this book is intended for a broader public: for other Peace Corps volunteers, past, present and future; for volunteers going abroad with other development organizations; and for anyone interested in glimpsing life "in the field" a generation ago when international development itself was in its formative stages.

Thirty-five years ago few people spoke about "international development." Certainly I didn't. I was fresh out of Notre Dame, a twenty-three-year-old graduate student in philosophy at the University of Toronto. In fact, this story of the transformation of a scholar into a Peace Corps volunteer begins at the Notre Dame graduation ceremony on June 5, 1960, and with the friendship I had with a brash humanitarian, Dr. Thomas A. Dooley.

That commencement was one of the most stellar in the history of the university, thanks to its popular and charismatic president, Father Theodore M. Hesburgh. I saw the prop-driven plane carrying Dwight D. Eisenhower fly directly over the main quad of the campus an hour before the ceremony, bringing the President of the United States to give the commencement address. I saw Cardinal Giovanni Battista Montini celebrate the Baccalaureate Mass less than two years before his election as Pope Paul VI.

However, of all those receiving honorary degrees that day, Tom Dooley was the most important to me. He had left Notre Dame twelve years earlier (without graduating) and had gone on to work with refugees fleeing Communist persecution in Indochina. He was a prototype of the Peace Corps volunteer, although we did not know that then. His work in Asia, and his talent as an electrifying communicator, made him immensely popular in the United States. The Gallup Poll called him one of the ten most admired Americans in 1960. His book about working with Vietnamese refugees, *Deliver Us From Evil*, was a best-seller; he appeared on the Today Show and was featured on "This Is Your Life." Touring the United States, he raised millions of dollars for MEDICO, the organization he created that had established fourteen hospitals in nine Asian countries.

In the spring of 1960 I met Dooley (as he preferred to be called) and had the opportunity to work with him. He was to make an appearance at Notre Dame, and because I was chairman of the Blue Circle Honor Society, I had the task of organizing his visit. A previous appearance had been sparsely attended, and I vowed this one would be different. Rather than reserve a lecture hall or the campus theater, I decided that Dooley's "lecture" would be given at the Field House, the largest arena on campus, the place where pep rallies for the Fighting Irish were held.

Students packed the Field House, transfixed by Tom's stories about his work in Asia. When the thousands of idealists filed out, they found trash cans for cash donations at every door, and they filled them. The event was a great financial success and a moving expression of support for Tom's work. We became friends.

At four o'clock one morning the following October, I was awakened in my dormitory in Toronto. Passing through town on another fund-raising tour, Dooley was on the phone inviting me to join him for breakfast and take him to the airport. I called a student I was dating and invited her to join me. As she lived in a dormitory at St. Michael's College, this involved waking up the nuns, and such was Dooley's reputation that the sisters deemed it to have been a good idea. By six, we were in the coffee shop of the Royal York Hotel, where Tom resumed kidding me for being a philosopher rather than getting involved with the real problems and opportunities of the developing world.

I don't think he had slept that night. In fact, in those last months he was fond of quoting Robert Frost about having "promises to keep, and miles to go before I sleep." He was obviously functioning on nervous energy, and there was an even sharper edge to his humor as he joked with me about the words of consolation Cardinal Spellman had spoken to him in the hospital after his recent cancer surgery. "Remember, Tom," the Cardinal had said, "our Lord died at the age of thirty-four." Tom had not found that particularly consoling.

On the way to the airport, Dooley gave us a wry lesson in bipartisan politics. I asked him whom he was supporting for President in the election just a few weeks away. Seated in the front seat, he whipped around toward us and turned out the inside of one lapel where he had hidden a "Nixon for President" button. We groaned. Then, with a devilish look, he turned over the other lapel and displayed a "Kennedy for President" button. Dooley was for anyone who would support his work as he prepared to return to Bangkok, via New York, and to his hospitals. It was to be his last trip, and the last time I was to see him. Three months later, he died of melanoma at the age of thirty-four.

Tom Dooley had his detractors during his lifetime and afterward—for using out-of-date medical techniques, for having a big ego and a gift for public relations. Formerly a Navy officer and always stridently anti-Communist, he was accused of collecting intelligence, of accepting help from the U.S. government, of regularly briefing the CIA on happenings around his jungle hospitals. The facts remain: that he served humankind as a medical missionary; that in mobilizing support for his work he awakened thousands of Americans to the plight of people in distant Asia; that the Vatican sanctioned a group to investigate his cause for sainthood!

Tom's life reflected the geopolitical context of the 1950s. He responded to the world with energy, humanitarian concern and love of country. News of his death appeared on the front page of the *New York Times* on January 19, 1961. Between his obituary and a photograph of Jacqueline Kennedy preparing for the inauguration was a speech by Nikita Khrushchev in which he predicted the defeat of capitalism and establishment of Communism throughout the world. Typically—and persuasively, many of us feared—Khrushchev claimed that the Communist bloc was the true supporter of liberation throughout the developing world. In urban slums, and rice paddies, and remote mountain villages, ideological battles were being fought and the Soviet Union was winning as impoverished people prepared to make the Faustian bargain of trading their human freedom for material progress. Dooley had a profound understanding of this and acted accordingly.

My transformation from philosopher to Peace Corps volunteer continued six weeks later. I had applied for a Rhodes scholarship and was invited to Philadelphia where over thirty candidates participated in a competition that would choose two representatives to compete against ten candidates from the other five states in the Middle Atlantic Region. Four Rhodes scholars would be chosen from these twelve.

When the lengthy interview process in Philadelphia concluded, a young medical student named Gil Omen and I were chosen, and we traveled to Baltimore for the finals. A reception was held on a Friday evening in the home of Milton Eisenhower, the president of Johns Hopkins University and chairman of the selection committee. Dr. Eisenhower and his colleagues engaged us in pleasant but scrutinizing conversation, weighing our responses carefully and eyeing our social demeanor.

I had good reason to believe I had done well when I was invited back for a second interview on Saturday afternoon. As my second interview ended, Dr. Eisenhower asked a few casual questions about my academic schedule in order to assure the committee of my availability to go to Oxford in the fall. Things looked awfully good as a few candidates had dinner together and the committee deliberated. The best thing, I thought, was that the process was over; the interviews were done.

When we returned at the appointed hour, however, Dr. Eisenhower announced that the interviews were not entirely over. The committee had chosen three Rhodes scholars but not the fourth. Committee members wanted to interview two candidates one more time, myself and a classics scholar at Fordham by the name of Brian Daley. Each of us went back before the committee for an hour-long interview. Late that night, the committee emerged with its decision. I had come about as close to a Rhodes scholarship as one can—without becoming a Rhodes scholar. Daley was chosen and I was crushed.

Had the committee emerged from the room that December midnight and uttered my name, my whole life would have been different. It was one of those setbacks which, though devastating at the time, turns out to be fortunate. There was no way I would have turned down a Rhodes scholarship to join the Peace Corps, and I would have continued my studies in philosophy and gone on, most likely, to a career in higher education. (As for Daley, he did go on, became a Jesuit priest and now teaches theology at Notre Dame!)

The idea of teaching philosophy at a university didn't seem as bad to me as it did to Tom Dooley. I was more interested in teaching than scholarly research. My exposure to truly great teachers at Notre Dame had awakened a desire to share what I learned with others. Besides, I was good at philosophy. I was attending Toronto on a Woodrow Wilson fellowship and, with a heavy summer reading program and an oral exam, I was allowed to finish a two-year master's program in one. Soon I was accepted in the doctoral program at Yale University, and I intended to go there.

My transformation to a Peace Corps volunteer became complete during a long walk around the Toronto campus one cold afternoon in February. Dooley had died less than a month earlier and my graduate studies, while stimulating, were leaving a very important part of me unfulfilled. The University of Toronto and the Pontifical Institute for Medieval Studies, where many of my courses took place, placed strong emphasis on scholarly analysis of historical texts. Discussion of the ideas in these texts was played down. I can remember the conversation I had with myself that day (we philosophers do a lot of that kind of thing); it went like this. "Let's face it. I'm not happy. Everything here is logical skeletons. There's no flesh and blood." "OK," I continued, "what would make you happy?" "I would like," I said to myself, "to do what Tom Dooley did; to be with people of my own age and motivation, to help needy people in a foreign land."

Two weeks later, President Kennedy announced the creation of the Peace Corps. I had already decided to join.

Breaking the news to my parents seemed harder, a phenomenon so common that the Peace Corps later issued a pamphlet called "Over My Dead Body" to help potential volunteers address parental opposition. I sat down and wrote my dad a letter—to his office, not home—telling him that I wanted to volunteer. A few days later I was speaking to both my parents over the phone from Toronto and Dad exclaimed that he thought joining the Peace Corps was a terrific idea. In the end my concerns that my mother would be opposed were unfounded too. In a flash I applied.

The next step came after the spring semester ended and I had returned to my hometown of Scranton, Pennsylvania. A telegram from Washington informed me that I had been selected to go to Ghana with the first Peace Corps group that would begin work overseas—as teachers. A package followed containing the paperwork for enrolling in the Peace Corps, including requests for letters of recommendation. Delighted with the success of my application and fully committed to go to Ghana, I picked up the phone and called Father Hesburgh at Notre Dame to ask him to recommend me. To my surprise, he turned me down. "There's no way you're going to Ghana," Father Hesburgh said. "Notre Dame is organizing a group for Chile and you're going with us." I answered that I would be happy to join his group but I would not turn down the Ghana invitation unless I had the Chile invitation in hand. Very swiftly, it arrived.

Yes, that's the way things happened in those days, when the president of Notre Dame had a special connection with the

Peace Corps—though that had nothing to do with the fact that Notre Dame was a Catholic university and John Kennedy was the first Catholic elected President of the United States. (Administration officials and Kennedy himself pointedly avoided any kind of overt or special relationship with Notre Dame or its president.) Father Hesburgh had been "present at the creation" of the Peace Corps because he had been friends with Sargent Shriver since the days when Shriver was chairman of the Chicago Council for Inter-Racial Justice and Father served on the U.S. Civil Rights Commission. Another link was Harris Wofford, a close associate of Shriver's on the task force creating the Peace Corps and previously a Notre Dame law professor whom Father had personally recruited from a Washington law firm. Most important, Father Hesburgh helped the Peace Corps get off to a quick start. A few weeks after its founding, he and a representative of the Indiana Conference on Higher Education, Peter Frankel, went to Chile to set up a Peace Corps program there. They identified the private institution with which the volunteers would work and developed the Chilean government's invitation to the United States to send a contingent the following summer.

Not only at the beginning, but throughout our service and in the thirty-three years since then, Father Hesburgh has remained close to our Peace Corps group, called "Chile I"—the first in that country, of course, and the first to go abroad after Congress passed the Peace Corps Act.[1] We counted ourselves blessed that we were adopted as special family by this remarkable individual, the man who served as Notre Dame's president for thirty-five years, who is today the president of Harvard's Board of Overseers, who has received the Presidential Medal of Freedom, who has served fourteen Presidential appointments and received 130 honorary degrees—more than anyone else in history according to *The Guinness Book of Records*.

Father Ted became a priest to all of us, Catholics, Protestants, Jews, agnostics, and atheists. Over the past three decades years he has seen us through personal crises, helped us find jobs, married us

[1] Three Peace Corps groups were "the first" in different ways. The first to enter training was a contingent of engineers bound for Tanganyika (now Tanzania). The "Ghana I" group of teachers was the first to take up its assignment overseas.

and baptized our children. This summer, Father Ted hosted a reunion at Notre Dame for the Chile I group, thirty-five years almost to the day after we gathered there for our training program to become what we soon called *Piscorinos*. I was there with my wife, Faith, and our children, Cashel and Garrett.

Waiting for the Snow contains four kinds of papers which emerged from my Peace Corps experience. There are "hello-goodby" letters which I wrote in the field and which my dad's secretary, Mary Kiesel, transcribed and mimeographed to send out to fifty or sixty friends. These generally positive accounts describe the excitement and challenges of our early experiences as volunteers.

Also, there are extended letters to my parents and my brother, Jim. These contain the details of more personal experiences and provide a narrative of some of the difficulties we encountered that I did not want to broadcast to "everybody."

There are two sets of talks to new Peace Corps trainees, one about cultural adjustment and the other about our work in rural development. These talks discuss what I regard as the most difficult tasks that all Peace Corps volunteers must face: adjusting to the culture and making a meaningful contribution to the country where they serve.

In addition, there are two lengthy letters to two distinguished persons, the first to President Kennedy. Yes, I wrote a long letter to the President after hearing that he, in welcoming remarks to government interns, had told a story about me in Chile! The anecdote he told gives this book its name, and is quoted in the epigraph. It was told to him by the other distinguished individual, who had visited me while on an inspection tour of "Chile I" operations in April, 1962. That, of course, was Father Hesburgh.

My original purpose has been to weave all these papers together and tell the story of an early Peace Corps experience in a novel way. I have tried to tell what the Peace Corps was really like and to demonstrate that its real accomplishments were different— and even more important—than those described in the success stories that Peace Corps/Washington communicated so effectively.

The papers were first compiled in approximately their present form after I returned from the Peace Corps in 1963. During the next four years I sent them to at least a dozen publishers, all of whom rejected them as not appealing to a general audience. Then I put them in a box where they lay dormant for over half my life.

The papers, intentionally left very much as they were originally written, have undergone only very mild editing for publication. My editor and I reordered material in order to make it more reader-friendly three decades after the fact, and we have reorganized a number of passages—in some case combining actual letters, in other cases splitting them up—to make a smoother narrative. However, we have not deleted language used in the sixties in favor of terms that sound more "correct" today. For example, both men and women used the word "girls" in those days to denote adult females. Likewise "gay" meant lighthearted, happy, and had no sexual connotation. To sanitize such expressions to suit the tastes of the nineties would undermine this book's value as a verbal snapshot of the past. Likewise we retained passages that may appear to some readers today (myself included) as overly earnest. This was done to provide a more accurate impression of how things seemed to me then, a self-assured idealist in my early twenties.

In order to give an accurate description of what it was like to be an early Peace Corps volunteer, I have allowed many of the smaller and more mundane details of our experience to remain in the manuscript—details which one reader a quarter-century ago warned would interest "only Mom." These details and some entire sections may be of wider interest now, because we live in a different world. Also, they allow me to give the full flavor of the experience.

I know better than to think that some things have changed much since receiving those rejection letters thirty years ago. Now as then, a universal complaint of Peace Corps volunteers is that few people are interested in hearing about their experiences when they return home—experiences which we found so incredibly vital and unique. Yet, last fall as I reread my contemporaneous accounts of those years, I began to hope that this book might reach other circles besides my immediate family and friends. Perhaps some people will be interested in it as a contribution to the early history of the Peace Corps because it describes how things were for us, the fortunate first few. Predictably perhaps I believe it was the volunteers themselves, not just officials in Washington, who defined what the Peace Corps was and what it could do. Also I hope that other former volunteers—of whom there are now over 140,000!—will find the book interesting and affirming. Finally I will be gratified if those who are considering a Peace Corps term, or who are Peace Corps trainees, find it helpful as they prepare to embark on what will be both great service and a great adventure.

One fact I realized in 1963 was that I had just returned from the greatest adventure in my young life, and that may have been one motive for compiling a book back then. In the course of working on this edition three decades later, I have developed a greater hope for it. In rereading these papers after so many years, I discovered that they are not only about the Peace Corps and about me. They are about the rural people with whom we worked in Chile. This was the ultimate purpose of Peace Corps service: to work in behalf of persons who were desperately poor; to share their lives and their humanity. Publishing these papers will be more than justified if it allows me to share this experience while reminding other Americans that more than 800 million persons around the world today live in similar poverty—and that we can do something about it. For as Harris Wofford said at a Peace Corps dinner during my first week of training, "If you have the means, it follows as day follows night that you have the responsibility to assist the poorer nations of the world."

We no longer have the threat of Communism to motivate the Dooleys, Kennedys or Peace Corps volunteers of today. But we do have a continuing sense of common decency and altruism. This should make our country remain a part of efforts like the Peace Corps, and other international development programs, that aim at reaching the poor throughout the world with hope and the promise of a better life.

Over the years I have met many outstanding individuals who wanted to join the Peace Corps but did not for one good reason or another. To these people I want to offer an invitation: Come along and share the experience with me.

—Washington, D.C.
September, 1996

Chapter 1

TRAINING AND EMBARKATION

Our group of volunteers, dubbed 'Chile I,' sets sail for South America—the first contingent to go abroad after Congress passed the Peace Corps Act. The three-week voyage provides time to reflect on the training program at Notre Dame in a long letter to my friends at home.

At Sea—September 1961

Adios Amigos!

This is incredible! Here I am a member of the U.S. Peace Corps, fit to burst with excitement after two months' training at Notre Dame and after friends sent me off as though I were going to war, and I am cruising to Chile, our group's destination, aboard a Grace liner. After the training program I thought we might walk to Chile, toting our baggage on our backs. Now we are taking about the same amount of time but doing it luxuriously. Don't be deceived by our ship's being a freighter, the *Santa Isabel*. It's plenty comfortable in the passenger areas. Some of the men in the group say we had to go by freighter because all the girls'[1] luggage would never fit on an ordinary passenger liner.

Mr. Shriver was opposed to this idea. In fact, he has already decided that our contingent of volunteers will be the last to go by

---

[1] Truth to tell, we used that term in those days, as in the phrase "men and girls." Even "girls" talked that way then.

boat. He wanted us to go to Puerto Rico for three weeks to an
Outward Bound camp where we would scale cliffs and float in the
water with our hands and feet tied, and when our administrators
were presented with this alternative, they became even more committed to their own plan for the trip. In this we heartily concurred.
I registered a stiff dissent to the idea of playing Tarzan. Whatever
Puerto Rico is like, I am sure of one thing now: a twenty-one-day
cruise on a liner equipped with pool, sun decks and exquisite cuisine is not the best way to begin two years in the bush.

Do you know that we are the only ones aboard this ship?
There are no passengers who aren't in the Peace Corps; just us,
forty-five volunteers with our directors and their families. Now
the good sense of our directors has kept the situation far from
anarchy, so the problem is not lack of discipline. The problem is
the very luxury of cruising with only your friends through distant
waters to intriguing ports in utter privacy. We would have to work
hard and save skillfully for years before we could afford this.

Of course the captain and the crew are aboard, but from
the very beginning we have perplexed them a great deal. The
captain says all our talk about nutrition for the poor people in
Latin America is just a new fad; he says they can live perfectly
well down there on bananas and rice. Many of the crew are
Latin American and although they speak English well, they are
surprised to find us babbling a few new words of Spanish to
them every morning. I'm sure it's the first time they have been
asked so many questions about standards of living in their
native lands, and I know the captain never had to issue so many
announcements pleading with the passengers to stay out of the
hold of the ship, to use the stairways to climb between decks
rather than climb up over the side, and to refrain from sitting
on the railings.

The most confounded members of the crew are the bursar,
the waiters, and the deck steward, whose duty it is to provide passengers with a pleasant voyage. They refuse to admit that we
should have a different schedule of activities than passengers in
the past, and in the end I'm not sure who has won out. At night,
the bursar shows movies when we try to study Spanish in the
lounge. When I try to avoid the heavy and too-frequent meals, the

waiters come ringing their gong outside the door. In the morning, as we begin to do calisthenics, the deck steward arrives with consommé. These men are happier now than at the beginning of the trip. Our talent show was livelier than what the usual octogenarians put on and our crazy hat contest and King Neptune party were among the best they've seen in years. They say we are finally entering into the real spirit of the trip. Wish you were here.

The original idea behind traveling to Chile by ship was that our training program could continue here. In most senses, this has been the case. The prediction that the boat would be a floating language laboratory has also been true, Then there is another advantage to this ship. It is an opportunity for us to get to know each other better. I am terribly impressed by the diversity in interests and backgrounds of my fellow volunteers. If we didn't have the Peace Corps in common, we would probably pass each other by because at home we travel in different orbits. Included in our group are farm folk and city folk from all sections of the United States. Aboard ship in the free hours of the afternoon you pass by a cluster of people listening to a short wave radio with its antenna extended over the ship's railing like a fishing rod. They are listening to Spanish broadcasts about politics. Seated in a deck chair, someone is reading a novel which you never thought of reading, and in the shade of the lounge two people are discussing poetry. At night on the top deck you can reminisce with new friends who represent the variety of American life itself—murmuring sessions in the heavy breeze, warm air and full moon while the ship rolls from side to side or lurches out of the sea and then crashes down hard again creating much spray and foam.

It seems years since we volunteers first met each other at Notre Dame. Our Peace Corps training program there was a great prelude to the coming two years. It was a worthwhile experience in itself, an adventure into new fields of interest for all of us. If some time is being lost aboard ship, our long summer at my alma mater compensated for that. It is hard to imagine how more could have been attempted or accomplished in the training program. This is what went on:

I arrived at Notre Dame on Thursday, July 20. Heavy bag in hand, I was wandering through the third floor of the Arts and

Letters building, familiar territory from days when I had been there for another purpose. I stuck my head in a classroom where I expected to find a Peace Corps office. Instead, I found my least favorite and most pompous professor, who once taught me Spinoza. He was conducting a class and luckily he didn't recognize me. "Where is the Peace Corps?" I asked sheepishly. He looked startled and then growled slowly, "In Chile, where it belongs." With this, I saw early that the coming two months at Notre Dame were going to be very different from the four years I had completed there a year ago.

That night the members of the Chilean Peace Corps Project assembled for the first time at a dinner given by the University. Present were fifty men and women, most of them recent college graduates, from twenty-five different states. Also present was the staff of the training program, six Chilean "native speakers," three professors of Spanish, two Fulbright scholars who had been in Chile, two Notre Dame coaches, and the University physician. The main speaker at the dinner was Father Hesburgh, president of Notre Dame and a man I'm proud to call my friend, whose Easter excursion to Chile with a representative of the Indiana Conference on Higher Education had been the real origin of our project. The Indiana Conference, through Notre Dame, is administering the first university-sponsored project in the Peace Corps' short history.

Father Hesburgh told us of his drive through the central valley of Chile in a bright yellow truck and of talking to the small farmers who are known as *campesinos*. In Chile, Father was advised that there are two groups now functioning effectively in impoverished rural Chile, the Communists and the Institute of Rural Education.[2] He saw the Institute as the Peace Corps' ideal "counterpart" organization—that is, our organizational host. It was young, organized completely by Chileans, and (most important) it wanted us. However, the Institute placed one qualification on its request for volunteers. It did not want an all-male contingent. A group of men and women would be less susceptible to charges of imperialism, the Institute maintained. Besides that, the girls

---

[2] Still operating throughout Chile, the IER is a private voluntary organization that promotes rural development; it has ties to the Catholic Church.

would have easier access to the kitchens of *campesino* homes where the roots of many problems lie. As a result of these discussions in April, nineteen girls and thirty-one men came to Notre Dame that summer night to train for a rural education project in Chile.

For the most part we were strangers to one another, having in common only the desire to belong to the Peace Corps (and the uneasiness of the situation). Half of us had never spoken a word of Spanish in our lives, and the other half had studied Spanish in a college or high school somewhere—hardly qualifying them for conversation in the language. Most had to start very close to the beginning as far as training in conversation was concerned.

At the banquet we were spoken to in Spanish for the first time, giving us a taste of the experience ahead and our first frustrating realization of how much we had to learn before we could function effectively in Chile. From the description of the training program, which had been sent to our homes in large brown Special Delivery envelopes, we knew that more than language study had been prepared for us. We were to study about Chile and about the complexities of representing the United States abroad. Many of us were almost as deficient in this as in Spanish. I remember the expression on the face of Mr. Pat Kennedy,[3] Washington's representative at the dinner, when he overheard the table conversation of one of our recent graduates from Purdue. "After Kierkegaard, Sartre is blah," she was saying. I am sure Pat reported to Mr. Shriver that our group had a long way to go.

The next day we began the fingerprinting and passport application processes, the psychological tests and the medical examinations—the latter putting our nurse and dental hygienist volunteers into action immediately. By Monday we were ready to begin the seven 60-hour weeks of class, and within a week it seemed we had been at Notre Dame a very long time. These days contained four and a half hours of class in the morning and four more in the afternoon. Evening sessions sometimes lasted until ten-thirty. If evening sessions ended early, there would be spontaneous groups

---

[3] No relation of the President, Padraic Kennedy headed the Division of Volunteer Support at Peace Corps headquarters.

working on Spanish, practicing Chilean songs, or enjoying bull sessions with members of the staff back in the dormitory. Our weekends began at noon on Saturday and were usually a frantic attempt to catch up on things neglected during the week, leaving only an afternoon or evening for a party or movie.

What we learned at Notre Dame cannot be adequately described by listing our courses. These were of an original design and, as had been expected, they overlapped considerably. The results of this intensive series of encounters with the staff and guests who came to speak were fourfold. We prepared to sustain our health in a foreign country, to speak the Spanish language, to understand the Chilean people, and to represent our country in Latin America.

The Peace Corps anticipates that mental health will present as many problems as physical health when we are working in strange circumstances. Mental health was carefully considered during the testing in the first weeks and in the training courses. Each of us was interviewed by a psychiatrist for an hour, and along with lectures on the symptoms, prevention and treatment of any disease we might contract went a helpful series of talks on the dangers of "culture shock." This is the uneasiness and fear which a person experiences when transplanted into a different culture. The lectures were not supposed to prevent culture shock, but to help us recognize the problem as it sets in and apply the best-known remedies immediately: patience, understanding and a sense of humor.

Our first class in the morning Monday through Thursday was dedicated to the pleasant topic of disease, and on Friday to the uncomfortable matter of receiving shots. We received fourteen in all. Dr. Began, the university physician, reviewed each shot in class, noting its preventative power and how long it lasted. Personal hygiene hints and an extensive list of what food and drinks to avoid were added as cautionary measures. In case accidents or sickness should occur, we were given training in first aid, and a medicine kit as big as a briefcase.

Our health classes were complemented by a physical fitness program. Under the supervision of Notre Dame's swimming and tennis coaches, we ran, did calisthenics, learned soccer and played baseball, basketball and volleyball. This was the only recreation scheduled during the long day of classes, and despite the fact that it had a serious purpose, the hour-and-a-half class was a source of diversion. The presence of seventeen sophisticated young ladies guaranteed many humorous moments. The first day, when the usual gym class call to "dress right" was given, the girls thought Coach Fallon was making a derogatory reference to their attire. Usually they got the giggles during pushups. Once Coach Stark was umpiring a girls' baseball game from behind the pitcher, who went into an exaggerated wind-up and a loud rip pierced the air. The coach finished umpiring behind the plate. After the girls began taking the class seriously, however, they developed a surprisingly good game of soccer.

Volleyball and basketball were part of the program because they are becoming increasingly popular in Latin America and we expect to teach them in the schools there. We learned soccer because a Chilean takes it as seriously as Green Bay does football, and we wanted to be able to understand the game. After seven weeks of continual sports activity, we were not trained for specific physical tasks but we had developed enough flexibility and fitness to make whatever physical adaptation should be necessary with a minimum of difficulty. Evidence of progress was visible in the mile run. At the end of the summer many of the men ran it in less than five minutes, and most of the women ran a fast half-mile.

Our second objective was to learn to speak the language. When people find out that we have been speaking Spanish for less than three months, they always remark at our "facility" for learning languages. In Spanish this noun comes from the adjective *fácil*, which means "easy." For this reason, I make it a point to disagree. Learning a new language is never easy. It is grueling, frustrating work. If we speak good Spanish now, it is because we worked in our four daily Spanish classes, at meals where Spanish was the only language allowed (a rule enforced by teachers who sat with us) and in whatever spare moment presented itself as an opportunity to practice pronunciation, copy down new names for things or study word lists.

Conditions for learning a language were ideal. At least ten people working with the forty-five volunteers were "native speakers" or instructors. We were taught with the help of the most

modern equipment and methods. Most important, we had the
motivation of knowing that in a few short months, Spanish would
be the language in which our affairs would be conducted.

Still, the process was difficult and even humiliating at times.
In class, a woman would hold a huge picture of a man and say five
or six times "¡hombre!" to a class of young adults as if she were talking to a three-year-old child. We would repeat the sound six
times, rest satisfied in the knowledge of a new word and ten minutes later be asking, "How do you say 'man' again?" Sometimes I
felt that I was being brainwashed and that the flow of new words
was pushing all the old ideas out and leaving new ones in their
place. Such is the matter of finding new phantasms for old ideas.

But the problem of knowing individual and discrete words
was nothing compared to isolating them in a spoken sentence.
For a few weeks any new sound—even a bell ringing or an object
falling—could have signified something to me. This reflected a
kind of linguistic broadmindedness, I guess, and it was only with
the help of Spanish Lab that we came to distinguish Spanish
words from ordinary noises.

The lab was held in the heart of the summer afternoon in the
sleepiest time of the day. It subjected us to recordings of properly
enunciated Spanish expressions, gave us a mercilessly short time in
which to mock the sound and then, in the replay of tapes, afforded us the distasteful opportunity to compare our voice to that of
the master. If this wasn't frustrating enough, there was always
Claudia Benavides, the five-year-old daughter of a Chilean professor who playfully used her knowledge of all the Spanish tenses
while asking us questions in her Spanish baby-talk. I avoided her
in terror, especially after she mocked my trilling of the Spanish 'r,'
a very touchy matter for all of us. When Claudia was in the lab and
the weather was especially warm, the best escape was sleep.
Usually it was possible to enjoy two or three minutes of drowsy
relief before the instructor opened the circuits connecting his
voice to your earphones, and gently but firmly reminded you of
your responsibilities to the microphone which protruded from
your language stall like the head of a curious snake.

As the weeks passed by, progress could be noted during
meals. In July we came to believe that we ate not for nourishment

but to learn the names of the dishes; and that if we could identify all the foods with their Spanish tags there was really no sense in staying for lunch. By mid-August, our language exercises at meals ceased to be the mere acquisition of new words as we began to put words into sentences. Soon we could tell time, and table conversation was a matter of asking each other what time it was as each minute passed. That made the conversation a little more interesting. Even when we combined nouns with verbs and made sentences, there were always a few English words thrown in. No matter what landmark was reached, however, the desire to learn more was greater than the sense of accomplishment. At the end of this important second week in August, Janet Boegli, a volunteer from Texas, complained, "How can we teach the *campesinos* to prepare for the future when we can only speak in the present tense?" It has been that way with everything we have learned in Spanish. It seems we will never know enough to use the language without effort. Even the Chileans our age have a twenty-year headstart on us.

Through sports and language alone there is a basis for a relationship between peoples of two countries, but the training program went further than that. Courses in Chilean culture and Chilean history occupied ten hours of our class time each week. The culture course was directed by Ricardo Benavides, father of Claudia, and Homero Castillo, a Chilean expatriate and a professor at Northwestern University. They related the folklore and superstitions of the country people and demonstrated the *cueca*, Chile's national dance. For the first time we encountered vicariously the Chilean *huaso* (cowboy) and the *roto*, his laborer counterpart in the city. In the evening, we practiced Chile's national songs and although we never could master the difficult national anthem our attempts were oft-repeated and sincere.

Señores Benavides and Castillo were themselves representatives of Chile. Like every Chilean I have met, they possessed a strong national pride and were obviously pleased to speak of Chile's heroes, customs, national institutions, natural wonders and Indian subcultures. Whenever possible, the impression was made clearer with slides. We emerged from the training program with a more panoramic view of Chilean society than we have of our own. There is still much to learn about Chile from actual experience, but the course gave us an appetite for these experiences and a ready-made framework in which they could be related to each other meaningfully.

Chilean culture brought insight into Chile's heart, but there were more serious aspects of the country to be discussed. We had to learn what was on Chile's mind at this point in her history, and this meant discussing the problems which Chile faces today. For us, Chile became not the land of the *cueca* or *huaso*, but a country experiencing development. An understanding of the fundamental economic social and political dilemmas facing the small nation became as essential to the training program as learning the words for "good morning" and "good evening." Most of these problems were discussed in the history course.

Chilean history was taught by Mr. Donald Bray of Los Angeles State College, who had been in Chile for two years as a Fulbright scholar. Extremely well-informed and with a perceptivity which gave him a phenomenal control over his material, he led us through the early years of Latin American history—the eras of the conquistadors, viceroys and wars of independence. He reviewed each step in the political development of the Chilean republic comparing it to other Latin American countries and examining under the impulse of our questions the origin of contemporary social and economic problems. This class alternated between revelation, fascination and hilarity depending on the topic. Professor Bray used the same facial expression and inflection when talking about the cat which Brazil sent into outer space and the housing problem in Santiago, not even grinning when he announced that the cat died.

Through Mr. Bray we learned that Chileans are thinking primarily about two things today: how to achieve economic growth which will raise the $425 average annual income, and how to deal with the political and social upheavals which accompany economic development in this decade. Chile has many untapped resources upon which this economic growth could be based.

For example, only 58 percent of the arable land has been cultivated. To develop agricultural resources, however, Chile

Training and Embarkation
21

needs tractors, education and loans. Recently farm matters have become worse instead of better because the increase in agricultural production has not kept pace with population growth, and Chile, which previously could supply herself with food, has begun importing wheat. Rather than fight a losing battle on the farms, thousands of poor farmers are pouring into the major cities each week, and slum areas surrounding the cities are surging and growing larger.

The new arrivals, frequently unemployed, live in *callampas*, neighborhoods of crude wooden structures providing neither adequate space or protection for a family. Today 40 percent of the population live in homes which do not meet minimum sanitary standards. Nothing adds to the *callampa* dwellers' problems more than inflation. Since 1950, the cost of living has often risen more than 20 percent a year. In 1955, it rose 83 percent. Since wages cannot be adjusted completely to the higher cost of living, the value of a worker's small salary declines more each year. The sad plight of both the farmers and wage earners in Chile is compounded by the fact that wine is cheaper than most foods, and Chile has the third highest incidence of alcoholism in the world.

Many Chileans, especially students and intellectuals, believe that the causes of these unacceptable social conditions lie in an outmoded social structure. They feel that more land would be farmed if it were not concentrated in only a few hands. At present, 9.7 percent of the landowners own 80 percent of the arable land. Furthermore, intellectuals see the need for better distribution of the national income through a more equitable system.

In 1958 a remarkable development at the polls indicated that the need for reform was felt by more than the intellectuals. The present conservative president, Jorge Alessandri, was elected by a margin of 35,000 votes out of 1,200,000. His nearest competitor was Salvador Allende, who heads a Socialist-Communist coalition. A defrocked priest running on a Socialist platform polled 41,000 votes, and if he had not run those 41,000 votes might have placed in the Chilean presidency a man openly sympathetic to the Communist cause in Latin America.[4] The elections of 1958

---

[4] That happened later, of course. Allende was elected in 1970; in 1973 he was overthrown by Pinochet's military junta, which ruled for twenty years.

indicated not only restlessness for reform but a willingness to experiment with radical Marxist methods. This then is the complete context of Chilean political life: there is a growing dissatisfaction not only with their own society but with American values and with the United States.

Our fourth objective at Notre Dame was to learn to represent our country in such a situation. We were not given any line to follow in defending the United States, nor told to present official U.S. views, but we were taught certain facts about inter-American relations and how Latin Americans view them.

For instance, I was surprised to discover that 65 percent of Chile's exports are produced by three U.S. copper companies. These firms have done a great deal to develop the Chilean economy and were invited by the Chilean government. But such a powerful foreign presence in any country will provoke the fear that its best interests will not always coincide with the best interests of the nation.

Chileans fear that these foreign enterprises, backed by our government, might interfere in their internal affairs. We learned that in the early part of the century the United States did send Marines to intervene in Cuba, Colombia, Nicaragua, Haiti and the Dominican Republic when the interest of some U.S. investors were threatened; however, the "good neighbor" policy of President Franklin D. Roosevelt saw the end of this kind of intervention. Still, many Latin Americans interpret our actions against Communism in the hemisphere today as a return to the diplomacy of the old days. President Eisenhower was greatly troubled when this insinuation was made to him by some Chilean university students during his trip there in 1961. The students asked whether U.S. opposition to the Castro regime was based on the fact that as a social revolutionary he would expropriate American property.

For many people in Latin America the fear of Communism is less poignant than the need for social change. They believe that our efforts to block Communism in Latin America are based on a desire to maintain the status quo. We have contributed to this misconception by associating with reactionary and dictatorial regimes simply because they were anti-Communist. Men like

Trujillo, Batista and Jiménez[5] were decorated by the United States while they were detaining in prison students and other dissenters in favor of real democracy. Statistics show that in the past decade, the United States has been more interested in the negative task of thwarting Communism and Communistic subversion in Latin America than in the positive program of developing prosperous, democratic neighbors. Between 1945 and 1960, only 6 percent of U.S. economic assistance to all parts of the world went to Latin America.

Among the arguments which some Chilean and Latin American thinkers make against the United States, there are exaggerated claims and hasty fears, and each volunteer will answer them in his own way; however, there is a consensus on two points among the volunteers. First, we believe that our country cannot be indifferent to the actions of American firms in a Latin American country. Second, we believe that the future of Latin America is so closely linked with ours that we have the responsibility to bolster economic development and internal reform throughout the hemisphere.

Preparing to represent the United States in a developing country was not a pleasant task. I sometimes felt as if I had been thrown into a cauldron which had been boiling for years without my knowledge. Our professors and guests spoke to us of poverty in other parts of the world, of the extent of Communist propaganda, and of the misconceptions of American life which citizens of foreign countries garner from our movies and from certain individuals who have not represented us well in the past.

But the final impression given by the training program of the role which our country can play in the developing world was not dismaying. Many maintain that our people have lost contact with people of poorer nations; however, within one week at Notre Dame we were visited by three men who demonstrated that Americans can understand the needs of countries in different stages of development.

The president of the Rockefeller Foundation spoke to us of his foundation's development of new crop varieties in Chile. Chuck

[5] Dictators of the Dominican Republic, Cuba and Venezuela respectively.

Vetter, from USIA, subjected us to six hours of haranguing as a would-be Marxist antagonist, putting questions to us that made us draw on all our resources and recently acquired knowledge. Harris Wofford, special assistant to Mr. Shriver, spoke some words at a Peace Corps dinner that have remained with me ever since. "If you have the means," he said, "it follows as day follows night that you have the responsibility to assist the poorer nations of the world."

That week was so stimulating that I abandoned my study of Spanish altogether. These men were not just presenting fancy ideas. They were realists. I became convinced that our country possessed a whole generation of individuals who are not satisfied with simply enjoying material prosperity but are anxious to appraise what they can do for those nations just beginning their development.

I suppose it sounds as if the summer was as intense as the South Bend sun and that we had little fun. But it was impossible to bring so many individuals together without raising a few roofs. I think the most important thing about any summer is the people you spend it with, and in those terms last summer was the greatest I ever spent anywhere.

Gradually the volunteers developed more than a common interest in Chile. They developed a bond among themselves. Class was not a mere academic exercise and the project did not loom as something in which each would perform his duty independently of the other. It was a group preparation for a group effort. We would succeed or fail together, and our hours in class and the moments relaxing together allowed us to know each other well and to formulate common assumptions and objectives. Although our backgrounds were disparate and each volunteer was immensely individualistic, there was harmony in goals and a pride in what each person stood for as well as in the contingent as a whole.

I wish I could describe all these individuals to you. One of everyone's favorites, Amos Roos lives as if he yearns for Rousseau's state of nature (or had already found it), but has a sociability all his own and a social consciousness which is deep and sincere. Kay Partridge, a nurse from Colorado, could beat

the boys on the playing field and then come into dinner looking like a Spanish señorita. Gerry Garthe, a Californian, is
expert at everything from planting trees to playing American
folk music on the guitar. Fred Morgner is a tall, stocky ex-foot-
ball player with the mind of a quarterback and the compassion
of Santa Claus. Jacques Seigler is a charming, freckle-faced live
wire from Cove, Arkansas. Ed Tisch is a poet, farm boy, and sci-
entist who chased bears around the Dakota hills for two years
while doing his master's thesis on their eating habits. Dan
McCarthy possesses a hilarious sense of humor which emanates
from a soul which is sensitive and intense. Kathy O'Connor, an
efficient and high-powered intellectual, was a student body
president at St. Mary's College across the way from Notre
Dame. I could go on. There are forty-five in all.

Outside of class, the lounges in the dormitory served for folk
singing and brainstorming sessions. The hideaway room at
Giuseppe's restaurant was discovered the first Saturday night we
were in town, and we met there frequently for a beer and the tele-
casts of some important sports events. The volunteers were out of
class enough—walking the seminary paths or swimming in the
lakes, playing football on the lawn or appearing in shorts in the
most sedate corners of the campus—to make Notre Dame administrators and the three thousand nuns on campus conclude that for
good or ill there had never really been anything like the Peace
Corps before within those sacred ivy walls.

At home, while I was preparing to leave for Chile, a friend
asked me, "What are the girls like who volunteer for the Peace
Corps?" My answer was that they have about the same amount of
talent, good looks and brains as any other group of seventeen
American girls—with a generous dose of independence and
strong will to throw in. Though they were outnumbered, there
were enough girls to make socializing a recurrent activity in the
program. On the first weekend a trip to the Michigan dunes was
arranged for us, and I have never had such a good time on a picnic. With our future teachers, a vice-president of the Ford
Foundation, and the president of Notre Dame, we played touch
football and baseball, hiked up the dunes and swam. Later we sat
among piles of box lunches, our backs against huge mounds of

sand, and sang while the sun went down and left heavy black
clouds in the north. The land was all sand and dark pine trees, a
study in green and tan. Then we made the long ride home and
began our classes in earnest.

One Thursday morning, almost a month later, it was hard to
concentrate on the lectures. By noon I wasn't relishing the idea of
four more hours of classes. We were watching slides of Chile
when our assistant director came in to announce that we would
take *another* ride that afternoon—*another* because the week before
we had traveled to Elkhart, Indiana, for inoculations against yellow fever. As I was trying to decide which was worse—the four
hours of class or another dismal journey for shots—Dr. Smith
added that we should bring bathing suits along. Our directors had
scheduled another outing for us, this time at a wealthy alumnus's
estate only a few minutes from campus. It was perfect timing. All
of us were pooped. The class of forty-five adults whooped it up
like children given a free day from school.

Within an hour we were at the estate where we separated
into teams for baseball, football, volleyball and water soccer.
Father Hesburgh refereed the water soccer game and was
splashed enough to make his trip to New York later in the afternoon uncomfortable. Some of the girls went to the set of swings
facing the swimming pool and made so many trips over the heads
of the swimmers that they were sore the next day. After dinner we
danced the marimba, the cha-cha, and the mambo as evening settled over the estate. Then we rested in the grass, talking and
singing songs. Despite the itch of a thousand mosquito bites, I
slept well that night.

We really have a wise directorate. They don't ask us to make
sacrifices for the sake of show. They understand that you can
become stale and saturated with too much information and that
you can tire of the routine. Their ability to be so human, even
paternal, is often comical. They remind us to write home and
things like that. When our group director, Mr. Walter Langford,
arrived after a quick trip to Chile, the group converged on the airport to welcome him in Spanish. He and the other teachers have
entertained us in their homes. One volunteer remarked that sometimes it is like being at Boy Scout Camp; but it is comforting to

know that the Peace Corps and Notre Dame feel responsible for us while we are volunteers.

Our last social event came in September and was a spontaneous celebration of an important event. We began the evening as guests of the mayor of South Bend and ended fearing that some of his more brawny civil servants might arrive uninvited at the party. This was the day that the final selection of volunteers was made; those who were going to Chile were told so and the few who were to remain behind were informed also. That night we released the pressures that had accumulated during the weeks before selection. Many called home with the good news and were surprised when their parents weren't so excited about their selection as they were. As the last stragglers came back to Notre Dame, the campus cop who had been imposing midnight curfews on the undergraduates for the last forty-five years said, "Gee, I wish I was in the Peace Corps." He didn't know how appropriate his statement was.

If anything had threatened our *esprit de corps* and our close relationship with the Notre Dame and Peace Corps leadership it had been this matter of selection. From the beginning we knew that some would not go to Chile. Then came September. The flies were getting pretty pesky and night was sneaking in before the lamps along the campus walks were lit. It was autumn in Indiana and springtime in Chile, and the decision had to be made. That day on the basketball court, rebounding became rougher and a few elbows flew. Even the girls began pushing each other occasionally. But these slight outbursts were an outlet for tension which we avoided showing in any other way. In the main, there was little talk of selection, and I know of no instance where the volunteers were criticizing one another—even though each of us filed secret ratings on every member of the group. The only vocal criticism was of selection itself. Was it necessary? Did it have to be held so late and in such a drastic fashion?

The climax came on the afternoon of September 5. We were in language lab with the most demanding of our professors, whom we had affectionately named "Ivan the Terrible." He screamed phrases for us to repeat—a phrase every two seconds or so. The exchange continued for a half-hour without interruption; to pro-

nounce the words quickly enough one had to speak as loudly as
he. Our mouths labored incessantly; our ears strained to hear the
lead words above the din, and our eyes watched fearfully for the
ambassador of bad news who would descend the steps from the
third floor where the selection committee was meeting and tap
some of us on the shoulder. No one felt secure.

The news of the outcome of the selection procedure circulated during gym class. We were playing volleyball while the class
was assembling—passing around the soiled white ball with *Phy-
Ed* written on it. Everyone would try to spike it, most with little
success. There was little interest in the game that day. The names
of those eliminated spread slowly, with no informant being certain of his news until the names on his list jibed with those who
did not come to class. This indirect notification of our acceptance
brought quiet relief, little open rejoicing and a lot of feeling and
questions directed toward the trainees who have been dropped.
How are they taking it? What reasons were given? What are they
going to do now?

The next week was anticlimactic. Everyone attended the
eight o'clock class the morning following the selection celebration even though they might not remember it. Judy Grant wore a
bright red dress that glared in the sun; she said she chose it intentionally to wake people up in class. By then, however, classes were
becoming repetitious. We felt rambunctious and busied ourselves
preparing for this voyage and making plans for the last eight days
before sailing.

At home, I tried to explain to my friends why all of us were
so anxious to arrive in Chile. My friends were glad I had joined
the Peace Corps, yet they seemed uncertain about what I could
do or what effect the Peace Corps can have in the long run. This
is an important question. Learning about Chile to work there for
two years would be easier if we were assured that the problems
would be less grave. The idea that we would have a tangible
effect and join a frontal attack on poverty did operate as a vague
stimulant during training. Any kind of reflection reveals, however, that we cannot even be the proverbial drop in the bucket; we
are more like a drop in the Atacama desert of northern Chile. It
will be hard to convince ourselves that we have any lasting effect

at all. Nonetheless, Americans should learn the needs of the people in undeveloped countries at first hand. Americans must show that we are still the friend of the common man, no matter which continent he lives on.

Congress approved the legislation creating the Peace Corps the day we readied our departure from New York.[6] As we were signing our contracts with the Peace Corps that morning, President Kennedy signed the bill that made the Peace Corps a permanent institution of the United States government, and we became the first Peace Corps group to leave the country with the official authorization of the U.S. Congress for the American people. This news was presented to us personally by Mr. Sargent Shriver who arrived in New York to send us off. Though weary from a Congressional battle, he gave a fighting speech. As a model of dedication to a cause, he told us of Mao Tse-Tung in the caves of Yenan before the Kuomintang lost control of China, and he asked us to match his enthusiasm. He offered us help "not to make your work easier but to make it more successful." The impression Mr. Shriver made was electric and one that will not be lost quickly, because he speaks for the Peace Corps ideal and we have made that a permanent part of ourselves.

The ship stayed in the dock longer than scheduled and farewells were drawn out for hours. Finally, a little before nine that evening, we began to edge from the pier waving to families, friends and fiancées who were staying behind. The noise of the ship drowned out what they were calling to us. Soon we found ourselves in the Hudson River surrounded by the towering shapes of well-lit buildings, and we watched the slow movement of the boats on the busy river. We passed Long Island, Staten Island, the Jersey Shore. "Isn't she beautiful," someone gasped as we steamed in front of the Statue of Liberty.

Everyone was on the top deck, gathered in groups of two or three. The moon was so bright that jokes about moonburn were in order but the mood was quiet, broken only by intermittent explanations of the clusters of lights along the shore and some

---

[6] Until then the Peace Corps functioned on the basis of the Executive Order signed by President Kennedy in March.

muffled cheers for the harbor pilot when he left the ship. In this solemn mood we grew aware, perhaps for the first time, of the distance our mission would take us from home. So far this had been the greatest sacrifice. Amos Roos' voice penetrated the stillness and expressed our feelings. "I don't know about you," he said, "but right now I am in church."

The lights of New York were an architect's model of what they were before—ever diminishing until they were a dull haze in the background. Soon they were enveloped by the expanse of sea and sky that merged on the horizon. The dark sea and sky represented the uncertainty which surrounds our mission, for what will come of this two-year journey of ours is something which we simply just don't know.

Cheers and keep in touch,
Tom Scanlon

Chapter 2
COASTINGS: INTRODUCTIONS TO LATIN AMERICA

Aboard the steamship Santa Isabel, *'Chile I' volunteers are introduced to the southern continent.*

At Sea—October 3, 1961

Dear Mom, Dad and Jim,

The opportunity to visit large cities along the coast of South America is the best justification for these days at sea. Other than a short stop in Panama, a late afternoon trip through the locks of the Canal and a passage at nighttime through the still lake waters and floodlit jungles of the Isthmus, our first real sight of land was in Guayaquil, Ecuador. Some sightseeing was done from the ship because Guayaquil is an inland port. Chugging quietly up the river on a beautiful Sunday morning, we saw an inactive scene: the homes of people who live off commerce on the river. It was an initial glimpse at our reason for coming to Latin America, and I think these homes excited our curiosity more than thoughts of Guayaquil itself. The radio blared uninterpretable Spanish and then "The Anniversary Waltz" and Frankie Avalon's latest hit. Our ways of life are merging and affecting each other more than I had realized.

When we entered the inland harbor, we were met by banana barges carrying loads which our freighter would transport to

Chile. Waiting for the launches which would take us to shore, we watched the laborers stew chickens on the decks of their barges and carry two banana stalks at a time up a ramp and into the bowels of the ship. They raced in short, quick steps and hesitated momentarily under the weight of their loads with the slightest rolling of the ship until they regained their balance.

In Guayaquil we saw the elements of a typical Latin American city for the first time: the cathedral, the cemetery, the markets where the poor buy and sell, and the hotels where a few fortunate members of society are waited upon. We visited a factory and talked to the workers milling around outside. They were on strike. Just above them were their homes, thousands of squat, unpainted houses that looked like cardboard boxes from a distance. Many volunteers went into these areas and entered these homes after becoming chums with the children. Some of us heard Mass. Later aboard the ship I learned that 60 percent of the population of Guayaquil live in homes like these.

Two days later we arrived in Chimbote, Peru. The crew advised us that there was little to interest a tourist there, no fancy shops or historical monuments; yet in many ways it was ideal for our purposes. Chimbote seemed unaccustomed to tourists, as if it were not prepared for us. We caught the city engaged in its normal day, the fishermen draining their boats in the inner harbor, the fish fertilizer factory in full activity with a stench which was strong and metallic, and the parish priest making his daily calls on a motor scooter.

Some of us engaged the priest in conversation. He described to us the life of the people who live in the bamboo homes which cover acres and acres of downtown. Tuberculosis is frequent. Death often comes in childhood and those children who live must frequently depend on charity or state relief programs. Some of the girls went to the hospital and asked the nurses to show them around. Others went to the school and talked to the children and their teachers. Another group found a fellow American who was studying social changes in Latin America as a Fulbright scholar. He explained the phenomenal changes which had taken place in Chimbote in the last ten years.

Today there are more than 100,000 people in Chimbote. In 1951, there were only 5,000. The sudden migration is explained by budding steel and fishing industries and the new opportunities for work which they created. The migrants provide themselves with shelter by arriving en masse during the night, constructing their homes on factory property and presenting the owner with a fait accompli the following morning. Unfortunately the growth of public facilities has not kept up with the population. There is still only one hospital, with beds for sixty, and a medical center which treats a few dozen persons a day. Although Chimbote is an extreme case, it is typical of the convulsive changes shaking all Latin America today and of the challenges now being made to governments to deal justly with the large members of people who are forcing entry into the modern world.

The important thing to know about Chimbote is that it is a prosperous town. There is work there. "Boy wanted" signs in store windows are commonplace. The factories are expanding and probably more jobs will be created for future migrants. Perhaps the people live better now than previously, and this first step toward modernity is a cause for satisfaction because it means that the country is industrializing. Yet when we returned to the comfort of the ship we left something of ourselves behind. If we lived three hundred years ago it might not have fazed us, but somehow it seems incongruous for electric light bulbs and automobiles (all with American names) to exist besides acres of human beings living in primitive conditions. We are sufficiently endowed with a sense of American optimism to believe that technology means a better life for all.

At Sea—October 6, 1961

For Lima, Peru, some conventional sightseeing was slated. In our two-day stay, I wanted to capture much of the famous flavor of the past which lives there. I saw the old mansion of Victor Haya de la Torre, the Church of San Pedro and the University of San Marcos where tradition hangs heavy in the air. But there is no escaping contemporary problems in Lima, least of all at San Marcos. Some students drew us into conversation. They were convinced Castroites and on the student bulletin board I saw a colorful portrait of Mao Tse-Tung and the schedule of Radio Peking broadcasts.

"Why can't we be friends with Russia?" the students asked. Didn't we know that "the only practical way" out of the misery in

which their country finds itself is the Marxist way? I suppose I was
shocked by the extent to which our ideas on progress and freedom diverged. My fear of the aggressive nature of Communism,
its materialistic nature and its disregard for human rights meant
little to them. They told me it was better to suffer the abuses of
Communism than continue under present circumstances.

That night many of us returned early to the ship, anchored
twenty miles away in Callao. The day left little strength for
evening activities, so a surprising number of volunteers stayed on
the ship's veranda and talked. Their discussions were what I imagine most teachers dream about. Animated and informed, they
compared notes on a difficult subject which had assumed great
meaning for them. Of all the day's escapades I heard discussed,
one very funny anecdote emerged.

My friend Amos Roos, a volunteer of very unorthodox ways
with an insatiable curiosity for the details of any piece of construction and an abiding cynicism toward Latin American clergy,
found himself a new church being built in a wealthy section of
Lima. With the priest in charge, he went up the scaffolding a hundred feet or so to inspect the lavish works and then began asking
the good father if the money might not be spent on the poor. A
heated exchange took place and the scaffolding swayed to and fro
with the argument. Amos's companion, watching from below,
concluded that as always Amos had chosen an inopportune time
to enter into a discussion. Thanks to the patience of the *padre* and
the grace of God, they descended friends and Amos pedaled off
on his rented bicycle satisfied.

For their second day in Lima, some volunteers planned on
seeing the museums which hold keepsakes of the age of the Incas
and the times of Bolívar. They had made friends with an artist in
Lima who offered to be there, and they invited me along. Their
friend proved as interesting as the relics themselves, and in the
museums we would pause between the cases which held Bolívar's
gun or the flags flown round San Martín[1] and talk about modern

---

[1] Simón Bolívar (1783-1830) was, of course, the great liberator of northern
Latin America from Spanish rule. José de San Martín (1778-1850), called the
"Liberator of the South," defeated Spanish forces in Peru and Chile; he assigned
power in Chile to one of his ablest soldiers, Bernardo O'Higgins (1778-1842).

problems. Our host had been in the United States as a Guggenheim fellow. Besides being an artist, he was well-informed on many issues. He spoke English as well as Quechua, (one of the Indian dialects in Peru),[2] German, French and of course Spanish. Again I was impressed by the difference between him as a Peruvian intellectual and the intellectuals I had known in the United States. His views weren't so radical as those of the students, yet social and political conditions dominated his thinking. Even his theory of art was that it should provide a social function and serve the nation's needs. His appreciation of the natural culture, art and civilization of Peru was deep and proud.

If social problems preoccupied our friend, it was because he was surrounded by them. He told us of remote communities in the highlands of Peru where the people don't even know the word for bread, of babies born twisted by congenital diseases, of the injustice of the wealthy who built a club on the exact location where they had been asked to make social improvements. The reaction of some people toward our friend was to call him a Communist, but I think he gave us a hint of the real dilemma in his mind as we were parting. We were in the city square watching an old woman place her child in rags and hoist him on her back. He reeled away to say good-by and added, "I can no longer even look at the poverty of my people, but I do not know what to do." His look seemed to beg forgiveness for a step he was about to take—or for taking no step at all. I would guess that even the students at San Marcos, for all their baiting of us and despite their Marxist protestations, would admit that the idea which will both unite Peru in the work of the future and resonate its spiritual past has yet to rise to the surface of the national consciousness.

At Sea—October 9, 1961

As I write you this letter, we are between Antofagasta and Chañaral, Chile. Our visits to Arica and Antofagasta, two cities on the northern coast of the Chilean desert, have impressed us with the extent to which Chile is different from other countries we have seen. There is a minimal Indian population there, 200,000 out of

---

[2] Quechua is not a dialect, as I later learned, but an indigenous language, indeed a family of languages.

over seven million. The homes appear more prosperous and well kept, the shoeshine boys are less insistent and the poor seem to have an extra set of clothes. When people pass, they wave in a manner which is more open and friendly than in other countries.

Some volunteers are asking now whether it is right to come to Chile to work when other countries are more in need. The average annual income of Chile is almost three times that of Bolivia. Sixty-five percent of the population is literate. Some say the threat of Communism is greatest where there is wide discontent, where the social conditions of the people are most backward and depressing, and that this is where the Peace Corps ought to be. However, we learned at Notre Dame that beneath the more pleasant superficials, Chile has social problems of major proportions. Also, Communist activity in Chile is greater than in any of the poorer countries. One would think that the Communists would work where the need is greatest also, but they are more pragmatic than that. With a higher standard of living, Chile has tasted progress and is desirous for more. With greater literacy, the population is more accessible to propaganda from Havana, Moscow and Peking. It is naive to believe that a country will avoid misery and then try to go no farther. The major part of Chile's development still lies ahead, and the Communists still feel that they have the best way to hasten the process. The issue is joined in Chile, and I don't think that the United States will abandon a friend once she has ventured into the stream we helped convince her to cross.

                    Love,
                    Tommy

Chapter 3

DISCOVERING CHILE: THE TOO-LEISURELY LIFE AT LO VÁSQUEZ

The volunteers settle down for training with our host organization, Instituto de Educación Rural, and encounter an unexpected difficulty: The IER is not really ready for the Peace Corps!

October 12, 1961

Dear Mom, Dad and Jim,

A t 6 A.M. yesterday morning, I awoke suddenly. The stilling of the ship's motors—like a noise—roused me from sleep. I dressed quickly and rushed to the top deck in time to watch us drift into the harbor of Valparaiso. Very few volunteers were on hand to witness that moment because it was so early. At first, it was dark and the hills of the city were lit like Christmas trees left burning through the night. Then the sun rose over my shoulder, above the point where the hills and sea met at the edge of the cove, and we knew this would be the first sunny day we had enjoyed in a week.

Some government officials and newspapermen came out on a launch to meet our ship and accompanied us to the dock. Until 10 in the morning, there were interviews with them. When our papers were found to be in order and all luggage had been removed, the ship's gangplank was lowered and the group descended quietly to the land. There were no fanfares, no heckling, no confusion. We filed past a curious and friendly crowd into an waiting bus, and we waved from there. When the last member of our party was off the ship, the gangplank was raised and the bus roared away.

We went through customs smoothly, in part thanks to Don Jaime Larraín, who is president of the Institute of Rural Education with which we will be working and who was once a candidate for the Chilean presidency. He ran through the customs house with the frenzy and solicitude of a mother hen caring for a brood of forty-five. Unbelievably soon, we were on the road to Lo Vásquez and the school of the Institute where we will live for the next six weeks. It was the first time we were on the road and not at sea or in a coastal town for over a month, and the valleys and trees were green and exciting, especially because they were part of the central valley of Chile where our work will begin.

We arrived in Lo Vásquez in time for a quick look at our new surroundings before lunch. The school is situated on a hill which slopes up into a high mountain. Next door is a Spanish church and courtyard. In back of the school there is a *campesino's* house (*campesino* is the word used for the poor, small farmer). This man keeps the animals and grounds belonging to the church. His adobe home is without floors; and his children, while friendly and healthy looking, seem to have very few clothes.

A richly rewarding exercise which we all enjoy a great deal here is to climb the mountain. At different levels along the way there is a shrine, a pasture for horses and endless species of flora and fauna which we have not seen before. Once on top, we can view an entire range of mountains, and the school, the church and the highway look tiny down in the valley. It is the end of the rainy season now and the landscape is very green, reminding me of the countryside of home except that the mountains seem taller, contain palm as well as poplar trees and their slopes are less marked by farms, homes and roads.

The school at Lo Vásquez is built on one level and is rectangular. At each end of the building, there is a dormitory with bunk beds. In the center are two open-air courtyards leading from the dormitories. The two courtyards are separated from each other by classrooms, offices and the dining hall. The girl volunteers have one of the dormitories, the men the other. Both sleeping quarters lack room for storage, Twenty-eight men must find space for themselves and their luggage in a room which is 100 feet by 40 feet. I live out of a suitcase and a briefcase stashed under my bunk bed. The bathroom adjoining each dorm is large and resembles those you find in bus stations in the United States, except that the bus station usually has hot water.

I am writing this letter in one of the classrooms. Tonight it is 40 degrees here at the base of the mountain. Because there is no heating of any kind in the building, the temperature inside matches the outside air. I am seated in a heavy coat at a row of unpainted wood tables. A dim, bare light bulb dangles from the ceiling, and I am feeling a great affinity with the monks who worked in the cold preserving the sacred texts in ancient monasteries. Life on the "new frontier" in the Peace Corps is also similar to life on the frontiers of the Old West. There is no hot water. Drinking water is dangerous, and beer or coffee takes its place. The comparison could go further. The community effort at chores, the bunkhouse atmosphere with trunks arranged in the center for card playing, the style of dress and the guitar players recall our country's past.

Tonight Mr. Langford made it clear that the boat trip had ended and that a new, more important stage of our experience had begun. This is fine with me. In the Peace Corps I would rather live simply than in the luxury of an ocean liner. The sense of purpose of the entire group is reasserting itself tonight. The other volunteers also made the adjustment from the ship to Lo Vásquez gladly, from too much food served in exquisite style to the chow line of the school; from heated cabins cleaned twice daily by a steward to a barracks lacking any source of heat but the sun which is sometimes stingy in the early spring and which puts in only a twelve-hour day.

And so our in-country training begins. In six weeks' time, I must learn some skill of which I am ignorant at present and teach it in a language which I seem further from mastering each day. I really hope that we can accomplish something tangible so that our mission does not result in an empty gesture of friendship.

October 26, 1961

It is difficult to find time to write a letter. Chileans are constantly interrupting the day with meals. They have a light breakfast of coffee and bread and a very time-consuming, full course dinner at lunchtime. Around five in the afternoon, Chileans serve *onces*, a snack similar to English tea. *Onces* (literally "elevens") includes a hot drink, bread and eggs, cheese or whatever else is available. Many times *onces* could substitute for the evening meal, though it rarely does. Between this 5 o'clock meal and dinner is the only free period in the day here. Yet we never know how much time we have. Dinner in Chile can be served at 8:30, or even 10:30, and there is no way of telling which it will be on any given day.

Other than the meal schedules and what can be learned from a few casual friends, we have learned little about Chile here at the school. The first two weeks of the training program have been slow, and the best opportunities we have had to learn about the people and the Institute of Rural Education have come when we left Lo Vásquez for the neighboring cities. We all make occasional sorties into Valparaiso, and from there Viña del Mar is only a mile away. "Valpo," as Americans conveniently dub the port, is a city of hills, a sailor's harbor, enchanting to look at day or night. From many points within the city a complete view of the harbor is attainable, and the traffic of the ships always seems close at hand. Viña del Mar is just north of Valparaiso's city limits. Some of Chile's finest beaches, best hotels and most beautiful residential sections are there as well as the world-famous Casino where millions of dollars are gambled away each year.

The trip to Valpo, a twenty-mile run, takes an hour by bus. Even aboard the bus, I enjoy observing the people. The other day I learned that Chileans have little regard for fixed schedules. The bus driver jerked to a halt every ten minutes, sometimes to talk, sometimes to pick up someone in the middle of the road. Then he stopped before a small restaurant and nodded to two men seated in the front of the vehicle. One descended to buy a pack of cigarettes; the other to use a little room in the back, and none of the other riders complained of the delay.

Another way to travel to Valparaiso is on the back of the truck entrusted to the Peace Corps by the Institute. I traveled this way one day along with some girl volunteers attired in cocktail dresses, thin high heels and stylish coiffures. The girls jumped down in the main street of town, causing a stir; and I was explaining all day that this was really not the normal way for girls to travel in the United States. On the return trip that evening, the cold night air had settled and the girls had been replaced by a flock of chickens. That night I decided that going by bus was a better way to observe the people.

Most volunteers have become friends with individual families in Valpo and Viña and visit them when they can. The basketball coach at the Catholic University in Valparaiso, Juan Yovanovich, came to visit me the other day. He is also biddy basketball commissioner in Chile and since biddy basketball[1] originated in Scranton, he was anxious to meet me. When some other volunteers and I repaid his call last Saturday, he introduced us to his students, who sang and danced for us all evening.

Yesterday was our first visit to Santiago, the nation's capital. Early in the morning we began a bus trip along winding paved roads and crossed the mountains separating Santiago and Valparaiso. We could view the scenery from over a thousand feet; and farms, irrigation systems and livestock stretched before us for miles and miles.

Our first stop in Santiago was La Moneda, Chile's White House, where we tried unsuccessfully to see the president. However we did tour the house, reputed to be the most beautiful building in Santiago. Our bus tour of the city continued past the country club, the racetracks, and factories, the homes of the rich, and the homes of laborers. It ended atop San Cristóbal hill and, from the patio of a restaurant there, the entire city of 1,500,000 people came into view. In the restaurant, the Institute treated us to Chilean wine for the first time, and I made my first attempt to digest an *empanada*, a tart of meat, olives and onions cooked in grease. It is the symbol of Chilean cuisine, but in my opinion is far from the best item on the list of delicious national foods.

On the way down San Cristóbal hill, the Andes came into view and the sight of Santiago hemmed in by massive dark blue hulks of earth coated with snow sent a ripple of "ohs" and "ahs" down the bus. Then we rolled into an agricultural show in Santiago where many interesting facets of Chilean farming were demonstrated. I enjoyed especially the exhibit of Chilean prize horses with their stocky bodies and short legs, supposedly ideal for the terrain. But the most interesting attraction at the fair was the exhibit of the Institute of Rural Education (IER). It presented a model home for *campesinos*. Luxurious for them, it looked like a log stable to me. The home was furnished with chairs, tables and cabinets built by students of the IER. Skirts and sweaters woven by the girl students

---

[1] Biddy basketball is analogous to Little League baseball.

were also on display. Outside were wheelbarrows, a spinning wheel and chicken coops, all made by hand, and a model vegetable garden was planted economically and scientifically in the back. Periodically members of the Institute staff would appear on a raised platform and perform the *cueca*, Chile's national dance.

A great throng of people gathered to see the Institute's exhibit. It seemed that the displays of farm machinery and heavy equipment bored many people and that the human touch of the Institute provided the best show there. The staff of the Institute was extremely interested in meeting the *voluntarios*, as we are known. They were patient with our poor Spanish and anxious to show us around. I think I will enjoy working with them for the next two years.

After the exhibition, we traveled to a small town named Malloco and the IER school where future staff members are trained. The students there are eighteen and nineteen years old. They gave us a heartwarming welcome and then trounced us in volleyball. (Wait till we get our sneakers!) Then they served an *onces* of hot chocolate, a rare beverage here, in a room decorated in our honor. After *onces*, the students presented a prepared entertainment. Two comedians bantered back and forth in incomprehensible Spanish, but they were very funny anyway. A Peruvian boy with a long reserved face and a beautiful voice sang Indian folk songs. He was followed by a combo of accordion, guitar and bongo drums. It was a rare chance to observe real folk culture. We reciprocated with the Charleston and Rock 'n Roll, and soon the students were rockin' with our girls. When it was time to leave they sang the theme song of the Institute, *"De Pie Campesino,"* (roughly translated, "Arise, Farmer" or "On Your Feet!") of which I understood only one word, *amigo*, but that was an encouraging one. We shook hands, and called *hasta la vista*. As the bus backed out of the school, at least twenty people ran alongside yelling directions from the ground. Then we were on our way back home.

Experiences like these preoccupy us in these first days, and each day brings promises of even richer ones. So far we have received more than we have given. Except for several bouts with dysentery and a constant case of shivers, we have paid little. Most importantly, we have gained a better understanding of the Chilean people.

We have learned that more than a common interest in Chile's social problems is necessary to have successful relationships with the people. Chileans are more interested in showing you the sights than discussing the plight of the *campesinos*. They are more strongly nationalistic than we are. Although they do not resent our coming, or deny that Chile needs programs like that of the Institute, they seem to regret that Chile needs a Peace Corps in the first place. Consequently it is best to speak of our goals in terms of increasing understanding between the two nations. When we arrived, Ed Tisch made a statement to a reporter that the American people, especially students, were interested in Latin America and wanted them to understand us. This remark made headlines. Another volunteer spoke of fighting misery and this statement warranted only discreet mention in the press.

One of the best ways of gaining the confidence of the Chilean people, as strange or natural as this may seem, is to accept their hospitality. The Chilean's inborn solicitude for guests will make it impossible to live in circumstances as difficult as we had envisioned.

Finally we have learned that someone interested in helping a nation to modernize must appreciate the quality of the people's lives as they live them today. There are many aspects of life in Chile which we can envy. They are less dependent on modern conveniences than we are and many of them know how to care for animals and till the land. Without television, Chileans entertain themselves. There are plenty of skilled guitarists in Chile and almost everyone sings respectably. Children have hobbies based on inexpensive items like stamp collecting, and they make toys from pieces of metal or boxes which we throw away. There is a fierce interest in languages in Chile, and teenagers from lower middle class homes have thrown American slang in my direction as well as fully formed sentences pronounced with a British accent.

Above all, Chileans allow more time for visiting each other. They are generous with their friends and a meal for one or two persons seems to require no sacrifice of them at all.

November 8, 1961
There is very little good news to report for the past two weeks. To begin with, our in-country training program has suffered from lack of prolonged contact with the Chilean people, and I fear this has led to a lack of understanding of the Peace Corps in Chile.

This morning we were visited by two students of the Chilean-North American Cultural Institute, and they made it clear that there are questions which Chileans would like to ask about the Peace Corps. Were we hypercritical of Chile? Were we more interested in helping the people or in making good impressions? Were we trying to Americanize the people? These questions come from friend and foe alike. A few days ago, a group of volunteers gave an interview to some reporters from *El Siglo*, the Communist newspaper, after they claimed they represented a different publication. The reporters asked pointed and difficult questions, saying that the Peace Corps had come to deceive the people and spy on them. However, they did quote the volunteers exactly; and one who read the account of the interview in *El Siglo* could see that there was no basis for the charges made in its headline. The volunteers simply insisted that they were there to help the people and when a politically explosive question was asked, they declined to express an opinion.

Another problem here is that the course is not well-organized. The Institute intended to prepare us for positions on its staff during these days and was supposed to arrange the course and to instruct us in the crafts and technical knowledge which we will need in the field. However, arrangements were made for only a few speakers a day; and these are one-shot affairs which do not constitute a complete course in anything. Rather our speakers repeat each other endlessly, and they invariably arrive late, upsetting our schedule for the day without seeming to care. Some do not come at all.

Even though these speakers repeat themselves, we are anxious to hear their lectures because they are the best class in the Spanish language which we have all day. Otherwise, there is little to advance our knowledge of Spanish. Classes in Spanish are conducted; but the Institute and Peace Corps all failed to see the need for "native speakers" as we had at Notre Dame who lived with us and spoke Spanish constantly. Here in Lo Vásquez we lapse into English whenever we are speaking to each other, which is the major part of the day.

This poorly organized course is a setback not so much in time as in spirit. The group is restless and wants to go into the *zona* (the Institute's word for the rural areas). We want to accomplish something after being talked to for four months. Despite gallant efforts by Mr. Langford and some volunteers to keep things moving, it is hard to avoid boredom. Review sessions of what we learned at Notre Dame were organized, as was a Halloween based on Chilean mythology and spooks, but generally spirit is at an all-time ebb.

The main problem with this training program is that no hint has been given to any of the volunteers as to what their work will be. This makes even preparation on their own difficult. The Institute maintains that we do not have to be experts in any one thing. In fact, it fears that the distance between the United States farm technician and a small farmer working with primitive means would be too great to allow for communication. According to the Institute, anyone with a good capacity to learn could carry out the work assigned to him after brief but intensive training. However, the work of the Institute ranges from graphic art for a magazine to inoculating hogs, and before we know which function we will perform we cannot train ourselves for anything.

Sometimes the volunteers' disenchantment with the poor administration of the Institute reaches the point of rebellion. Strangely enough, it was our girls who acted first. As a result there is a vast difference between the food we had today and what was served a week ago, and a very interesting story lies behind the change.

For the first month in Lo Vásquez we did not eat very well, and a general malaise settled over the entire group. The only milk we had was in tea. Only at lunch was there a small piece of meat. Potatoes, rice and bread made up most of every meal. One supper consisted of two soups, and the main ingredient in one was bread. The home economists and nurses studied the diet and decided that the men were not receiving enough protein and that no one was getting enough vitamins. This was not a matter of poor care by Chileans, because the Peace Corps was responsible for our food budget here; it was poor administration and planning by the particular member of the Institute staff in charge of the kitchen. The girls were extremely reluctant to offend this individual. Certainly they did not want to see American food served. In fact they themselves wanted to learn to shop and prepare Chilean meals. Using this as a pretext, the girls moved into the kitchen. And things have improved! With the same budget, they have prepared smaller meals which leave us satisfied. Fred Morgner lost twenty pounds since arriving here, and he is already regaining his normal weight. It was his girlfriend, Ramona Marotz, who led the expedition into the kitchen.

The lesson is that you cannot serve a poor diet to nutrition experts and expect them to do nothing about it. It also means that when Chile has an immense shortage of forestry experts and only one nurse for every four doctors, graduate nurses and foresters should not be expected to fritter their time away. It also means that immense damage will be done to the enthusiasm in non-skilled volunteers who came here to do a job and are asked to sit on their hands.

At the moment when we needed encouragement most, Mr. Sargent Shriver arrived in Lo Vásquez during his tour of Latin American Peace Corps projects. In an hour-and-a-half session with him yesterday, we discussed our relationship with the Institute. Mr. Shriver stressed the Peace Corps policy that all volunteers serve under national institutions and take orders from them. We replied that we certainly wanted to be a part of the IER but that there were further questions to be asked. Did the Institute have a place for us? Must we do nothing when the Institute fails to provide work or prepare us for it? We believe we will be effective within the Institute only if it respects the potential contribution we can make and not if it regards us merely as an increase in manpower or as helpers without a mind of our own. In the opinion of some, the best way to gain the respect of the Institute is to show that if they do not use us properly we will find use for our time.

Mr. Shriver's visit accomplished a great deal yesterday. Underneath his gay, urbane veneer, he is a very practical and inspiring leader. He understood our problem, yet he encouraged us not to make any final judgments at this early stage. When he left, the spirits of all the volunteers had been buoyed. Mr. Shriver suggested that these might be the days when culture shock was setting in. According to one definition, culture shock is when the faults of the national character bother you more than they should. The inexact, easy-going Latin American way of life has some advantages over our precision schedules and sense of rush, but it can be disconcerting. One day last week, none of our scheduled lecturers were present for their classes, yet twenty unexpected guests arrived for dinner. When these things are more disconcerting than they really should be, when the cold sets in, when we are unduly bothered because no one has arrived to fix the water pump, it could be our own failure to adjust.

November 15, 1961

I am afraid that in my doldrums last week I failed to explain that this course does have a bright side. The mere fact that it is in Spanish prevents its being as tightly organized as the one at Notre Dame because listening to a foreign language is a doubly frustrating and exhausting effort. To show you how trying it can become: The other day Mary Ellen Craig was talking to a Chilean friend when she suddenly burst out crying for no apparent reason. Her friends rushed up to her and an embarrassed Mary Ellen admitted that she was so frustrated by her inability to express all her thoughts in Spanish that she could not control her tears.

Our ability to understand Spanish has progressed noticeably during the lectures. We also learn new words and verbal constructions from our speakers. When the speaker of the day does not show, volunteers have time to study those parts of the language where they are weak. This is important because learning a language is really a very personal affair, a contest between mind and will. The will is filled with the desire to learn but the mind is vacant of the nerve connections and reflex actions which turn thoughts into Spanish words. No course, no teacher can assure a person's victory. Basically it is up to the individual.

When I find someone to talk to in Spanish, someone who does not understand English, I consider this my most important class of the day; now I can communicate almost anything to anyone who has patience to listen. When there is no one to speak with, I talk to myself out loud. I find a place on the mountain where no one can hear me, and I speak the same phrases over and over again, loudly, until I have mastered a new form of the past tense, a new word or a new idiom. One day I became so absorbed that when I put down my book to rest my eyes and throat, I found myself surrounded by a group of curious cows standing there chewing on their cuds and staring at me as if to say that even a cow shouldn't moo unless there is another cow around.

Another redeeming feature of this training program is a course organized by Mr. Langford and Ed Tisch. They gathered all the Peace Corps technicians and prepared a series of talks for the non-skilled volunteers. These talks sometimes last for two hours and are so interesting that everyone comes to them. The nurses are learning about watersheds; the foresters about cattle and the husbandry experts about root crops, soils and grapes. For the volunteers who have no skills, the talks give a general orientation to the terms used in farming and an appreciation of farmer's needs. If I do not have a specific assignment for which to train, this kind of preview is the next best thing. Listening to our experts talk about farming makes me appreciate for the first time the highly developed state of United States agriculture. When I return home, I want to visit one of those fabulous American farms to which I have been living so close all these years.

One very faithful teacher in this training program has given me an idea of what I might do in coming months in Chile. Mr. Winifred McElroy from the United States AID Mission in Santiago has been giving a course in community development theory to us. "Community development" work involves encouraging local groups of *campesinos* to work together on common problems. I sincerely believe that my most fruitful work could be done in this kind of endeavor. Working in community development, I could learn about farm matters gradually, as I need to know them for each specific project. And I could put into service whatever experiences I had in the United States. Needless to say community development requires real proficiency in the language, but I believe that this will come in time. The other day Mr. Langford hinted that I will be given a community development assignment.

Life at Lo Vásquez has provided some interesting experiences with the *delegados*, the community development workers whom the IER sends into the field. This has helped us to appreciate the Institute more. Lo Vásquez is near a rural sector served by the Institute, and *delegados* stop at the school for rest, supplies and for meetings. I attended one afternoon session which they held under a tree on the mountain. They were planning activities for the "week of the *campesino*," which the Institute has succeeded in making a national occasion in Chile. This year's event is scheduled for next week when I will make my first visit to the *zona*.

On the agenda of that meeting were other items of Institute business. The *delegados* discussed a campaign to sell the *campesinos* better seeds for corn. A plan through which *campesinos* can purchase radios and sewing machines at cost was also reviewed. The *delegados* prepared to sign contracts with rural schoolteachers who will utilize the broadcasts of the Institute's "radio school" in their classrooms. Finally a drive was outlined to allow more farmers to subscribe to the Institute's educational periodicals.

I was impressed by these *delegados* and by what their programs would mean to the people if they were successful. Later that day, I met the national leader of the organization of *delegados* within the Institute. Juanita Carrasco is a young woman with a strong body, beautiful face and clear, dancing eyes. She has a logical and supple mind which is not unladylike. Juanita is a very gracious and polite daughter of *campesino* parents. She is not just a Chilean *campesino*; she identifies with the rural masses all over Latin America. She has visited her rural counterparts in Colombia, traveled with them on foot through the highlands of Peru and attended international conferences convoked in their behalf. Juanita has seen misery in her travels and in her home. She knows that not all attempts to help her people are sincere. Yet she is not bitter or extreme. While she is dedicated to raising the standard of living of her people, she appreciates their life as they live it today. She said she is glad that the *campesinos* are strong and have to work hard.

Finally, these weeks at Lo Vásquez have included excursions into the *zona* to meet the rural people. The volunteers travel with the students who are being trained as future *delegados* in Malloco. My turn has not come yet, but I have benefited from the visits made by others. When the volunteers come back on Sunday night, tired, dusty and happy, they go into session with the entire group and describe their experiences.

Jim Coleman, one of the first to go into the *zona*, recalled being very impressed by the Institute workers with whom he traveled. On Friday night, he and his counterpart met with a sparse crowd of farmers who would not listen to each other talk. By Sunday, the students had shaped the farmers into an earnest group in the process of organizing as a community. Emory Tomor proudly counted fifty flea bites. Dan McCarthy told of drinking wine mixed with sheep's blood offered to him in an intimate gesture of friendship by a *campesino* after Dan had helped him slaughter some sheep. Gerry Garthe described his difficulties vaccinating chickens. This is difficult on a farm where there are no chicken coops because you have to catch the birds before vaccinating them.

One universal impression of these volunteers is that the *campesinos* think Americans are know-it-alls. The other evening a woman brought a child sick with an incurable disease here to the school because she felt sure our nurses could help her. The *campesinos* also think that we sing like the singers on the North American records they hear. When Emory Tomor arrived at a meeting, he discovered that his appearance had been advertised in advance and that he had been billed as a North American ballad singer. Emory is one of those people who knows neither the music nor the words to songs. Undaunted he invented his own lyrics and plucked the guitar a few times feeling he had wormed his way out of the situation until the people requested translations for those "beautiful songs" he had just sung. After hearing experiences like these in the *zona*, I look forward to my first adventure there with some trepidation.

November 22, 1961

Yesterday I received my assignment. I will be stationed in the province of Osorno in which the city called Osorno is the capital. I will be in an Institute school located in Rupanco, some thirty miles south of the town. Although I will live in the school, my work will be in community development. The Peace Corps volunteer accompanying me is Gerry Garthe. He will teach in the school. Gerry is an expert forester and knows a great deal about vegetables and animals as well. He will be my source of technical information. Gerry will be a fine person to be with in Osorno. The only drawback is that he belongs to a different political party in the United States than I do, but that seems to matter less and less as we get farther south.

I could tell you a great deal about the province of Osorno and the work of the Institute already, but on-the-spot descriptions are better and there is plenty of time. Suffice it to say that Osorno is in the southern lake region where water is more plentiful because it rains constantly. Here in the north, the land is so dry that it seems to be turning to sand. Yet the poverty of the small farmers can be worse in Osorno than around Lo Vásquez, so I am not expecting a paradise.

Some people have advised me not to write home about the hardships of our work, but I am not sure this is a good idea. If there are any real discomforts, I am ready for them and anxious to learn from them. You have been very understanding of my intentions all along and know that the Peace Corps entails difficulties, so I'm not going to paint any rosy pictures. If I go without a shower for a week or sleep in a hovel, I'll tell you about it. Somehow these things fit into a different perspective down here. In achieving this perspective, our understanding of human nature can grow.

Let me tell you about my first experiences in the *zona*. Twelve volunteers left Lo Vásquez around four o'clock last Friday for

Malloco, and I was among them. When we arrived, the students were still going through their daily routine. Attending a class on cooperatives with them, I noticed that no one was taking notes and that there was a constant undercurrent during the class because the students were buzzing with enthusiasm for the coming weekend. After class, each volunteer talked with the students with whom he would be working over the weekend. Then we ate a dinner of barley, peas and bread and drank water from a community glass.We stayed at the school Friday evening and, after a closer inspection of the grounds than during our last visit, we retired for the evening. All the volunteers slept in sleeping bags on the floor of two rooms about the size of a freshman's room in a university.

On Saturday morning we rose at six o'clock and took the cold shower which is a tradition at the school. (Not only do cold showers make you miserable, they do not make you clean.) Then we waited two hours for breakfast. After a bowl of hot rice, some cheese, and a cup of green tea mixed with milk which had been burned, we were off for the *zona*. The sixty-five students and volunteers were packed into a bus, and teams of eight were dropped off at various communities along the way. As we wheezed along this backcountry road, the group dwindled to the eight of us going to Loica Arriba for the weekend. There were six students, a fellow volunteer from Tennessee named Larry Forrester and myself on our team. We were led by a short, hunchbacked fellow named Pedro who is "Don Pedro" to the local residents because they respect him very much.

Just before lunch we arrived at the home of one of the most prosperous small property owners in the area, our headquarters for the weekend. This independent small farmer had a three-acre lemon orchard, some chickens, cows and sheep, many crops and even a truck which is the real sign of prosperity among the *campesinos*. His home, made from adobe, was without electricity or hot water but was big and roomy. He immediately took us on a tour of his farm and it was there that I had to endure the most difficult moment of the entire weekend. When we arrived in his lemon orchard, he promptly offered me the biggest lemon I had ever seen—to be eaten right there. I tried to eat the lemon with a straight face and pretend I was really enjoying it. This would have been impossible without the pressure of onlooking faces. I ate all but two sections without squinting and then my friend from Tennessee arrived and I generously

offered him the rest of the lemon while raving how delicious it was
to my proud host.

Since this was the *"la semana del campesino"*—the week of the
farmer—throughout Chile, the people were gathered at the local
schoolhouse in fiestas, and it was difficult to visit them in their
homes. However, we were able to visit two families. By our standards, their homes were extremely depressed. They were poorly furnished, with cheap drawings and plaster of Paris artifacts on the
walls. The rooms in the home were not all connected to each other;
and a separate, shack-like structure contained the kitchen. Yet the
people could not have been nicer. They offered us white wine mixed
with strawberries, *borgoña*, a favorite drink in Loica Arriba.

Later, six girl students of the Institute arrived with dishes and
food for lunch. The girls prepared noodles, peas and the strongest-
tasting fish soup I have ever had. Their dishes resembled basins more
than dinnerware, and there was no liquid chaser. But the lemon had
quenched my thirst for a few days to come. After lunch, we waited
for an hour (hour delays are as common in Chile as coffee breaks in
the United States) and then began walking to the school where the
afternoon's festivities would be held. As we passed the home of
another property owner, we were invited for more of the strawberry
drink (it sounds less potent that way) and then transported the rest
of the way to the school on the back of our host's truck. During the
trip I saw proof of the drought afflicting Chile this spring. The dust
on the road was inches thick and the truck left behind a screen of
dust which hung over the road like a heavy fog.

On Saturday afternoon the crowd was composed mostly of
women, teenagers and small children. This was not because women
enjoy fiestas more than the men, but because the men had to work
in the fields during the day. It is said that the *campesina* women are
very difficult to lure away from their homes. They spend fourteen
hours a day working and become lost in a rut of drudgery. Although
they had only a passive interest in the happenings of the day on
Saturday, they definitely did enjoy themselves. However, I noticed
very few women speaking at great length with each other. The men
were different when they arrived later on. They enjoyed talking to
each other but were not comfortable discussing their problems in a
group. Probably the main objective of the Institute is to break

through this individualism. It is as difficult as it is well-advised.

Entertainment was scheduled to begin at three o'clock in the afternoon. It began at five. The show included a comedy act by Don Pedro, a local girl reciting a Spanish poem beautifully and resonantly, the gusto singing of the girl students of the IER and the discordant chorus of the local gentry. Afterward there was *onces* where I had my first taste of *aguardiente*, a strong Chilean liquor, and a very rich cake called a *torta* baked by the schoolmaster's wife—local people, local dress, local foods and Ray Conniff's "Serenade in Blue" coming from the radio on the table.

In the evening, the men came in from the fields and danced the *cueca*, the national dance which the Institute is trying desperately to preserve. The students started the dancing, and to my surprise the people joined in. The *cueca* is a flirt dance in which the boy and girl skip around each other delicately waving a handkerchief to the music. The steps are geared to the singing, which on this occasion sounded like an African funeral chant. I think it was just the singers. A complete *cueca* consists of three disconnected parts and in none of them do the participants join hands. Nonetheless, it is a very graceful dance; and it isn't until you attempt the *cueca* that you realize how difficult it is. I tried later in the evening and my lack of success was the *campesinos'* delight. Anything for my country.

The couples danced into the night which is a little more noticeable where there is no electricity. Soon you could see only the hint of a white handkerchief waving in the air and the red glow of cigarettes fixed tightly in the dancers' lips. They then lit three candles and continued dancing as we went outside where the trucks that bore the people to the fiesta were lined up like hay wagons outside a jamboree. We climbed aboard our truck and headed home and the party continued.

We had dinner with Padre Domínguez, who had come to say Mass in Loica the next morning. The *campesinos* in Loica have a priest to conduct church services only once a month. We reviewed the events of the day with him and discussed what could be improved in the following day's activities. Everyone was obviously pleased with the success of Saturday of *la semana del campesino*. Because it was late, our conversation ended with the meal itself and Father left the table for a sofa in the adjoining room while we unrolled our sleeping bags on the dusty floor beneath the crumbs of bread and empty wine bottles left on the table.

Sunday is not spent that differently in the *zona* than anywhere else. Just as on so many Sundays at home, I awoke, washed, dressed and became a little bored waiting for the trip up the road to church. It was the same ritual you were performing, probably at the same time. However, this trip was made in the back of a truck, the services were held in an outdoor field, and people came on foot, horseback and in carts pulled by oxen. This open-air Mass was part of the festival and the most colorful moment of the weekend. Loica Arriba (Upper Loica) and Loica Abajo (Lower Loica) merge for religious services. The *campesinos* came in opposite directions up and down the narrow road until they approached each other as if they would collide and turned into the entrance of the field. The cowboys, *huasos*, rode in on short, well-groomed horses. They dressed in their distinctive attire: a bright striped *chamanto* or half-poncho, covering their shoulders, and a black, broad-brimmed sombrero on their head. Singing *campesino* families arrived in carts pulled sometimes by two teams of oxen. The oxen were unmanageable and dumb and had flowers in their horns. They wanted to go anywhere but forward but the people in the carts didn't seem to mind. They left everything to a small boy who ran ahead with a long pointed stick and egged the animals on.

During Mass, the people clustered before the altar and the rim of the crowd was formed by the *huasos* who remained on horseback. They reminded me of the ever present group of men standing in the back of our churches, except that they were more attentive. Padre Domínguez preached a sermon I secretly entitled "Christ and Community Development." The Lord wants people to come together, he said; that is why there are community religious services on Sundays. When people get together, they should find solutions to common problems. After church, breakfast was served from community pots cooked over an open fire in the field. I watched *campesinos* bring their tools to the priest to be blessed, and it seemed, for a minute, that I was living hundreds of years ago.

The weekend continued with a feast in the schoolhouse that afternoon. Three sheep had been slaughtered the day before, and the wine was so plentiful that there were more jugs than glasses. Certain men were designated to keep circulating through the crowd with a pitcher of wine and one glass, filling and refilling the glass until everyone had had a healthy swallow. I managed to avoid them most of the afternoon but when I looked up and found an arm extended to me with a glass at the end of it, it was impossible to refuse. You do not have to drink much, a sip if that is all you desire, and then pass the rest to the fellow on your right.

Since our community was the farthest away from Malloco, we were the first to climb aboard the truck. This meant leaving the party early in the afternoon. At each stop on the road back to the school, we were greeted by crowds saying good-by to the students and volunteers who had spent the weekend in their communities. Some communities were engaged in soccer matches, others were inside dancing or reclining around improvised tables set up outdoors. By the time we approached the school, sixty-five of us had clambered aboard one truck. The volunteers jumped off at a point on the highway where we could wait for a bus to Lo Vásquez some two or three hours away. A midnight supper was waiting for us there, served by friends who didn't seem to mind our soiled clothes or unshaven faces.

How's that sound for a weekend? Fascinating? Well yes; but I must admit that it was an effort every inch of the way—to meet the people, to speak the language and to adjust to strange customs. It is not easy for me to understand the *campesinos*. I have been in the habit, subconscious though it might have been, of assuring myself that if I were in their situation I would be different or find a way out. Now I realize that any one born in the same circumstances would have the tattered clothes and the dust of the road caked on his feet. He would have the abscessed tooth which had to be pulled because there was no dentist, leaving him with dark gaps in his smile for the rest of his life. Now when I see a toothless mother and her child together, I realize that their relationship is the same as between my mother and me. This is the difficult and important first step. Otherwise our work would be motivated by pity not by human respect.

Love,
Tommy

Chapter 4

JOURNEY TO THE
PROVINCE OF OSORNO

*The volunteers disperse throughout the country. Our team goes to
the Osorno region where we meet our future co-workers and
encounter the stunning beauty of the landscape. And I, the philosopher, encounter for the first time my limitations in the practical
world of farming.*

Christmas Week, 1961

Dear Mom, Dad and Jim,

In this week between Christmas and New Year's we are working
so hard that we forget it is a week of celebrations in the United
States. Mr. Langford is interviewing all of us personally and at
great length. In my two-hour session with him, I made two requests:
that he send me back to Osorno and that he send a girl with me. A
girl is needed because only a woman can talk to the people about
health, diet and cleanliness. In this culture, a man does not talk
about these matters unless he is a doctor or health specialist.

This week the volunteers are recognizing that the original
Peace Corps idea of working directly under a national institution
and with a counterpart from the host country will not be as easy
as planned. We also realize that we will be made use of only if we
assert ourselves more often and make some demands. All this has
come out in the reports we are making to Mr. Langford and to the
Institute. The volunteers who were teachers in the schools have
stressed that the schools should exemplify good hygiene and diet,

but that they do not at the present time. The community development workers are preparing a critical statement about the organization of the Institute effort in the rural communities by the *delegados*. Even the nurses have complained that the Institute still has
no clear idea of how it will use them in the future and that,
although we were received very kindly at our work sites, our uti-
lization as part of the Institute team had not been prepared. This
does not mean that the policy of working with national institutions seems unwise or that we regret being with the Institute. After
the past month, we are proud to associate ourselves with IER and
especially with the individuals within it.

An issue which loomed important but not divisive when we
returned was a religious one. Many volunteers, especially the
Catholics, were concerned that the Institute seemed heavily dominated by the Church or at least oriented toward Christianity.
Even though many of us possess the same orientation, we were
very fearful of giving the Peace Corps any religious overtones
whatsoever. It was the non-Catholics in the group who understood the situation most clearly. They argued that in a country
which is 90 percent Catholic, you cannot avoid working side-by-
side with Catholic churchmen, but that we should not need to
worry as long as we do no religious proselytizing ourselves and
assist the Institute in its function of giving material support and
organization to the people.

My main worry is still how someone with no agricultural
background whatever can be of help to small farmers. This month
a lot has been learned and some fundamental adjustments have
been made, but there were enough experiences to show that it will
not be easy to teach simple improvements in farming as I lack general familiarity with the subject.

My first impression of the Chilean southland came after an
all-night ride through the central valley. At the break of dawn
Gerry Garthe and I had breakfast with the volunteers who were
destined for the Island of Chiloé, a point further south than our
own. Other volunteers had boarded the train in Santiago and
been dropped off during the night at the towns nearest their duty
stations. The sun rose that morning over terrain that was remark-
ably green, and rivers ran alongside, beneath and away from us.
Everything seemed much more alive than in the dry valleys of the

north. As we watched from the train window, we saw a white horse trotting unperturbed in a shallow brook and a bevy of horses cavorting together in a field filled with fog.

Gerry and I were met at the Osorno station by two men whom we were to see often in the month to come, a tall blond missionary priest from Holland named Gerald Aukemans, and Fernando Guevas, a short, middle-aged Chilean with a beard. Father Gerald is the parish priest in Rupanco, a large *hacienda*. He is very young; in fact, we celebrated his thirtieth birthday during the month. I soon discovered that Father is highly esteemed by his parishioners who think he looks like President Kennedy. He is one of those men who always seems in a hurry, delaying little over meals and anxious to return to his work, yet he never seemed rushed around the people. Don Fernando is a rather pessimistic bachelor, very sensitive and kind. He was apologetic about the state of the school although he had been there for only a short time and there had been little he could have done to improve it.

Because of their experience in dealing with rural people, Don Fernando and Father Gerald became our best teachers. The long hours at the dinner table became something to look forward to because we would sit and talk endlessly about Chile and our work. Afterwards, we might continue the conversation in Father's room, which is sparsely furnished but well-equipped with Dutch cigars, a phonograph and Bach recordings.

The school in Rupanco is one the Institute hopes to replace. The building and land belong to a large *hacienda* and are loaned to the Institute. A faded yellow color, the building is almost hidden from the road. To enter, you turn right at a sign proclaiming "Instituto de Educación Rural" in sticks of white birch against a dark oak setting. Then you cross a small wooden bridge and climb a stony incline which Father Gerald's Citroen never makes if there are more than two in the car. The day we arrived, the little red bug started stalling and sputtering halfway up the hill, and twenty screaming students came running down the road to give us more of a push than necessary, and we rolled easily to the top.

This boarding school is really an old farmhouse, stuffed with sixty students and five staff members. The students sleep in two very odoriferous rooms, one downstairs and the other in what was once an attic. They have a bathroom which I never really had the courage to enter. Most used the outhouse and washed in a stream nearby. The facilities for the professors were better. Our quarters were roomier and our bathroom had running water when the electricity for the water pump was working (there were quite a few "dry" days). Gerry and I shared a small room which looked like it was attached as an afterthought but was just as cold and damp. It was really someone else's room (whose we did not know) because his trash was on the desk and his coat hung on the wall. This made it rather difficult to unpack.

Most of the activity in the school went on downstairs. The small hallway was a gathering place for assemblies, dances and chapel. Two side rooms were offices, recreation rooms or class-rooms depending on the hour. The kitchen was the meeting place for the teachers when they were not in class because it was warm and contained a round table where they sat and sipped an extra cup of tea. A very impoverished couple manned the kitchen, and their two illegitimate children, scantily clad and gobbling pieces of bread, hovered around the stove all day. Four times each day the seventy of us managed to crowd along three long picnic tables which filled the narrow room. There we were served our meals which were the usual carbohydrates but with vegetables from the Institute garden thrown in. Our real treat at meals was to spread farm butter on hot bread, until I noticed that only the table of the *profesores* had butter on it; I spread it more sparingly then.

Every morning it was an effort to come out and face this strange world. The best part of each day was when it came to an end and the fight with the cold and the language was over. Then I could crawl into my sleeping bag, which was really the most comfortable place in the house, and lose myself in sleep. Other volunteers here say the sleeping bag was the best escape. One claimed that he walked around all day with his and that when an unpleasant moment occurred, he withdrew inside, zipped it up and went to sleep.

Even the peace of sleep, however, was not uninterrupted. In the dormitory on the other side of the wall, a student had an all-night cough which made us all concerned. Also there was the harmless yet bothersome scratching of a rat which lodged itself in the crevice of the wall and scratched—inches away from my ear. When I left my room in December, this pest had become a family of scratchers, and I was glad to leave for fear that the wall would not hold out forever.

The school building was poor beyond redemption but the little farm on the Institute grounds offered great promise. In front of the school were rows of vegetables, grasses and cereals planted experimentally. Behind the kitchen, there were chicken coops, rabbit huts and shelters for ducks and geese close to a small river. Beyond the stream and up a hill was a hog house; sheep, a cow and her calf roamed in a pasture nearby. This small farm provided the students with subjects for observation and experimentation. To me, it provided a frustrated peace. I was fascinated and happy amid these rustic surroundings, yet embarrassed by my own clumsiness in an agricultural setting.

Although I read extensively on farmer's cooperatives, chickens, bees, etc., my total lack of farm experience loomed more and more. When we went up the hill to see the hogs for the first time, I strained my memory to recall if I had ever seen hogs before. (I think I did, once.) Yet I remembered very little about them and when Gerry jumped into the pen I was sure they would bite his leg off. I studied the principles for selecting good laying hens and weeding the nonlayers out of the flock, but this came to naught when I was unable to catch one for inspection. The worst moment came when a professor decided to impress me with his skill at castrating pigs. After witnessing half the operation, I grew pale and almost fainted. It was an hour before the blood had flowed back to my head.

Gerry and I wanted to begin work immediately. This was difficult because Don Fernando had not heard of our coming until the day before we arrived. The course was well in progress and would end in three weeks. There seemed to be little we could do. Gerry taught some classes and worked to improve facilities for the animals. I helped him by translating some extension service pamphlets for his courses and assisting him to construct a rabbit hutch, a good record for someone whose only experience in building consists of a few stabs with an erector set. The only direct contact I had with the students was teaching them basketball on the dirt court outside the school.

During the few days I spent with them, the students impressed me as being extremely courteous young men who were not accustomed to being in a large group or with foreigners. They asked Gerry and me questions about the United States as though an answer from us was something special for them. At the same time, they watched us constantly, until it seemed that their favorite pastime was to observe *gringos* (a word for foreigners, especially North Americans). But this was because they are accustomed to waiting and staring a great deal anyway, and we were just a convenient target for them in their idle hours.

However, my work was not meant to be with the students or in the school. Whenever possible, I would travel through surrounding rural areas, making observations and formulating plans. Here in detail is the area in which I will do community development.

The Institute carries on community development work in three different zones in the province of Osorno. One is the Hacienda Rupanco itself, and this is served by one *delegado* of the Institute who has organized several small community organizations around the *fundo*. The other two zones to the west are Río Negro and Riachuelo on the coast. A *delegado* is assigned to each of these.

Thus, the Hacienda Rupanco, in the southwest corner of the province near the Andes, is part of my bailiwick. This *fundo* or large landholding ranges over 150,000 acres and employs 250 men. The laborers and their families are dispersed into small communities along roads which encircle and divide the *fundo*. These workers are poor and neglected. The owners of the hacienda live in Santiago, 400 miles away, and they are represented here by an administrator who is close to the people but hasn't the power to make necessary changes. Nonetheless, the hacienda does provide the people with some benefits. Schools with the first few grades are spaced conveniently throughout the *fundo* and the school in the center teaches all six primary grades. Most of the homes have electricity and are well-painted, but they are small nonetheless and two families are often crowded into one house.

Despite the poverty of the people, Rupanco has a physical beauty which is breathtaking. The cone of Volcano Osorno is plainly visible from anywhere you stand on this immense property, as is the *cordillera*, the chain of snow-tipped mountains running uninterrupted in the east. The *cordillera* and the volcano are far away, but there is nothing between you and them except open fields, lakes and more mountains.

Our school is a few hundred yards from the hub of the hacienda, the *administración,* and the road from the school is lined with pines. At the *administración* are the offices of the salaried "employees" (as opposed to "laborers"), the offices of the *fundo,* a cheese factory, large warehouse, and the homes of employees. A large home for the owners has been built but is rarely used. Finally, Father Gerald has his church at the *administración,* a barn-like structure of unfinished wood with the rims of the windows painted white. Inside the church is plain and rustic, and the odor of raw wood along with the simple colors of the altar make it the most charming religious setting I have ever seen.

On a weekday in any community in Rupanco there is a steady stream of workhorses pulling milk carts, of men on horse-back and children walking barefoot to school. On Sundays, people stroll in the open air, seeming to acknowledge that their greatest gift in life is the beauty of the place where they were born. They walk to church in the morning and to a soccer match in the afternoon. Everything is done on the *fundo.* Rupanco is a world all its own.

I traveled with Father Gerald because he knows the people and manages to combine community development with his own work. One day he introduced me to the *maestros* in the carpentry shops, old master craftsmen who were making him some candle-sticks and soldering the bell for the church. While he talked with the men, Father mentioned a cooperative; there was great interest in the idea—and in what I might do to help form it.

Helmut Seeger is another guide for me here, the head of the Ministry of Agriculture office in Osorno. With Don Helmut, I traveled beyond the hacienda into the skirt of the volcano itself, visiting the small farmers whom the Ministry organized to receive loans and technical assistance. Señor Seeger is an ener-getic Chilean of German descent, highly nervous and over-enthusiastic. However, he is a truly inspiring character and has motivated and assisted the small farmers in the area with great success. Unfortunately, he does not have a high opinion of the

Institute, and it seems that the Ministry of Agriculture and the Institute of Rural Education do not work well together in the province of Osorno.

Río Negro and Riachuelo are both small villages made up of dirt streets, shabby homes and small stores. Río Negro has 2,000 inhabitants; Riachuelo 900. Both have surrounding rural districts divided into twenty or thirty tiny communities—actually neighborhoods where twenty or thirty families live together in a place. In the villages there is bus service, light and government. It is in the outlying areas where the really abandoned live. The *delegados* of the Institute work almost exclusively in the rural neighborhoods rather than in the villages themselves.

On December first, Don Fernando, Father Gerald, Gerry and I packed into the car and made for Río Negro. "This is your territory," Don Fernando kept repeating as we buzzed along. "This is your home," he said as we drove up the calamity-stricken streets of the town. Visiting both Río Negro and Riachuelo, we called on the American missionaries Emil Schuwey, Richard Woytych and Rocco Constantino. In Río Negro, two fathers were living in three large rooms on the top floor of the school because the recent earthquake had destroyed their home.[1] In Riachuelo, one lone pastor lived in a house beside the church; his home looked like a hunting lodge inside. These missionaries have tremendous responsibility in their towns. They must run a high school and grade school, service the religious needs of an entire village and reach thousands of farmers who hear Mass only if the priest comes out to them. They have little time for nonreligious projects in community development, and we will be working separately.

Nonetheless, the fathers reviewed all the rural communities in their parish and showed them to us on maps. To that they added some very helpful advice. For instance they warned us against giving things away. As missionary priests, they receive abundant supplies of U.S. surplus food for distribution to the people. The fathers are unsure whether handing out this food does more harm or good because the people become dependent upon it and learn to expect it. Father Eugene Stiker, the pastor of

---

[1] The earthquake that shook the south of Chile in 1960, one of the strongest and most devastating in history, reached 8.3 on the Richter scale.

Riachuelo, has his own way of circumventing the difficulty. He bargains with the people. "You build yourselves a school," he says, "and I'll come up with the grain." While it's hardly a perfect community development technique, he claims it gets results.

When the visit with the fathers ended, our party journeyed to one of the rural communities in Río Negro, Buenaventura. Don Fernando dropped me at the home of Don Hector Bittner, the Institute's best friend in the community; and after a brief delay, he, Gerry and Father returned to the students in the school. I was alone in the *zona* for the first time. Now I am happy that Don Fernando chose Buenaventura for my first solo stay in the zone, because of all the communities I saw in my first month in the south this is the one to which I am most sure to return.

Buenaventura is a very productive dairy *fundo* though small in comparison to Rupanco. The twenty-five families who live there are well taken care of, and many of them live in homes constructed since the earthquake in 1960. The home of the *patrón* or estate owner is a gorgeous and spacious mansion with red roof and white sides arranged in perfect symmetrical lines. A drive leads to the house which is beautifully landscaped with shrubs, trees and patches of flowers. The business entrance to the *fundo* passes a school, social center and chapel, all built for the people by the *patrón*, and leads to the center of the *fundo* where the warehouses and administrative offices are all constructed on a single motif. Don Roberto Urisar, the owner of this *fundo*, is a professional architect with exquisite taste. He has made Buenaventura a place of beauty and peace.

In talking with Don Hector Bittner, the gate-keeper for the *fundo*, our conversation would invariably return to the *patrón*. Not only had this *patrón* built social centers, he showed movies there on Sunday. Not only did he provide vehicles to take the sick to the hospital in Osorno, he also supplied transportation on Saturday when they went to buy food. Don Roberto had even organized social clubs for the men and women where they could work together on common problems. It was assumed that I would work in the clubs.

One Sunday, I dined with Don Roberto and his wife in the "house of the *fundo*." Their home was filled with souvenirs of trips to India and Japan. There was so much silverware on the table that for a while I thought I should use a different spoon each time I swallowed some soup. Don Roberto and his wife were excellent company, cultured, informed and most accommodating. After lunch Don Roberto and I followed a custom of pacing up and down on the outside lawn while we conversed. This is a very pleasant Chilean custom. You walk for a span of fifty feet or so and then gracefully, almost without noticing it—certainly without interrupting the thought—you turn and walk back. The first few laps, I kept on walking until I was out of earshot and then turned, saw my host walking in the opposite direction and rushed back.

In our conversation Don Roberto gave me an insight into his own position vis-à-vis the lower classes. He was certainly concerned about social problems; he favored some land reform and wanted the people to act toward him as an equal. On the other hand, it cannot be said he had much confidence in the people because, from his viewpoint as *patrón*, he had been struck by their weaknesses, especially by their lack of a fully developed sense of responsibility. This was my first contact with a member of the rural aristocracy, and I certainly did not enter into our discussion with many prejudices in his favor. However, Don Roberto did point out the problems which must be faced realistically by someone trying to help the *campesinos*; and, more importantly, he showed that a *patrón* can have a constructive attitude. Our main disagreement, which remained inarticulate because of my nationality, was that I have more confidence in what the people can do for themselves once they are given new opportunities and responsibilities. Obviously one task for a community development worker in Buenaventura is to request that the *patrón* leave something undone so that the people can do it on their own.

On that first visit to Buenaventura, the time was spent making friends with the people and my lack of technical ability did not show through. However, there were two close calls. One was when I became anxious to put into use my vast horseback riding experience (twice around the ring at Rocky Glen Park), and I rode on horseback across the *fundo* accompanied by one of the youngsters who was too young to work in the fields. That day I demonstrated an excellent ability to ride a horse which is walking slowly. Then, however, I foolhardily made him gallop and found it impossible to keep my feet in the stirrups. They dangled freely in the air bruising themselves and the horse. Later I explained to the disenchanted lad that the Indians in our country rode not only without stirrups but without any saddle equipment at all.

Another embarrassment which I barely avoided was when Don Hector decided one Sunday morning that it was time to castrate sheep. He insisted that I observe his method and make comments on how we do it in our country. (Perhaps Don Fernando set me up for this.) I followed him to the barn like a doomed man walking the last mile until we met fifteen men playing soccer in a field. They yelled for me to be the sixteenth and I accepted "reluctantly." Then I played a porous but earnest defense while our teams clashed to the pitiable baying of sheep in the barn next door.

After my stay in Buenaventura I hitchhiked into town and met the *delegados* in Río Negro. Until then, I had done extensive traveling alone. This was probably a mistake because it gave neither the *delegados* or myself the chance to make a good first impression on each other. Everywhere there had been unfavorable reports on the *delegados* from people who were both friendly and hostile to the Institute. They knew they had been placed on the defensive and resented my being taken into their zones without their company.

Even after we worked together, we remained estranged. (Here in Lo Vásquez other volunteers report the same difficulty.) They had been working completely independently until then and they feared that I had been sent to take over. The *delegados* did not feel that they needed me on their team, and there was little hope of demonstrating my usefulness immediately. On the other hand, their way of working was so inefficient that I wondered if they got anything done at all. The *delegados* would schedule their days loosely—leaving an entire weekend to travel thirty miles. In their communities, they worked slowly and with small groups. Three weeks after I arrived in Río Negro, the year ended without any satisfactory understanding between the *delegados* and myself about how we could help each other. However, our relations were friendly and provided hope.

On my return trip to Rupanco, there was final proof that I was not a "natural" for a rural education project. All month there had been indications that I had a poor sense of direction. Even after I had been to the same rural place three times, I would still need a guide to get there again. However, returning to Rupanco, I discovered that really I had no sense of direction at all.

The trip was made urgently because Professor George Smith, our assistant director, had arrived at the school and sent for me through the fathers in Río Negro. They found me out in the hinterlands and brought me back to town in the jeep. Not knowing why Dr. Smith had come, the fathers and I thought it was an emergency. So they loaned me their jeep and pointed out on their maps the zigzag roads that should take me to Rupanco in forty-five minutes. I double-checked the maps, threw them under my arm and took off. A mile outside of Río Negro, I missed the first turn and an hour later I was twenty miles south of Río Negro and Rupanco. Rather than chance it on unknown roads, I backtracked to Río Negro, conferred with the fathers and took off again, this time on a route which was less direct but easier to find. This new route led me to the long gravel road which runs a straight course between Rupanco and Osorno. I had seen this road many times in the past month, but did not recognize it, so instead of turning I went straight, heading for the Andes mountains. The road became smaller, then an ox-path, until I was driving across fields and stopping to open gates in fences. Still no Rupanco.

Once the jeep was off the gravel and onto dirt roads, the dust rose. Soon there was mud on my face; my eyelids were heavy with dirt and a thick cloud of dust hung between the windshield and me making it hard to see. Knowing something was wrong, I would stop at each *campesino's* home and inquire: "How do I get to Rupanco?" The women would eye me carefully, let a little slack in the chains with which they held their dogs and say, "Rupanco is a little bit up the road, *Señor. Un poco más allá."* After asking directions from the fifth *señora* and running out of road, I decided to have it out with one of them. "How can you say it is up the road when there is no road left?" I stammered angrily. "But *Señor,"* she replied, "that's just it, you are at the lake now." Rupanco is more than a hacienda, I was reminded that day. It is also a lake at the foot of the Andes, fully as far east of the school as Río Negro is west. And so I had to start the trip over again, this time with an empty tank of gas.

I was finally rescued by a friendly *patrón* who pointed me down the right road and gave me enough gas to get there. From then on, however, I stopped every four miles to make sure I had not strayed. Four hours after the frustrating journey began, I arrived at the school black with dirt, nervous and tired. "What's the emergency?" I asked Dr. Smith as we met at the school. "Oh, nothing," he said, "I just thought you and Gerry might like a night off in Osorno."

Dr. Smith had his own frustrating experiences getting to Rupanco. None of the taxis in Osorno wanted to make the trip, and when he tried hitchhiking on the road, only one truck came by and that was going in the wrong direction. He finally paid a cab driver what seemed more like a bribe than a fare. He was very glad to see me, and my borrowed jeep, and so we all went to Osorno for a steak.

I hope going to Osorno for a steak does not sound incongruous with being in the Peace Corps. Too often people at home think of the Peace Corps only in terms of leading the hard life, forgoing privileges or giving things up. Actually we have as many very pleasant, very funny moments as you do, and there are opportunities to have a good time which we never think of denying ourselves. They, too, are part of the story of my first month in Rupanco.

There were good times even at the school. The last week a drawn-out departure ceremony included an outing to the lake for Gerry, all the teachers and the students. The day of the outing my tired body behaved in the oddest way. Whether from slight illness or mere exhaustion, I managed to sleep all day. I slept on the back of the truck driving to the lake in the chilly morning air. After arriving at Lake Rupanco, I slept on the rocky shore. Someone woke me at lunchtime for some barbecued goat meat; then I went fishing with Gerry and slept in the bow of the boat.

Gerry's day was no more productive. He had wanted to go fishing all month and brought his tackle to the picnic. Then he made the mistake of inviting some students along. Once when I woke up that day, I looked out on the lake and saw Gerry propped up glumly in the back of the boat, his line cast uselessly in the water while five students hung over the sides, three arguing over who would row and one strumming harshly on a guitar.

Gerry caught nothing that day but made up for it later. After the students had been sent home, he coaxed Father Gerald and me to join him on a fishing trip. Father borrowed from the hacienda the key to a cabin perched on a cliff on the lake shore. This fisherman's haunt is accessible only by launch. We arrived in the black of night and fished the next dawn. This fishing was good; even I caught one to contribute to our salmon brunch.

Besides fishing trips and outings, volunteers still like to go to town. This is even more enjoyable for me because Osorno is the town where Father Haske and Father Nugent are stationed.[2] Since all bus lines, business dealings and government activities originate in Osorno, I must go there often; and whenever I am delayed in town, I have a place to stay—at the Jesuit residence. The first day I visited Osorno with Don Fernando, we paid a call on the Jesuits and they gave me a key to their home. This treatment is reserved not only for me. Volunteers of all religious stripes have stayed at the Jesuits'. Even before the Peace Corps came to Chile, their home was known as a way station for travelers.

Father Haske is still the stocky, athletic, kindhearted terror of local schoolboys. Father Nugent is still the very priestly gentleman who won the hearts of Scrantonites four years ago. With four other Jesuit fathers, these men are building a school that is really a transplanted Scranton Prep. I suppose people in my hometown would be surprised to hear that 7,000 miles away a group meets regularly around a potbelly stove and talks about the news from Scranton.

On December 22, Gerry and I were to travel to Osorno and then to Santiago, and the fathers invited us to have dinner with them while we waited for the train. As usual, it took a whole day to travel to Osorno. First, the truck which was to take us had to transport a corpse instead. Then another man promised to drive us and he forgot. Finally the administrator of the *fundo* took us and our luggage to town just in time for dinner. Again stressing the more pleasant aspects of the experience, Gerry and I bought

---

[2] My parents knew that Father Henry Haske, my high school Latin teacher and junior varsity basketball coach, had already been assigned to this post. They also knew Father Frank Nugent, who had been a key administrator at the University of Scranton.

reservations on the first-class *rápido* train which leaves the south for Santiago three times weekly. On the ticket, the departure time was written as 20 o'clock. We both counted off twenty hours and figured we would be leaving at nine. So we talked well into the evening at the dinner table, enjoying the chicken dinner. At 8 P.M. the whistle in the station blew, reminding us that we had an hour to get our luggage to the station down the block. At that moment, seven Peace Corps volunteers whom we were to meet on the train, were frantically searching the station for us. An hour later, we arrived at the station and asked if the *rápido* was on time. "*Sí Señor.*" the dispatcher replied, "*se fue hace una hora*—it left an hour ago." We were doomed to make a twenty-four hour trip on a mail train the following day and we finally arrived, haggard and late, in Lo Vásquez at 6:30 P.M. on Christmas Eve.

We did not spend our first Christmas in the Peace Corps with Chileans because the Institute had begun its summer vacation; we were away from our work sites and the people we knew. Besides, Christmas in Chile is strictly a family festival, and the Peace Corps is our family here. Although I missed the mincemeat pies, the music on the stereo and that special mood which captures the darkness as everyone goes to midnight services back home, Christmas in the Peace Corps was a very joyful affair. When Gerry and I arrived in Lo Vásquez, the volunteers were gathered in a darkened classroom, elegantly dressed and singing Christmas carols around a beautifully lit tree. Somehow, Mrs. Langford had scraped up the ingredients for eggnog and fudge, and there were cookies and sweets of all sorts spread on the table. In the middle of the Christmas Eve celebration, she brought me a belated birthday cake with red and green candles burning on it. We all received Christmas presents from the Institute and we gave Mr. and Mrs. Langford a gift from all the volunteers. Then couples, stags and mixed groups headed for church or to see friends in Valparaiso, while I tumbled into the first bed I had seen in days.

On Christmas Day the high spot was a dinner prepared by the home economists who had returned early to Lo Vásquez. It seems there will be a repeat performance today. It is early Sunday morning, New Year's Eve, as I finish this letter and begin a general one to all my friends. Soon a huge hog, now snorting madly in the courtyard, will be unbound, strung up and butchered. Then we will dig a barbecue pit while the girls make pineapple sauce for the pork chops and bake doughnuts for desert. Japanese lanterns already have been hung outside the school where we will welcome the New Year in the warm summer air. Should it turn cold, a classroom has been decorated, where hats and horns sit unbroken and unused in two boxes on the table. This New Year's Eve will be a special occasion for us, for it is no secret that tonight Fred Morgner and Ramona Marotz will announce they are engaged. So you see that in this welter of strange circumstances, some things are preserved.

Love,
Tommy

Chapter 5

YEAR-END REPORT: A RESPITE IN THE CAPITAL

Summarizing these first months abroad, my letter to a wide range of friends finds its way to Peace Corps headquarters in Washington. There it is selected to be printed as the opening of the agency's first official funding request to Congress. Sargent Shriver calls this in itself a first.

Santiago, December 31, 1961

Hello Everybody,

I t's the weekend of the New Year holiday and the Chilean Peace Corps project has a few days of rest from its work. At last I have a chance to write you about my work with the Peace Corps in Chile. I hope you won't mind that one letter is being sent to all of you. So many have asked me to write and have written me that it would be impossible to say something worthwhile about our work to everyone. I feel that a major part of my responsibilities to the Peace Corps lies in what I can teach my fellow citizens of the United States about the problems facing the peoples of other nations in the world. For this reason, I want to write one letter as well as I can, which will include some of the most illustrative experiences of my months in Chile; and send it to all who have expressed an interest. From the first day of Peace Corps training I have learned enough to fill books, and deepened my understanding of things I thought I knew before. Thus you must forgive me if this letter becomes long; it is really only an abbreviated account.

You must also forgive me if it becomes serious for we are trying to play a real part in a seriously grave reality.

Officially, I have just finished the Peace Corps training program. After the two months at Notre Dame, we spent another two and a half months training in Chile—six weeks at Lo Vásquez, a small village some twenty miles from Valparaiso, and five weeks dispersed throughout the rural areas south of Santiago and in on-the-job training. A few of the volunteers have been asked to serve in the Santiago offices of the Institute for which we are working as photographers and artists for its magazine, agents for the educational radio service, or coordinators of its present program for cooperatives. Most of the forty-five were in the field—four as far south as the windy, damp island of Chiloé, some seven hundred miles and two days' journey by boat and train from the capital. I was in the rural areas surrounding Osorno, the second most southerly point in the distribution of our group.

In every instance these final days of training were spent in outposts of the Chilean Institute of Rural Education. The work of this Institute is as diversified as the needs of the *campesinos* themselves. It has many media for reaching the *campesinos*—radio broadcasts, publications, rural schools which offer three-month courses, and one-hundred-fifteen young men and women called *delegados* who travel village-to-village vaccinating animals, constructing looms and teaching sewing techniques to the men and women who are willing to gather in some community meeting place such as a school, chapel or centrally located home. Because of the direct and broadside approach which the Institute takes to the rural problem in Chile, it is harder to describe the purposes of our Peace Corps mission in one project definition. Secondary teachers are sent to Ghana and the Philippines, and a group of engineers to Tanganyika to build a road. In Chile this month, the Peace Corps has: fifteen volunteers teaching everything from mechanics to food canning in rural schools; six nurses and a dental hygienist in these same schools keeping records, teaching and examining the students; two men working in credit unions and cooperatives; four in the Institute headquarters, and eighteen volunteers "in the zone" working full-time on community development. During the weekends, the nurses and teachers in the rural schools also enter the zone for community development work.

Obviously this was more than training. For the first time we started our work in behalf of the Chilean *campesino*, yet the emphasis was still on preparation: learning the area, making contact with the people and seeing with our own eyes the needs of these peasant farmers. Now we are in Lo Vásquez again, making recommendations to the Institute, which is a young organization and very anxious to improve its operation. During the summer month of January, we will share our technical knowledge and ideas with them. In February we may return to our assignments.

It is clear to all of us that our most important work in Chile is to render the Institute itself a more effective instrument for the education of the *campesino*. Already our six home economics graduates are in charge of all the food served in the Institute's schools. Our nurses are examining, treating and keeping records on all the students. Our mechanics are setting up the one well-equipped mechanical plant which the Institute owns. And our men and women "in the zone" are helping to transform the present work of the *delegados* from community service to community development.

The term "community development" is extremely important though frequently misunderstood. It is also the term that best describes my role in the Peace Corps. Our mission is to develop the most important resources a country has, its people. Until now, the Institute's *delegados* provided important services to local people by staging vaccination programs and teaching carpentry classes in my area of Río Negro. More important than providing these services is teaching the people to do something for themselves, and that is an extremely difficult enterprise. The farmer's attitude of acceptance, his lack of education and the national tradition of poor living conditions combine to mean that these people need a stimulus to work cooperatively for progress. We must find a way to lead them to a solution without giving it to them, for the experience of a progressive step engineered by the community itself is the important thing. Once the people have confidence in each other, and are convinced through experience of the advantage of group activity, they need no one but Father Time. I am convinced that the most important meaning of the word "underdeveloped" when applied to a segment of a country's population is that the people themselves don't realize their own potentialities. Community development is an attempt to get a very long process started. Inevitably the first step is the hardest.

So that you can understand the possibilities for community development in the rural areas of Chile, I want to describe the conditions of life among the *campesinos*. This raises a touchy question (even though I'm not writing this on a postcard).[1] Suffice it to say that everything I have learned about Chile's social problems has been taught to me by the Chileans themselves and that the intelligent interest which millions of people here have in the *campesinos* shows that a large percentage of the population is not "underdeveloped" at all. I never use the word when talking about the country in general. There are great numbers of educated people, large cities and industries at high levels of development. What no one can deny is that at least one segment of the population is very "underdeveloped" indeed—the 45 percent who live as *campesinos*. It is their life which I want to describe to you.

First of all, *campesinos* are almost completely without money. They are without purchasing power for food, clothing and farm utensils, having only the land they live on to support themselves. One of our community-to-community campaigns, intended to demonstrate how to build a good loom for making their own clothes, was severely hampered because most of the people had neither hammer or saw. One type of *campesino* has a little more cash than another. The small property owner has about forty acres of poor, hilly land and nothing more, while the *inquilino* [local farm worker—almost a serf] who works on the large hacienda or *fundo* makes a small salary, which may add up to $150 a year. (The legal minimum wage is 70 cents a day.) This does not mean that the *inquilino* has a great advantage over the small property owner. He doesn't own his own land but uses an acre or two of the *fundo* and a small ramshackle house given him by the *patrón*, or owner. On the contrary, I believe the small property owner is better off than those who work on the *fundos* if for no other reason than he owns his own land and has more initiative.

---

[1] This refers to an international incident in Nigeria where a volunteer wrote about "squalor" and primitive conditions on a postcard which she lost on a street. It was picked up, copied and circulated widely by critics of the United States.

These homes are poor and unsanitary. They are usually one-story, unpainted houses with two or three rooms, one of which can be made warm in the wintertime with a stove. Sanitary conditions are always bad. During this past summer month, there were thousands of flies in every kitchen in which I sat eating or drinking. In the winter, Río Negro receives most of its annual rainfall of 80 inches, and these homes must become perpetually damp, a good explanation for the prevalence of tuberculosis. Despite the heavy winter rains, water is a summer problem for many because the soil is so porous that the land becomes dry. This worsens sanitary conditions in the home. The outhouses are poorly constructed if they exist at all. The Institute is trying to have one man arrested for going through a northerly area of Chile making a fast dollar by building latrines over irrigation ditches. Half of the *campesinos* drink from these ditches and all of them eat the crops which are irrigated with their contents.

In my area of Río Negro, the houses give an appearance of greater prosperity. Many are new. The explanation for this is not a cheering one. In May of 1960 the region was wrecked by an earthquake. Well-constructed buildings like hotels and churches were demolished. You can imagine what the earthquake did to the homes of *campesinos*. I have slept in the new house of a man who reconstructed his entire farm plant, including his house, without one helping hand from another person or agency. The favorite topic of conversation in Río Negro is still the earthquake; the help which the United States sent is always mentioned with real gratitude.

The *campesinos* are undernourished from the moment they are born. The most common baby formula I have encountered is a drink called *papal*, which is given the child until it is almost two years old. It is made from tea leaves, the water in which rice is cooked, flour and sugar. For the adults, the standard fare is bread, rice, noodles and potatoes—all carbohydrates. Fruit, meat and milk are very uncommon. Vegetables are plentiful enough now during the summer, but when the winter comes the *campesino* will have only the few animals he owns as sources of protein. He will kill almost all of his ten or twelve chickens, getting meat for that many days and leaving his family without eggs except for the few laid by the one or two hens left for incubating in the spring. The next to go will be the family pig or one of their few sheep. Without refrigeration, this meat lasts a very short time. They will have to eat it all in one festive day of abundance, and then go for weeks without meat.

Sometimes the paltry supply of food is enough for only one real meal a day. For breakfast, they take bread and a tea made from herbs and boiling water called *aguita*. For supper there is more tea and bread and the scraps from the large meal at noon. In San Juan de la Costa, a settlement near Osorno which we hope to reach with our Peace Corps jeep, a sociological study revealed that the people received less than 1,000 calories a day.

With poor living conditions and improper diet, the *campesinos* are subject to a storm of maladies and physical handicaps. One of the saddest experiences of my six weeks was a recurrent one that happened every time I boarded a local bus or climbed on a wheezing truck jammed with *campesinos*. The older men and women would show signs of a life's struggle with sickness, looking older than they really were with only a few teeth left and with a figure shaped by a lifelong diet of starches. The young children would be as cute and well-formed as grade-schoolers in the United States, but the only possibility open to them within their environment was to suffer everything their parents had and lose what we consider to be normal health. It is when this problem can be seen perpetuating itself that one becomes discouraged.

Most probably these children aren't really in normal health, but are marked internally by worms or by the infantile diseases which kill 25 percent of the babies in rural areas before they reach their first birthday. In San Juan de la Costa, 60 percent of all the deaths recorded last year were babies under three. In a settlement of about one hundred families where one Peace Corpsman was last month, six babies died within two days.

The older people suffer from pneumonia and tuberculosis. Typhus, dysentery and typhoid fever are also killers. The strain of having large families and little protein means early death for many women. The women also encounter difficulties from having babies in crude ways. In Chol-Chol, an Indian settlement to which two Peace Corpsmen will return in February, the woman is customarily left alone in an isolated shack as the time of labor approaches. In San Juan de la Costa there are worse customs. Although proper medical attention is available to all the *campesinos*, the problem is to reach a clinic or hospital. We took the *señora* of one man some fifty miles over dirt roads to a hospital in Osorno. He brought her to where we were from his home, a two-hour journey on horseback from the road. She was unconscious and had been that way for two days.

This problem of mobility affects the *campesino's* life in many ways. It means that he is unable to go to a market frequently or stay very long if he wants to return home the same day. He has to travel part of the distance on horseback and then hitch a ride on the back of a truck. To reach one meeting place, I had to drive a jeep for a half hour over oxen paths and then walk through pastures and climb fences for over an hour. The inaccessibility of the market means two things: the *campesino* can't buy economically and he can't sell economically. Instead of making the time-consuming journey, he will purchase commodities in nearby stores (*boliches*) where prices are twice the normal. To sell his crops, he'll hand them all over to a middleman in town who pays him little. We are collaborating with the Ministry of Agriculture in Osorno to bring the *campesinos* to a new free market where they can sell directly to the public. In another area, two Corpsmen spent the entire month carting the *campesinos'* lettuce to the nearest market in a truck. With a better market and greater profit motive, these particular farmers were already showing enthusiasm for better use of their land.

Although their land is poor and hilly, almost every farm could produce more than at present. The *campesinos* plant wheat and potatoes year after year, without rotating crops or using fertilizer, and cause soil erosion on a grand scale. Oxen pull their plows when workhorses would do twice the work in the same amount of time. Their trees are unpruned and the crops go unthinned; if pastures were fenced off, some sections could be used and others rested, but that is not the case. Pigs, chickens, turkeys and dogs run wild in front yards, and flowers grow alongside vegetables in the garden. The *campesinos* have no idea of farm finances. They will raise a turkey or two, then sell them for less than they invested in labor and feed. With a few new farming and husbandry techniques, and some elementary habits of calculation, the *campesino* could have a better life. It is this fact which makes our work more challenging than discouraging.

This point leads to the most important problem of all: lack of education. In the rural areas of Chile, the average child has four years of schooling. A successful educational system in the rural areas could diminish every difficulty I have mentioned. If they understood the connection between dampness and tuberculosis; between the fly, the outhouse and the baby's fever; between irrigation ditches and dysentery, they could avoid many bouts with illness. If they were taught that an egg is more nutritious than a potato the same size, they might spare more chickens and use their land for green vegetables instead of putting them all in potatoes. If they learned the real needs of a woman in labor or a child in its first few months of life, they could satisfy many of them with what they already have. With technical advice and a calculated investment in fertilizer or animal vaccine, they could build up a farming operation which would satisfy their own needs and provide them with goods for the market. It is in this area of "rural education" which the Peace Corps will concentrate in Chile.

We will use the direct approach of giving talks to the men and women gathered at the local *centro* or meeting place. In the first week of February, one of the Peace Corps girls will accompany me to Río Negro armed with pamphlets from the US Department of Health, Education and Welfare; a dictionary; visual aids, a background in education courses, practical nursing experience, and knowledge of home economics. Her name is Janet Boegli, a gorgeous blonde graduate of the University of Texas. She'll give talks and demonstrations to mothers in each *centro* once or twice a month. I'll do the same before the men, explaining the advantages of simple farming and husbandry techniques.

We must also use an indirect approach, for the most important thing we can teach the *campesinos* is what they can do for themselves. Through hints, discussions, sometimes outright suggestions, we will try to organize the efforts of individuals into community projects. The possibilities are limitless. In one area, the farmers are running out of firewood and in a few years will be using their floors or fences for winter heat. We want to encourage a community plan to buy seedlings of Monterey pine trees which grow so rapidly that they can be cut in ten years.

On one *fundo*, we are arranging a competition in rabbit care. I'll organize the youngsters, teach them about proper sanitation and feeding for the rabbits and arrange for them to buy a buck and a doe very cheaply. Janet will teach the mothers some tasty ways to serve rabbit and we might succeed in getting the people more protein during the winter. A project which could be started almost anywhere around Río Negro would be putting the unused land into cherry or peach trees instead of the trees that produce the small, green *chicha* apple which they use for a fermented drink and nothing more.

If the community as a whole could be convinced of their efficacy, medicines and vaccinations against animal disease could be bought and distributed with little initial cost and great dividends. Most important of all is the cooperative. By pooling their money, the farmers can buy in wholesale markets and in bulk quantities. They can run large-scale animal operations with better equipment and more profit for distribution to all. They would be in a position to receive credit for buying farm equipment, perhaps someday even a tractor. With cooperatives, both the direct and indirect approaches are needed; and once we have successfully suggested that a community form one, we have the responsibility of educating them in how to participate in it properly.

Lack of education can be a formidable foe, and many of our projects will not succeed as well as we would like them to. The director of the Chilean National Health Service has told us some of his agency's frustrations in San Juan de la Costa. Once the people used a powder designed to kill typhus-bearing lice on themselves instead of on their sheep. In another instance, they learned the reasons for boiling their drinking water, and they did, until they decided they didn't like the taste, so they stopped.

Even if we succeed in all our attempts, it would not mean a tangible amount of success in the overall fight against poverty in Chile. Therefore our group of Peace Corps men and women have accepted two very important principles. First, while in the *zona* we will work very carefully with a few communities hoping that word of highly successful activity will spread and more *campesinos* will be inclined to attempt it later. Secondly, we want to deposit in the Institute all the valuable things we know. Our nurses are trying to introduce new standards and courses in the health programs of rural schools. Our teachers want to improve the facilities of the schools. The "zone-workers" are asking for more efficient use of time and accurate records on the growth of each community organization. In eighteen months we will leave Chile, its rural schools and *campesinos*. The most permanent contribution we can make is to incorporate better methods and ideas in the structure of the indigenous Chilean Institute of Rural Education. For this reason we are spending January with the staff and *delegados* of the Institute in summer workshops, even though this takes us out of direct contact with the *campesinos* where we would like to be.

I am anxious to return to Río Negro because I enjoyed December there. My life was hectic but not unhealthy. In one period of nine days, I slept in eight different places, once on the floor of a chapel in my sleeping bag. I traveled from place to place on foot, horseback, bus, truck, and sometimes in the jeep of the North American *padres* in Río Negro. I ate well enough; and, although a great portion of the Peace Corps contingent has suffered from serious intestinal disorders and loss of weight, I remain one of the lucky ones.

Another big reason for wanting to return is that I like the *campesinos* and have grown to respect them a great deal—for their endurance and capacity for hard work, for their ability to live off the land without any of the things we call "necessities," for their love of music and the generosity which prompts them to slaughter one of their few sheep for the meal they are serving me. All this leaves me filled with admiration. They are simple from their lack of education, and this is refreshing even though it caused me one of the most difficult moments I have had with the Peace Corps. One long Sunday afternoon I attended a dance at a *centro* and had to rock'n'roll with every girl under forty and answer questions about Brenda Lee for six hours—all in a language I acquired recently and pronounce miserably, and while a bunch of microbes played havoc in my lower intestines. But it was worth it when one of the men asked me for my autograph and when, days later, one of these local jitterbugs approached me and shook my hand in the middle of the busiest street in Osorno.

The *campesinos* are usually flattered that a North American has come so far to work with them even though they know little about the United States. (One asked if we received those wonderful CARE packages in our country too.) The higher social classes haven't quite figured me out yet. One time an aristocratic couple saw me walking through Osorno in old clothes, caked with dust and with a sleeping bag on my back. The next time I was standing before them at a banquet in my Ivy League suit explaining our work. Some have been very understanding, however; and one *patrón* purposely avoided me in front of his *inquilinos* because he knew I wanted to associate myself with them. This same *patrón* only laughed a few hours later when I arrived at his mansion for Sunday dinner in clodhoppers and soiled working shirt. It was all I had with me in the zone.

All the Chileans have been extremely hospitable. They have an expression, *mi casa su casa,* "my house is your house," and when they use it, they mean it. Our Peace Corps group must have been in four hundred houses by now. They are all very patient with my language difficulty because although I can converse more or less fluently in Spanish, I make some atrocious mistakes. Once I told a *campesino* that an egg was better than a pope, instead of a potato. (I got my genders mixed). Another time I translated *camarada* as *camera* and offered to lend my spare one to a man who said his was in poor condition. In the country *camarada* means wife, not *camera.*

My work was carried on in a peaceful atmosphere without disturbance from any enemies of the United States. This is not to say that they aren't active here. There is an area called Catrihuala in the coastal mountains within my zone where 200 Indian families are living on land they claim for their own but which has been deeded to some large land owners by the government. They retain this land with arms, and refuse us permission to enter when we request it. Struggling for leadership in this "revolt" are two Communists, one of whom lives in Río Negro. They operate, as do all the 1,500 Communist agitators in Chile, by making themselves part of a local community and spreading dissension against the government. This is not an isolated case. I know of a more bitter revolt in another area. Both are dramatic instances of Communist influence in Chile—an influence which has already been directed against us.

We know that word has been sent to Communist members of labor unions to embarrass us at every opportunity. The daily Communist paper *El Siglo* has branded us as "45 spies." When our teachers arrived at one rural school, anti-Yankee signs had been posted on the gate.

Communism is a strong political force in Chile. In the last election, a Marxist candidate came within 35,000 votes of being president. In the 1964 election, it is very possible that one of the most democratic and prosperous countries in Latin America will elect a convinced Marxist.

Janet and I will request permission again to enter Catrihuala, this mountain colony, because we believe that part of the Peace Corps idea is to show the poor people in the world that the United States can be as interested in their problems as the Communists and that where they offer bitter slogans, we can offer deeds and helpful advice. Still we work not so much for the downfall of Communism as the elevation of the *campesino*. Communism is the symptom; poverty is the disease; and, if our work were motivated by a fear of Communism instead of by human compassion for those in misery, we would never succeed.

Somehow it is hard to end this letter. It has already become too long. This is because no conclusions or summaries are possible. Like the *campesinos* themselves, we are just beginning. Please remember us in your prayers.

                              Your friend always,
                              Tom Scanlon

Chapter 6

FIASCO Y CONVIVENCIA—
QUISCO AND HUALAPULLI

Told to go on summer vacation though we have not even started work, the volunteers revolt! My friends and I join a group of Chilean university students ministering to a poor Indian community in the Andean foothills.

Tuesday, March 1, 1962

Dear Mom, Dad and Jim,

January and February were months of wandering. We were busy, but we still have not found any permanent work.

New Year's Day was balmy with a gentle breeze that made me agree for the first time with the switch in seasons. Now that Thanksgiving and Christmas were over in the United States, I could stop trying to believe that it was really becoming colder. That day the summer weather was noticeable, and I was glad I could smell the moist ground outside the school in Lo Vásquez. However, I also awoke that day to some other realities of our predicament.

The Institute was on summer vacation. They had nothing planned for us in the first two weeks of January and insisted that we attend a summer camp in the third week. Then there were two-week summer courses for the teachers in the schools. For February also there was very little scheduled. When asked what the volunteers should do with their time, the Institute suggested dryly that we continue training or go on vacation ourselves. It opposed our returning to our work sites before its vacationing personnel.

So our stay at Lo Vásquez was prolonged for two weeks. Mr. Langford, our director, arranged many activities for us but there was little he could do to dull the pain of sitting uselessly in Lo Vásquez. I adopted my own personal project during that period, and completed the composition of the "Hello Everybody" letter which I began on New Year's Eve, feeling that if I could not pursue the first Peace Corps goal of helping the people, I could pursue the second and inform my friends about what I had learned. During the mornings, I would sneak away to an old water storage bin which had been dry for some time and sit on the concrete floor with stones keeping my papers from the winds. Then I could write on an old typewriter case sitting alongside the dried-out cow dung which some *campesinos* used for fuel.

This project carried me through those frustrating two weeks, yet I was as upset as the others and voiced my discontent in my sleep at night. Some of the volunteers who stayed up late would hear the others mumble in their sleep when they came into the dorm. One night I moaned (so they tell me) "Don't worry men, all this hullabaloo will be over in two years anyway." My final speech to the dormitory late at night was brief but inspiring: "We've got to organize those damn *campesinos*," I cried, according to reports.

A real turning point in our relations with the Institute came at the summer encampment. A very beautiful place had been selected for this head-on collision between the Peace Corps and the Institute. El Quisco is a small seaside resort and our tents were pitched in a grove of eucalyptus trees not far from the sea. We arrived by truck there one Sunday afternoon and found that the encampment was organized like a Boy Scout camp. We were to live in "patrols" and each morning we were to rise at dawn, fall in and face inspection, saluting when it was all over. We ate with our patrol mates, swam with them and were even supposed to spend our free time together. Meanwhile in a segregated camp across a gully, the girls were organized in a similar way. There were curfews at night and very few worthwhile activities during the day. Surely we had not come to Chile for this, we argued, and open rebellion broke out in the volunteers' ranks.

Some of us tried to be cooperative and organized sports activities and demonstrations of square dances and the Virginia reel, but most everyone was part of the rebellion. One way of showing disapproval was to ignore the entire camp system. I went canoeing with one of my favorite Peace Corps nurses. Others saw movies or went dancing. Mr. Langford had to rush up from Santiago to smooth things over and then even his patience reached its limit. After a hastily called conference with the Institute, it was decided that the volunteers could return to their work sites immediately. This was all we wanted, and by then even the Institute was glad to get us off its hands.

The incident in El Quisco is a good example of how cultural values can clash. We failed to understand that in Chile you are expected to give a great deal of your time to other people; that time spent laughing and joking with your fellow workers is not considered time wasted, as we certainly considered the week in El Quisco to be. We also failed to appreciate that the other staff members, especially the *delegados*, benefited from this meeting on the beach—as much as we suffered from it—because the mystique and comradeship developed there lasts them through the year. So far we had been acting toward the Institute as if it were a North American organization, expecting from it definite time tables and job assignments, which are not customary here.

In its turn the Institute's people assumed that we noted the passage of time in the same casual way they did and that we would enjoy a week at the beach under any circumstances. They expected us to be as docile in their hands as the *delegados* and failed to take into account that we were going to have minds of our own and a compulsion to get things done. The Institute should have realized that given little to do for three months, the volunteers would become restless beyond taming.

Janet Boegli and I made it a point to go south as soon as possible. Our first task was to set up the new headquarters for the *delegados* and ourselves in Río Negro. We feared that unless we did this during the summer, valuable time would be lost when the *delegados* returned in March. The Saturday morning after the encampment came to an end, Jan and I began the three-day journey in the jeep to Osorno.

Although I was glad Janet was going along, I must admit

that this whole matter of traveling with a girl, and of shopping for household items, made me very uncomfortable indeed. I would give the hotel clerks a "it's-none-of-your-business" stare when they looked at me doubtfully as I requested two separate rooms in the hotel.

Janet and I arrived in Osorno covered with dust and with a jeep caked inside and out with heavy layers of dirt. Janet operated out of the hotel and I stayed at the Jesuits'. We discovered the price of the homes in Río Negro and what it would cost to furnish them. All this information was forwarded to Santiago. Then we placed ourselves in the service of Helmut Seeger, the Ministry of Agriculture man who was fighting the forest fires raging in the mountains of the coast. At the end of the month we drove north again to a town a hundred miles away and made ourselves part of a program of social assistance organized for the small farmers by some college students from Santiago.

As the summer vacation project, sixty-three students from the Universidad Católica in Santiago had come south to work in the rural areas between three cities, Loncoche, Gorbea and Villarrica, where 24,000 poor farmers live. Like the Peace Corps, the students were to work with the Institute, and the Institute school in Loncoche became the headquarters for the project. The dining room of the school became the central station and the convocation point for all meetings and social gatherings. Square and spacious, it has walls of paned glass, a fireplace in the center of the room and a long table set in the end near a kitchen.

The Chilean students were organized into teams of two kinds. One resided in a particular community all month and was composed usually of a medical student, lawyer, teacher and veterinarian. The second kind was mobile and would travel to all the communities where the other students resided. One mobile team was composed of dentists. (They pulled over 400 teeth in that month.) Another was composed of student economists who set out to be community developers. A third group, the most popular, were entertainers. Peace Corps volunteers joined each of the student groups, except for the team of entertainers.

In the first week of the project, I helped drive the students into the field, and I had the opportunity to meet all of them and see their good work. Like all Chileans from the upper classes, they

were affectionate, urbane, witty and gay. They lacked the sullen-
ness which I find in some *campesinos,* and were very anxious to be
our friends. The girls were beautiful and dedicated; and for many
of them it was probably a greater effort to live among the
campesinos than it was for our girls.

It was interesting to compare these Chilean students and
ourselves. However well organized the students seemed, they still
possessed those national qualities which downgrade organization.
The requirements of a time schedule frequently were displaced by
an attack on a watermelon or a greeting for a friend. These students were highly idealistic, and they made plans and hopes for
the month-long period which far surpassed what could realistically be accomplished. They preferred the thought to the deed, the
spoken intention to the accomplished fact; and in this idealism
the Chileans surpass us, I believe. Many times they asked me to
articulate the philosophy of the Peace Corps—the idea that
makes thousands of Americans leave home and work for other
nations. I have to admit that so far there is no clear-cut rationale,
no elaborate explanation which all volunteers accept for their
own actions.

The Chilean students are proud people, especially proud of
being a good friend, and they like to talk with us for hours. Of
course, we discussed politics. Their penetrating interest in politics
gave them many criticisms of the United States. The important
thing, however, was the atmosphere in which these matters were
discussed. If you take time to establish a friendly, personal
ambiance, you can begin a give-and-take which becomes heated
and intense and ends with everybody hugging each other.
Without the proper groundwork, however, the same conversation
could produce enmities. Perhaps our country's biggest mistake so
far has been failure to just become friends with Latin American
countries.

In discussions with Chilean students, it is just as important
to give as it is to take, to respect their pride by answering their
assertions and establish your own human respect at the same time.
When students become hypercritical of the United States, I point
to blemishes within their own society—not to poverty but to the
rigid class system, to plans that are not completed and to work
patterns which undermine the economic potential of the nation.

When asked about Castro, I responded that if he had said or done to Chile what he had to the United States, there would have been a war between Chile and Cuba a long time ago. Not one of them denied it.

One evening I visited Hualapulli, a place stuck in the ribs of the Andes between Lakes Villarrica and Calafquén. This was the most distant and isolated student outpost and the only one where the students were working with Chileans of Indian descent. The students I met there were filled with stories of their escapades in the zone—of trying to learn some basic Mapuche words and of their bouts of dysentery brought on by a local brew made with fermented honey. These students lived in a schoolhouse and slept on the floor. (They claimed that you become accustomed to this soon enough and that only that part of you which protrudes the most hurts after a while.) They washed in a small stream which coursed by the school, and bathed in a river. This was the most spirited of all and I asked if I could join them and they welcomed me as a member of their team.

The Hualapulli students had already scouted the area when I arrived there and had begun working. Hector Aliaga had established a medical clinic in the school. Sonia Werneberg was teaching home economics there. Another was staging a literacy campaign. Raul Fuentes, a law student, was consulting with the people about their land title problems. Sara Mangamarchi, who had studied economic theory in Russia, was making a study of the agriculture of the area. Marla Carter, the first woman veterinarian I ever knew, was conducting a vaccination program against hoof-and-mouth disease.

A few days after I arrived, the students had their first meeting with the people. For this meeting, the troop of entertainers arrived on the scene, the men in *huaso* outfits and the girls in gay calico dresses. They performed a Chilean hat dance and skipped around a bottle skillfully avoiding knocking it down. They also staged a puppet show for the children, though all the adults, including ourselves, watched it too.

The owners of the throngs of horses tied to the trees outside the school did not come only to be entertained that Sunday. Marla exhorted them to milk their cows twice a day and feed them as best they could. Sara gave a demonstration of pruning a tree. Hector talked longest about the most serious health problem in Hualapulli, a tapeworm called *Echinococcus granulosus* passed from dogs to sheep to people. It causes cysts on vital organs, especially the liver, cysts which can be removed only by surgery. In Hualapulli, surgery for *"bolsas de agua,"* ("water bags") was as common as operations for appendicitis.

What will come of this meeting only time will tell. The people nodded in agreement when I spoke to them about working together. Certainly they all had the same problems, but social organization and real change is not acquired through one meeting. All of us urged the Institute to continue working in Hualapulli after we left there.

During the rest of the month, Marla Carter taught me how to vaccinate cows and we worked together. A man living behind the school had twelve cows. (He milked only two of them and only once a day.) His animals became the not-so-willing subjects on which I practiced. As payment, we vaccinated all his cows and sheep for nothing, even donating the vaccine. I learned to give the injection well enough, but never anticipated that cows would not like receiving shots any more than humans do; and there was no corral. The real art was to get in position to insert the needle. During the campaign, Marla and I worked in circumstances which were not ideal, and we were both kicked by bulls and oxen and received many an insult from the cows.

As we galloped from one part of Hualapulli to the next, the campaign became larger and larger. One day we vaccinated over two hundred head of cattle in one locality and had to agree to return the next day to vaccinate the remaining twenty-five. However, when we returned there the following morning, there were over a hundred cows, bulls, and oxen pushing, fighting and haranguing each other in a fenced-off field, their owners sitting on the fence waiting for us to arrive. It seemed that our supply of vaccine always needed replenishing and after spending the day on horseback or giving shots, Marla and I would journey at night to the nearest town, wake the local pharmacist and ask for more vaccine.

All of Marla's skills were in demand. She was called upon to test a cow's hide for disease after a woman who ate meat from the cow had died and two children were made sick. Another time a woman waited all day for Marla to return from her work and then pleaded with her to come and cure a sick ox. Marla was exhausted that day, yet the loss of an ox to a *campesino* family is very serious, and so we both walked through the mazes of roads, paths, and pastures which led to the little tract where the woman and her husband lived. The ox had the bloat, and Marla worked on it into the evening until she needed a lamp to work by. The woman's husband held the poor animal's head while it stood there moaning, and the woman held the oil lamp while Marla put her ear to the beast's side listening for symptoms. I helped when I could and watched the night close around us and wished I were a painter capable of capturing that scene. It was beautiful not only because of the mood and colors but because of the relationship existed between these people and their beast of burden. An ox is not an object, it is not dollars and cents to a *campesino*. It is something which lives and breathes, becomes sick and dies. *Campesinos* know something about animals which we don't know, how inferior they are to us and how they are similar.

I wish I could interpret all the beauty of Hualapulli for you—of the hills rolling in smooth, yellow curves and flanked by clumps of trees dry and plain in the sun. And of people too, and what they say, and carry, and do. One morning I saw a man on a black horse leading a pair of oxen with a long yellow stick that had a nail in the end of it. He laid the pole behind his saddle as he talked and looked up at me because his horse was in the oxen path down off the road. From time to time his wife, seated in the oxcart, added a *"si"* or *"no"* to our conversation. She called me *"padre"* because I was a *gringo* and drove a jeep, and I told them I wasn't a priest and we laughed at that. She was very pleasant and he was too, especially when I bent down to pick up the stick which had fallen from where he placed it on the back of his horse. That same day I met a very sad woman, dressed in black, sitting sideways on her horse coming from a funeral. She used the words *"Maria"* and *"Dios"* a lot and although she had no education, she knew what it was to be religious—to look for a meaning in life. Her life had great meaning for me.

So much could be learned about the people of Hualapulli by

observing insignificant things about them. Take, for example, the kind of teeth people have. One afternoon I drank *maté* (a green tea) with an old woman who had only six strong teeth left and one which wiggled all the time she chewed a piece of bread or pressed to her mouth the metal straw through which she drew the unnourishing mixture of leaves, sugar and hot water. The following morning I met three young girls with beautiful teeth and gaunt, lovely faces taking their cows down the path to the river. It was so dry that they had to fetch water even for the house from the river. "The animals drink but once a day and give little milk now," they said to me as they passed by. I dreaded the lack of milk because I liked their strong white teeth. In Hualapulli, those that have good cows have good teeth.

It was in Hualapulli in February that I felt for the first time that I was really living among the poor of Chile and seeing them as they really are as I experienced many aspects of rural life for the first time. This place was a "first" in several other senses, not all of them happy or pleasant. In Hualapulli, I was really sick with dysentery for the first time, thanks to "honey cider" which tore down all the impregnable defenses I thought I had. Now when I see someone coming at me with a glass of fermented honey, I gallop in the opposite direction. It is one of the few items which, when offered, I turn down with an absolute "No, thank you."

Also in Hualapulli I realized for the first time that in addition to bearing the terrible brunt of poverty, the poor in Chile suffer from other human hardships as well. We found a little blind boy, completely uneducated, living with his illiterate uncle. The eight-year-old child was extremely bright and glib, and he had a delightful personality. Now Marla has taken him to a special school for blind children in Santiago.

We came upon a husband and wife who fought constantly. The woman asked us to come vaccinate her sheep and the man would not allow us to when we arrived after a three-hour journey. The neighbors told us this marriage would not last. I had thought that for the *campesinos* marriage was such a necessity that people stayed together no matter what. The fact that reality surprised me shows that I had assumed that with all the problems and hardships that poor Indians face, they wouldn't have time for marital discord. How naive!

It was also in Hualapulli that I met a lonely *campesino* for the first time, and again was surprised. Life is so harsh in these remote areas that marriage and children become less a matter of choice and more one of necessity. Bachelors are few and far between, so I will relate a dinner we had with this man. He accosted Marla and me after we had vaccinated his cattle and he insisted that we come to dinner. We went along sheepishly yet curious about how this lone wolf could survive in such a remote place. He led us into his barn where a table for three had been arranged as in a dining room. A young girl, his niece, served us a piece of black meat which had no odor at all. Marla and I gave each other encouraging glances. Then I noticed that there was nothing to cut the meat with. Our host recognized my predicament and reached for his penknife in his pocket. Wiping it on the shoes he had worn all morning while rounding up cattle, he handed the penknife to me. Marla gave me a look that said "If you do it, I will" and I cut slowly, swearing to myself that if I were in his situation I would have been married long ago.

There were many occasions in Hualapulli to balance these eye-openers. A prosperous resident of the community threw a feast for us which was positively Biblical in its dimensions. Ordinary men serenaded girls and composed songs for us. At the end of the month, they played *chueca,* a game inherited from the original Indians of Chile which is similar to lacrosse which our Indians handed down to us. (The players hit a small hardwood ball toward a goal with the handle end of their walking stick, the *chueca.*)

Also there was a great deal of comradeship within the team. I would tease the students about their way of doing everything together. One week five earth tremors shook our little school and rattled the windows in the middle of the night. The students all ran out together. I remained, not because I was brave but simply because the tremors failed to wake me up. The final night the team became disgusted and manufactured a tremor which shook me out of the sleeping bag, and I joined them outside waiting for the earth to settle down again until they admitted that the tremor was a hoax meant to disturb my rest.

Throughout our month with the university students, we enjoyed Chilean *convivencia* (a word which I can translate only in five, "having a good time together"). On weekends, all the students would converge in Villarrica, a resort town nearer to

Hualapulli than Loncoche, and there would be a bonfire on Friday night and swimming on Saturday. At the end of the month, we all came to Loncoche for a send-off dinner. This was the most satisfying moment I have had in the Peace Corps so far. After the first hot shower, batch of mail and clean clothes in three weeks, we ate in the school dining room where everyone was buzzing with anecdotes about the month gone by.

The Peace Corps volunteers told the students that after working with them we would now work with better ideas, more enthusiasm and a greater love of Chile. In turn, they threw us in the air eight times—very demonstrative and spontaneous these Chilean friends of ours.

That night we sat until three singing and put the room in darkness and watched the moonlight creep through the panes of glass. I had a favorite song by then, "Las Aguas del Tolten," and they sang that too. The following night the room was quiet and the students were on the train heading north, probably awake. I went to bed early, heard them singing and dreamt that I saw some peasant women dancing to their songs and beckoning us all to enter their world more completely.

                    Love,
                    Tommy

Chapter 7
TO BE A VOLUNTEER:
WHAT IT'S REALLY LIKE

As my co-workers and I adjust to a new life in a new language and a new country, we find our lives more exciting and less romantic than often portrayed. How we enjoy it!

April 1, 1962

Dear Mom, Dad and Jim,

There is a need to talk realistically about the Peace Corps. So far the press in the United States and the Peace Corps itself have given an inaccurate view to the American people. They make us all seem like success stories when we really aren't. They make the immediate success of a few individuals speak for the entire group. They have been so interested in canceling out the image of the "ugly American" that they do not recognize the danger of creating a new type—less harmful perhaps but still misleading—unless the problems of volunteers are understood and dealt with. Not that the press or the Peace Corps willfully misrepresent. It is just that in their enthusiasm they cannot believe ill of volunteers, and they recount stories which reflect more their hopes for eight hundred of us overseas than whatever we have actually done. The danger is that unless the American people understand the difficulties and frustrations faced by volunteers, they will never understand the real success of the Peace Corps when and if it comes.

Let me tell you what it is really like to be a Peace Corps volunteer in Chile. To be a volunteer does not necessarily mean to endure poor living conditions. This is another way in which the Peace Corps has been misunderstood. Many people believe that to be in the Peace Corps, you must live in a slum. However, one of the first pieces of advice which experienced people gave us was *not* to live as the *campesinos* do. First of all, conditions of life among *campesinos* are not only poor but unhealthy; and they have resistance to cold, dampness and germs which we do not have. Secondly, it is not necessary to live like a *campesino* to be accepted by them. In fact, I suspect that they resent someone who is putting on a show of poor living conditions. At best, they would consider him odd. To be accepted by the people, it is necessary only to live simply, be yourself and associate with the *campesinos* as much as you can until they realize that they are your main reason for coming down here.

Some volunteers insist on maintaining the appearances of poverty, frequently to the point of being oblivious of the goals of the Peace Corps. First they run the risk of putting themselves out of commission. Then they forget that one goal of the Peace Corps is to raise the people's standard of living to our level rather than stoop to theirs. Finally and most importantly, these volunteers neglect the need to develop a constructive philosophy of action for themselves and to create reasonable expectations of what they can accomplish. If a volunteer feels that he is fulfilling his role in the Peace Corps just by "roughing it," he will spend so much time and effort setting up his grass shack and keeping up his image that he will precipitate very few changes among the people.

To live like the poor has a romantic appeal at the beginning, but after two weeks the glamour wears off and you become content with making just the sacrifices which are necessary. I make no attempt to pretend I am poorer than I am, and the Peace Corps has never asked me to. All that seems unnecessary now. I give three cheers for the volunteer in Ghana who wrote that every Saturday he "roughs it" by taking a blonde to the beach. On a train I go first class because I like to read philosophy along the way. My first five days on vacation were spent in the most comfortable hotel in the area where I read, ate well and took three showers a day. In Río Negro, we live modestly in clean, healthy surroundings and we frequently have a meal out when we feel that our reserves of vitamins are running low.

However, any perspective on living conditions in the Peace Corps must see physical discomfort as part of the overall picture. You are never as clean as you would like to be, and there is no escaping dangerous food. Many times I have been served delicious meals by the *campesinos* but other times they are really bad. Our group has had its share of food poisoning, hepatitis, appendicitis and dysentery. None of these are serious, but they mean that anyone who enters the Peace Corps must accept the risk of suffering from the conditions.[1]

To be in the Peace Corps in Chile is to struggle with the language, and I think it is a real accomplishment of our group that now we can do business and conduct our work in Spanish. Frequently, I do not have to translate before using a word; it just pops into my mind and runs over my lips in Spanish. The other morning I awoke from a dream as I have from thousands and suddenly remembered that the dream had been unique because all the characters were speaking in Spanish. In fact, many of us now have an opposite language problem and find ourselves stumbling around when we discuss our work in English. So many words dealing with our work were learned directly in Spanish that we must pause and think before remembering their English equivalent. I frankly do not know the English for some agricultural terms. When the Peace Corps volunteers are together, they speak a gibberish which only they can understand. It consists basically of English words and sentence structure but with Spanish verbs and nouns thrown in and frequently given English endings. "Spanglish," as we call it, would scandalize a language professor; but in our situation it is the only medium through which we can

---

[1] This remark reflects the tragic naïveté of youth. Kathy O'Connor, one of our group, seemed to take hepatitis in stride. But the disease so damaged her liver that some years later the strain of pregnancy was too much; her child was stillborn and Kathy died.

communicate with each other. We speak of *campesinos*, of course, and call ourselves *Piscorinos*.

Another challenge is to adjust to a host of changes which affect your daily life. There are signs that I am adjusting to Chile now. More mail comes to me from within the country than outside. I have grown to expect wine at lunch and to linger for a long time over my meals. Yesterday morning I caught myself putting hot peppers on my scrambled eggs, a cross-cultural act if I ever committed one.

I am used to seeing plazas in fine taste after driving past dirty strings of *callampas* (slums) where barefoot schoolchildren play marbles in the street soiling their white school gowns even more than they were before. My eyes don't flinch at unpainted, damp, cold houses, but focus on further signs of poverty or relative prosperity. The sound of oxcarts rolling by the house is as familiar now as the scraping of autumn leaves on the sidewalks of Scranton. Chile's national ballads and folksongs are as well engraved in my memory as the tunes from *Oklahoma*. Shabby grocery stores don't bother me now, and small modern buildings, common in the United States, catch my eye as something extraordinary when I see them.

Some things which were surprising to me at first, seem different now to me. Country roads are dirt roads; that's all there is to it. The only place for pavement is in the cities or on the main Pan-American Highway. A jeep is not a rough-riding auto; it is a phenomenal machine which allows one to travel to places in one day which many people do not reach in a year. Electricity and hot water are luxuries of the city. Horses and buggies are bulwarks of the transportation system, and only the twice-weekly *rápido* train deserves a diesel engine. Some quaint things will never lose their charm; and I never tire of watching a steam locomotive puffing through the countryside or of seeing the curved line of horses and buggies waiting at the station for the five o'clock train from the north.

The people who once seemed strange and far-off no longer appear so and this is a sign of adjustment. The man who works on the road and lives in the shack beside it is a friend of mine. The truck drivers who sleep and live in their trucks have told me

about their way of life. When a *campesino* comes into town walking his horse, covered by his long black *manta* which fits over his
head and hangs down so that you can see only his shins and
head, I look closely because it could be someone I know.

Above all, adjusting to Chile has meant slowing down. Here
you work at a much slower pace than in the United States, and if
you appear too rushed it is very possible to offend people. You
have to be interested in more than the work at hand—in the meal
over which your business is conducted, in friendship and in live-
ly (if idle) conversation. You must not raise a business matter for
discussion immediately, or slice it up into organized pieces.
Rather, you ease into the subject, talk by way of implication and
leave everything in a half-organized state. "When will I travel here
to meet you again?" You do not answer "This Saturday, at four
o'clock" but rather "Sometime this weekend."

In Chile we must spend more time than usual just being nice
to people and being involved in all kinds of time-consuming personal relationships. Chileans do not share our dedication to efficiency for efficiency's sake, or our desire to put things on a strictly business relationship, or our habit to wander off somewhere
and just be alone.

In retrospect, the major shortcoming of our Peace Corps
training program was its failure to explain the fundamental differences between our culture and Chile's. You might say we had
a personality clash with Chile at first. But they were very patient
and understanding and we worked at overcoming it and now we
get along quite well. We remain, however, very different; my
understanding of Latin American culture goes only as far as recognizing difference as difference and refusing to make a judgment about which culture is better—even though, because of my
upbringing, I prefer my own. Chileans and North Americans
have altogether distinct attitudes toward life and work, toward
themselves as individuals, toward others, and in numerous matters of taste.

The biggest mistake I have made so far has been in the matter of recognizing and following clearly defined social customs. In
Chile, a person who enters a small community like Río Negro as
part of an organization like the Peace Corps is expected to pay

calls on all local officials and prominent citizens, explain his work and request their assistance. I was anxious to get to work and unaware of this duty until it was too late; then I compounded the damage by calling on the mayor at his home in the country when I was visiting some *campesinos* around his *fundo*. Later I learned that such spontaneous social calls at country estates—and I had made many—are frowned upon. One of the weaknesses in my own performance as a volunteer has been in this secondary but important matter of maintaining good relations with the upper classes. I have almost no contact with them at all.

Despite the fact that the original adjustments have been made, we still need to know a great deal more about Chile. It is always a temptation to withdraw into a world of North American friends, North American magazines and other Peace Corps volunteers and to hold back from the people. You have to hold back something and cannot adjust completely; but the moment you cease making the effort to learn more about Chile and to increase your span of Chilean friends, you have left the real spirit of the Peace Corps behind.

There are mountain passes to Argentina to explore, descents from the coastal mountains to the sea. There are social problems of a different nature than the ones we know: unemployment, urban development, housing. By a perpetual curiosity and hearty interest in Chile, one can avoid reaching a plateau and going no further. This is especially true of the language. The minute my Spanish stops progressing it starts getting worse. Now that our grasp of the language is adequate for our work, it would be very easy to continue to rely on our basic vocabulary and tenuous grasp of grammar without a conscious effort to improve it, but that would be a mistake. Nevertheless, the most important challenge of the Peace Corps is not *conocering* ("getting to know about") Chile, or perfecting your Spanish, but performing a job.

Love,
Tommy

Chapter 8

BEYOND OUR REGION: VALDIVIA AND LONCOCHE

I find a Chilean mentor in a veteran organizer of cooperatives and enjoy the camaraderie of volunteers stationed nearby.

April 15, 1962

Dear Mom, Dad and Jim,

I have been in Valdivia all week. The idea for this trip originated in Orsono some time ago after I spent a long Sunday afternoon with the youth club and a friend advised me that Don Tito Steffens had arrived in town for the day. He is known within Institute circles as the best expert on cooperatives in the south of Chile. Although the ride was long and the hour was late, I decided to travel to Osorno and introduce myself to this man whom I now consider to be the most outstanding individual I have met here.

Señor Steffens was not affronted by the young upstart who came knocking on his door late at night to talk about cooperatives. This tall, slender man with balding hair and a blond mustache ushered me inside the home where he was staying. Don Tito possesses the bearing and mind of a college professor. He is, I discovered that night, an accountant. He explained that his work from Monday to Friday in Valdivia meant he could pursue his "hobby" only in his spare time. His attempts to form cooperatives in the Osorno area were hampered by distance and by lack of time. My desire to form them, I replied, was curtailed by lack of expert knowledge. That evening in Osorno we both saw the possibility of a coalition. Don Tito invited me to travel to Valdivia and see the cooperatives he has formed here. This opportunity has been the biggest break for me in my Peace Corps work so far.

During this week I have enjoyed talking with the whole Steffens family. Don Tito's wife is a beautiful, middle-aged woman—sensitive, sympathetic and with a somewhat sad tone in her voice. He acts toward her as though they were still courting. Don Tito has given all his children more education than he had, and his whole family shares his interest in cooperatives. His oldest daughter, Helga, is writing her thesis in law school on co-op law in Chile. Señora Steffens used to accompany him when he first worked with co-ops in Pucón, a small village in the Andes near the Argentine border. In many ways, the Steffens have never left Pucón. They return every summer and talk continually about their walks through the Andes and their life in the little mountain town where Don Tito once served as a government clerk.

Don Tito's personal accomplishment in Valdivia is that he has single-handedly nursed credit unions into existence in all the distressed areas of the city. This week he never seemed to tire, and hardly stopped for a bite to eat after work before going into session with one of them.

Our schedule has been to talk at breakfast and lunch at his house, work in the afternoon and evening and then return to his home for a late dinner and more conversation. Don Tito has taught me how to form a cooperative, and we have discussed each community where I am working. When we begin something together in one of them he will assume the responsibility as the expert and I will do much of the work. When it comes to cooperatives, he is my boss now.

Before coming to Valdivia, I performed another of my duties as a volunteer. The provinces of Osorno, Valdivia and Cautín make up an administrative region for the Institute. A local steering committee helps direct activities in all the "regions" of the IER, and Peace Corps volunteers have been asked to serve on these committees. I have been given the job for our region. Every other month I make the five-hour train trip a hundred miles north to Loncoche to attend the meetings. These have helped me appreciate the importance of the Institute in Chile and some of the problems it faces.

In our region alone, we will inaugurate four new schools in the next year. Around each school, new zones of community development activity are already being opened, and there are difficulties of a different kind in each area. A volunteer and a *delegado* are being sent to one zone where 70 percent of the people are openly Communists. In another area a particular clique of landowners is the problem. Rather than assist the Institute's work of hope, they store their money in a Swiss bank and work their laborers so hard that they can return home only once every week or two. In another town, the Institute faces a very hostile press.

The Institute is racing against time, and in the light of its rapid expansion and sense of urgency, it is impossible to expect orderly, step-by-step, organization. Nonetheless, the rush puts its staff members and the volunteers in extremely trying situations. I brought a case in point before the steering committee meeting this month. It had to do with the operations of the new school in Huiscape, a village just outside of Loncoche.

First of all, classes began at the school too soon. Forty students began the course with only two teachers before the director arrived to assign classes or outline the curriculum. Jackie Seigler, one of our outstanding "home ec" volunteers, was named nutritionist for this school as well as for the one in Loncoche twenty miles away. Jackie worked under the following conditions: There was no cook and only a small stove. The school had no lights, electricity or running water. Even the building was not completed until the day before the school was dedicated officially a month after the course began.

Somehow Jackie and two valiant Chilean staff members managed until the dedication but that day was the worst of all, when the IER expected a hundred guests but four times that many came. The water went off four times that day as Jackie was preparing a meal for four hundred. When the water came on, it flooded the floor. The large stove finally arrived, and the carpenter came to install it on the day of the dedication. Jackie had a hard time keeping sawdust out of the food. Gigantic quantities of food were needed for the luncheon yet someone, no one knows who, left the chickens in water all night and they were spoiled the following morning. No assistance came from Santiago until the day before the event, yet Jackie and the Chileans assigned to the school made the day a success anyway. We whisked Jackie back to Loncoche early in the evening because she looked glassy-eyed.

Although Loncoche is a five-hour train trip away, it is the nearest Peace Corps site to ours and Jan and I like to travel there for business, relaxation and technical advice. Gerry Garthe is stationed in Loncoche with Jackie because Mr. Langford decided to send no one back to Rupanco. As the volunteers live together in a boarding school, life in Loncoche is a little less lonely and a lot more fun than in Río Negro.

It is fun to watch Jackie as she surveys the floor like the headwaiter at Sardi's while meals are served. The students and staff respect her as being obdurately sensible in the matter of nutrition, yet there is a constant undercurrent during dinner of jokes about *vitaminas* and the zany idea of eating potatoes with the skins on. However, the school has kept within its food budget for the first time, and the students are eating more nourishing foods than ever. Some complain that they are eating less, but Jackie shows no mercy to anyone who wants to revert to the old custom of stuffing themselves with carbohydrates. She even replied tartly when the school director asked for an extra piece of bread.

Gerry Garthe is still the steady, hard worker that he was in Rupanco. He is starting a project which will supply six-week-old chickens to farmers willing to begin a chicken cooperative. Now he is building the chicken coops himself and installing a kerosene incubator. Meanwhile, he is meeting with the men in the countryside around Loncoche. Already there is real interest in the cooperative.

Gerry was president of his fraternity at college; and with his wit, folksinging and guitar he has the capacity to inject the atmosphere of a frat house on a Saturday night into his forlorn room in Loncoche where we gather. Jackie reads us "Uncle Ned's" column in the newspaper serving her hometown of Cove in Polk County, Arkansas, the *Mena Weekly Star*, and we roar at that.

But most of all we gather in Gerry's room to hear a different kind of news relayed to us by a friend whom we have affectionately named "Hepatitis" Partridge. Kay Partridge has also been assigned to Loncoche, but has not arrived yet because she contracted hepatitis and has spent the last three months in bed. Yet Kay has been a regular part of the life of Loncoche. Twice a week, a detailed account of Peace Corps news reaches us from Kay who, like all sick volunteers, is staying at Mr. Langford's house. Last month there were five volunteers recuperating there under Mrs. Langford's care. Can you think of a better place to get news? Everything happening within the Peace Corps is known in Loncoche within a few days. When Jan or I arrive, a special reading is arranged for us. There is no more interesting experience.

Last weekend, Janet, Jackie, Gerry and I came down to Valdivia from Loncoche after one of our regional meetings. It was the first weekend free for any of us since January. Two American AID contractors working in Valdivia had invited us down to meet some Chilean friends at a party they were giving last Saturday night. Coming to Valdivia on Saturday, we could be as casual about travel plans as our Chilean friends. While we were having lunch in the dining car of the train, the car was detached from the train to Valdivia and hooked up to one destined for Puerto Montt. Our bags, passports, and overcoats went on to Valdivia while we sat there conversing, not noticing the change. We became aware of it in time to avoid the trip to Puerto Montt but not to catch the bags. Luckily, when we arrived late in Valdivia the suitcases were waiting for us in the station master's office and our two friends were there to take us to the party.

Saturday night we met the Valdivians, drank *pisco* and made a foreigner's attempt at the American twist. Sunday morning Jackie and Janet made a North American breakfast of pancakes, bacon and eggs in the home of the AID contractor and his wife. For dinner they prepared southern fried chicken and hot biscuits. And then we parted.

I took my fellow volunteers to the train station and said good-by because I was staying in Valdivia. Then I made the long walk back from the station to the main part of town, smoking my pipe and thinking how glad I was to have this week ahead of me. I was content and happy with the only kind of happiness I know—a brief pause spent in the company of friends. Part of my work has been done and another is about to begin.

There is little more that I could want except my family itself, but through letters I can play the role of Hepatitis Partridge, keeping you informed of the news and waiting anxiously for the day when I'm in the circle again that drinks hot milk before an early bedtime in Scranton. With the rapid passage of time, I refuse to believe that that moment is far away.

Love,
Tommy

PHOTO ALBUM

Like the letters that make up this book, a box of slides and snap-shots had been put away and came to light again after more than 30 years. Here are the best of those souvenirs.

In addition there is a new photo, on page 123, taken in the spring of 1996 by my friends and fellow volunteers Elden and Judy Stang, which shows that the co-op in San Juan de la Costa continues to function today.

On September 23, 1961—the
day after Congress passed the
Peace Corps Act—I board the
Santa Isabel with forty-four other
volunteers, Peace Corps staffers
and families. Director Shriver
had brought the good news of
the law's passage to New York
and hosted a lunch for our
contingent, dubbed "Chile I,"
the first group of volunteers to
go abroad after the Peace Corps
became a permanent agency of
the United States.

"Chile I" volunteers and staff pose for a "class picture" at Lo Vásquez, a training center of the Institute of Rural Education.

First row: Liz Langford, Ann O'Grady, Sarah Patterson, Terry Atwood, Evadna Smith, Jackie Siegler, Irene Avila, Jacqueline Wallace, Larry Cartano, Glen Trebour, Jim Berkey;

Second row: Dit Langford, Bob South, Marty Ronan, Mike Curtin, Judy Grant, Ramona Marotz, Kay Partridge, Bill Fox, Kathy O'Connor, Ken Bartlett, Amos Roos;

Third row: Walter Langford (director), Joe Keyerleber, Wayne Wolf, Jim Fitzgerald, Bob Woodruff, Frank O'Hern, Gerry

Garthe, Emory Tomor, Sharon Pulchin, me (partly hidden), Elden Stang, George Smith (deputy director, wearing a tie);

Fourth row: Peggy Ahern, Jim Dungan, Mary Ellen Craig, Fred Morgner, Janet Boegli, Kathy Schoening, Larry Cornish, Joan Workman, Dan McCarthy, Larry Forrester, Jim Coleman, Larry West, Tom Paulick, Dave Coombs.

Not pictured: Roger Marshall is most likely behind the camera.

In Río Negro, Janet Boegli laughs
with her co-workers Carmen
Carillo and Maria Oviedo (above),
and with me (left). The Hotel
Central (top opposite) boasts the
best food and lodging in town.
A Socialist banner spans the
street and a Communist poster
promises "the victory of a people's
government" (inset).

Catrihuala 1962: Don Pablino
Melillanka holds forth on a stump
in a depleted forest. He was the
Marxist Indian leader who famous-
ly dared me to return after the
snow fell. The bridge (above
right) marks the boundary of land
claimed by the Indian insurgents.
The Huechuan family poses
proudly atop the mountain;

poverty persists there today and
ownership of the land is still
contested. Seen from the road
to Catrihuala, a sawmill stands
abandoned (opposite); the Indians
hoped Amos Roos (inset) could
rehabilitate it. Members of a rebel
band (below) guard alerce shingles
stacked for sale.

In Rupanco, members of the Yañez
family proudly display bumper
crops of carrots, lettuce and
cabbage—produce for their new
Plan Hortaliza, the "Vegetable Plan"
of 1962. Helping the farm workers
raise vegetables "from the furrow to
the fair" was a signal achievement
for our team of Peace Corps
volunteers, for our IER co-workers

here, and for the people of Rupanco as well. *Campesinos* who grew some vegetables for market had long been exploited by middle-men (and women) in the towns.

Co-ops like the one we founded enabled farmers to buy seed and fertilizer cheaper, then get higher prices for their crops.

Juan Yañez, his wife and other co-op members truck their crops to market. Community leader Alba Aquilar (with cigarette) haggles with market women. In sight of Volcano Osorno (opposite) another family shows off a garden, as does Guillermo Casas, one of our most successful growers (inset). Alvarado Valdovino, Juan Wierdervoll and his wife Marta sell their carrots in Osorno. Decades later I learned that Juan had died and Marta did not have a single photo of him—until I could send her a print of this one.

In San Juan de la Costa, a region without a town center, the landmark Mission church stands like a beacon. Helmut Seeger (left, with his wife) was my mentor in community development but later opposed our efforts here. In 1963, coastal residents gather for the charter meeting of their co-op and elect leaders from among proud candidates (inset). Three decades later Cooperativa Campesina de San Juan de La Costa still operates, as evident in this 1996 photograph taken by Elden and Judy Stang.

My friends and I: At the Colegio San Mateo in Osorno (above), Chilean students surround Father Haske, who had been my Latin teacher and JV basketball coach. In Atlantic City, my family—Margaret and James Scanlon, and brother Jim—(below) relax on the beach, where they took me after my return home in the summer of 1963.

My able coworker in southern Chile, René Borquez (top). Father Hesburgh shares a moment with me in Río Negro. I take to the saddle on a Pacific beach near Osorno. Back stateside, a television panel discussing the Peace Corps includes Art Buchwald, Sargent Shriver, Leo Rosten (host), me, Georgianna Shine (a "Ghana I" volunteer) and Holmes Alexander, Peace Corps critic.

PEACE CORPS

Washington 25, D. C.

February 21, 1962

Rev. Theodore M. Hesburgh, C.S.C.
President
University of Notre Dame
Notre Dame, Indiana

Dear Father Hesburgh:

Many thanks for sending me the letter from Tom Scanlon. I was delighted to read it, and thought it was a masterpiece. In fact, all the people here at Peace Corps Headquarters liked it so much we're using it as the opening section of our presentation to the United States Congress. I'll send you a copy of the presentation as soon as it is off the press, which should be within the next few days. Perhaps you would like to send it to Scanlon's parents. I'm sure they would be very proud, especially since, to my knowledge, it is completely unprecedented in the history of the United States Congress for a letter of this type to be used for the opening of a Congressional presentation.

Best regards,

Respectfully,

Sarge

Robert Sargent Shriver, Jr.
Director

Dear Mr. + Mrs. Scanlon,
I thought you
would enjoy having
this letter. I'm enclosing
one you can send to Tom.
Regards, Father Fred Hes.

A letter to Father Hesburgh from Sargent Shriver informs him that my "Hello Everybody" letter will be used as the opening section of the Peace Corps' first budget submission to Congress. In turn, Father Ted adds a note and forwards it to my parents.

Chapter 9

WE HAVE FOUND OUR
WORK AT LAST!
RÍO NEGRO AND BEYOND

After months of frustration, our team of volunteers and delegados *selects the communities where we will work, and we define the projects we shall pursue in the months to come.*

April 28, 1962

Dear Mom, Dad and Jim,

Since I cannot be in Scranton for your anniversary, this letter will be my gift, and it really contains good news because I feel I can say that at last, four months after leaving Lo Vásquez in January, I have found good, satisfying work to do. I believe that this has been my most important accomplishment in the Peace Corps so far—creating my work and defining my relationship with my Chilean hosts.

Over the past two months Janet and I have defined our role in the community development program of the Institute in the area around Osorno. We have even picked the communities where we want to concentrate our efforts and Don Tito Steffens will assist us!

March and April were months of frustrations and some successes, like music played sometimes in a major key, other times a minor. One of the first frustrations is that Río Negro is not a very appealing city. Maybe if we were working with the people there it would be different; but for us Río Negro is only a place to live and not a very pleasant one either. The main street in town contains many general stores, half a plaza and several canteens. Then it twists around a bend, passes some government buildings and dips down to the post office and train station. That is the main part of town. There is a hospital in Río Negro but no doctor; the dentist is in charge. Río Negro has no movie house and the water supply is turned on only three times a day. It has its share of nice homes painted bright colors, but there are many more decrepit ones, tilted by the earthquake or sunk into small crevices from which they have only partially emerged. On a public lot at the southernmost reaches of the town, the poorest of the poor live in a slum where five hundred men, women and children are bunched into emergency housing. All of these people draw their water from a single spout.

We live directly across the street from this shantytown in houses built by CORVI (Corporación de Vivienda), the government housing development agency. In this CORVI settlement, thirty small unpainted houses have been constructed with running water and electricity and with a small patch of grass well fenced-off in the back. At first sight, these wood homes seem intended to displace the slum across the street, and they would be ideal for that. However, these homes are way beyond the price of the unemployed. Those who can afford them—people with middle-class employment—find them small and cramped. Consequently these houses serve no one really well, and we were the first to move into them after they stood unoccupied for a year.

When we arrived in Río Negro, Jan and I discovered that, despite the work we had done in January, the Institute had not yet rented the two houses and that we and the Institute's *delegados* had nowhere to live. I had to hurry to Osorno and assure the CORVI director that the Institute really did intend to rent them, and he magnanimously allowed us to move in anyway. Then no funds were forthcoming to furnish the houses or to buy food. This placed Janet and me in a very difficult situation. As Peace Corps volunteers, we had access to enough money to make both homes comfortable and to supply ourselves and the *delegados* with food. However, we felt we should all live together as equal members of a team, and we realized that paying expenses for the Institute would alter our entire relationship with the *delegados*, remove our equality and distort whatever communication we had. The *delegados*, embarrassed by their lack of funds, were beginning to regard the homes as the Peace Corps' headquarters and were staying away until Janet and I explained that expenses would be divided among us equally.

Thus, for the first month and a half we all slept on the floor because we had no money for beds. Six of us had between us one knife, three spoons and three cups plus a small kerosene burner for heating coffee. When they discovered our plight, the fathers in Río Negro stripped their own spare beds of mattresses and made our lives considerably more comfortable. We ate from American farm surpluses and found the cheese and Spam sent down by CARE delectable. When our supply of food ran out, we insisted that the *delegados* eat with us in a boarding house, and we charged it to the Institute. Six weeks later, this "sleep-in" and "eat-in" paid off. The Institute rented the two homes, and funds arrived to buy a stove and some wood. Then came money for furnishings and food. Finally the Institute rushed to pay the bills at the boarding house before we ran up more.

Now, although we still have to fight the mud and cold, and struggle to keep things dry, our homes are very comfortable. I have the luxury of luxuries, a private room. The theme song of the Peace Corps in Chile so far could be "All I want is a room somewhere… Wouldn't it be loverly?" because the most distressing inconvenience for all the volunteers is their inability to be alone—to find a private place. Even that inconvenience has been removed from me now.

The girls occupy one of the CORVI houses, and the men occupy the other. We are all better friends now after undergoing the experiences of the last two months. Let me tell you a little about the members of our team.

First, there is Janet Boegli. She has a very sensitive make-up and prefers a few close friends to many superficial ones. Basically shy, Janet is one of those intellectuals who is constantly wondering, constantly searching for new meanings and for poetic glimpses into the lives of others. Very frequently, she finds them.

Jan lives with two other girls. Maria Oviedo is a conscientious and competent *delegada* who is known and liked by a great many people in each of the communities she serves. Maria is strongly principled and has a sharp sense of time. Her face is round, topped with short black hair; and she can flash a very winning smile when she wants to. More often her face seems glum.

Jan's other co-worker, Carmen Carillo, is more even-tempered and gay. Carmen is a rather stout girl with an extremely beautiful face and soft eyes. While a most competent worker, she does not take her work so seriously as Maria. Her moods, when she has them, are coquettish or even giddy. Jan constantly compares Carmen to her sorority sisters in the United States, and it is not hard to picture her as the hit of an American campus, especially when you see her chattering away at a party or sleeping late in the morning.

Of my two co-workers, one has been transferred, and I will tell you about him later. The *delegado* who will remain is René Bórquez with whom I worked in December. René is a kind young man—very anxious to learn. He has trouble organizing details, but he is very interested in doing things the right way. People who talk to René for the first time, instantly like him. He has the simple and sincere soul of a *campesino* and, I might add, a *campesino's* physical robustness and prowess.

This small group lives in harmony now. I am learning, however, that it is difficult to please three women at the same time. One night I drove Carmen to see her parents in the Hacienda Rupanco. We all went along, and I lingered as late as possible so that she could have a full day at home. When we finally drove back to Río Negro that night, Maria started to cry because she was afraid the neighbors would see how late she had stayed out.

Living so close to an American girl was something which I did not anticipate. How many young men who join the Peace Corps today realize that their co-worker might want to put curtains on the silly windows, or that they will return from the field some night to find a fellow volunteer in tears over a ripped skirt? Poor Janet was very upset when she ran the jeep into a horse-drawn milk cart. (It was nothing serious; Río Negro went for a day without milk is all.) She has had other unexpected problems. For instance, once the "Mothers for Breast-feeding of America" wrote her a nasty letter after *Time* magazine reported that she was teaching the *campesinas* how to use powdered milk; they thought she was promoting the use of formula. Jan wrote back that if the promotion of breast-feeding in Chile were our mission, we could all go home.

Janet and I felt we could help the *delegados* mainly in two ways, by creating greater expectations of what could be accomplished in a specific amount of time, and by emphasizing true community development methods in the communities. We wanted to make the people less aware that they were receiving services from the Institute and more conscious of the growing strength of their own organization as its members met, discussed problems and took action. However, we knew these suggestions had to be made indirectly because the *delegados* were extremely independent and resented anyone who set himself up as an authority.

In two short months, René has demonstrated many times the perceptivity and patience necessary for community development work. He has postponed meetings which seemed unlikely to produce results because not enough conversation in the community preceded them. The other day he very deftly yet firmly suggested to a *patrón* that he not make an appearance at a meeting which his workers had called to discuss their own problems.

The other *delegado* with whom I worked was entirely different. Fortunately he was called to another assignment and a new *delegado* will soon replace him. His tactic was to call a meeting as soon as he arrived in a community. Perhaps he would speak first with a few leaders or to some prosperous families in whose house he had lodged, but he did little personal canvassing of the community. When he agreed to make house-to-house visits, he and I found families who had never been advised of the community meetings. However, this did not dissuade him from having meetings for the sake of meetings; and wherever we went he would start off by presenting the "Institute's program" to an assembled throng and tell them all he was going to do for them. This *delegado* believed in exhorting the people to unite rather than in giving them their first experiences in working together. He did not start out at the level of the people's needs. For instance, when we found hog cholera to be a real problem in one community, he lectured on hoof-and-mouth disease in the first meeting. During these meetings the people sat, nodded their assent to everything he said, and did not participate. I was most discouraged when it seemed the people preferred this kind of meeting—preferred to come out and hear a ringing speech, then return home without any new responsibilities or intentions to change their conditions of life.

Even without the problems caused by this kind of *delegado*, community development work is difficult enough. It is never easy to walk into a community and start talking to the people about their problems. If we did not have the Institute as a way of introducing ourselves, it would be nearly impossible to avoid appearing as an intruder or just plain nosy. At least the people have heard of the IER and take our claim to be there to help them at face value. Nonetheless, I have never found the perfect formula for telling the people I am there to help them help themselves. First of all, they are not accustomed to such an interest. Then, some are uninterested or shy. Others are more openly conservative. "Cooperatives will never work here," they declare. "Clover does not grow here," they say abruptly as we try to focus on solutions as well as problems.

Charity or practical advice would have appealed to all, but the people were not willing to make many efforts to organize themselves and our mission sounded very nebulous to them at the start. They discovered that I was not an expert soon enough. That I had nothing to give them, I insisted from the first. That they could accomplish much through social organization, I never doubted; but to ask them to believe in the value of working together was like asking them to believe in something they had never seen before—something which this *gringo* who knew less about farming than they did was going to help them find.

The people always treated us with respect and reserve. When we offer our help, they interrupt us in the middle of a phrase with a polite "Thank you, sir." But I wondered if we were communicating with them. It is so difficult to judge what is in a *campesino's* mind, and I wished I could be one for a day so that I could anticipate their suspicions and fears. There must be more to them than the childlike innocence we see. One begins to believe that they suffer patiently and without hope, but I know there are things which trouble and unite the *campesinos* and that they are more aware of their deprivations than they reveal. For example, we had a lesson in the fact that these people mislead us. One schoolteacher offered us his strong support, protested he was a friend of the United States and even offered us the use of his school. Two months later he announced he was a candidate for the city council on the Communist ticket.

Visiting people in their homes was slow, hard work. It involved walking long distances and presented unexpected hazards. One morning our team set out to visit all the homes in a small community called Chahuilco. The second stop René and I made was at the home of a rather prosperous small farmer. This gentleman made his small fortune, we soon learned, by being a master brewer of *chicha* (hard cider). In his basement he had seven casks, each bubbling slowly through a small air hole opened in the top. These seven casks contained *chicha* in seven different stages of fermentation. There was "sweet cider," "hard cider," "strong cider" and "old cider," to name a few. So that we could appreciate his art, our friend offered us a sample of every vintage. "It does nothing to you," he insisted as he poured the champagne-like fermented apple juice into tall glasses. "Nothing at all; here help yourself."

When we managed to escape from the cellar, our host decided to invite us to lunch. "There is more *chicha*," he noted, "and as for the food, it is the luck of the pot because we didn't know you were coming." My luck was not good that day, because the pot was cooking the stomach and feet of the sheep he had slaughtered a few days before. I would never have been able to eat this dinner without the false courage of his apple wine. When René and I wandered away from his house after lunch, we were a little tipsy and ill. The girls were waiting for us in the jeep, anxious to move on in the community. "Drive us home," is all I said to Janet, realizing at last that I was an hour late. My day ended there.

Despite all our difficulties, this person-to-person combing of communities was a rich source of ideas for future projects. In each community a different starting point would be apparent. One whole community was not enrolled in the social security system through which they gain their right to medical attention in the hospital. All the crops in another area were ridden with plant lice. One rural neighborhood grew fruit and the farmers all had the same blight on their trees. Another community produced dairy products but their milk was being rejected in town because of its high bacterial content. In short, our experiences proved the basic tenet of community development: that communities have common problems which call for common action.

In the past two months we had experiences with good and bad community development. For instance, we opened the year in a place called Millantué after making elaborate preparations which attracted the attention of the local *patrón*, parish priest and schoolteacher. They all decided to come and encourage the people. However, there were so many supporting actors at the meeting that the people never received the chance to speak. When the next meeting was called, only four or five men showed up. On the other hand, in a community called Río Blanco, René and I organized a vaccination campaign in close collaboration with the community leadership. The community president registered the names of those who requested the vaccine and how many doses they wanted. When the time came to certify the vaccinations in city hall, the people even performed the paperwork. This community has responded so well to community development that it is ready for more ambitious steps, like starting irrigation projects or purchasing a tractor. One day in Río Blanco I even saw a man making his oxen run.

Most of the community development work in Río Blanco was greatly abetted by the Ministry of Agriculture, which is the only other agency, private or public, working with farmers in the area. The Ministry operates very differently than we do. It has a wealth of material resources, most of them provided through the United States AID program, and it makes these resources the basis of its activities in the community. The Institute and the Peace Corps, however, both put emphasis on working with only the resources of the people. The Institute and Ministry do not work together in this province, and one day last month the Ministry tried to impress us with what it expects to accomplish this year. In an hour-long meeting, a Ministry aide enumerated grandiose projects and the thousands of dollars available to him. The *delegados* claim that many of these plans are never accomplished; perhaps they are right, but the effect of that meeting on me was disastrous.

All the frustrations of the two months came together that day. I thought of our own paltry resources and of the lack of confidence which even the *delegados* were beginning to show toward the idea of community development. I thought how difficult the past two months had been—of pleading with the Institute to send us funds for the house; of the strain of living with people whose complete friendship or confidence we have yet to gain. Some of the habits of the *campesinos*—the way they slur their words, the time they demand to be spent in idle chatter—were beginning to wear. The rut of the *campesinos'* slow life seemed to be dragging me into it. There was mud on the floor that day and nothing seemed to dry. I wondered whether it would be wise to persevere, and it seemed that patience might be a vice, an imprudent stubbornness in the face of insurmountable odds when it would be better for me, for Chile and for the Peace Corps if I went home. What saved me from packing my bags was the thought that even though we were not an immense help to the *campesinos*, in most cases we provided the only help they had.

Fortunately I have gotten beyond that terrible moment of frustration and settled into our work. We have visited over a dozen places and talked to people until we found those we thought we could help the most. Now, although we will be concerned for the Institute's overall program in the area, certain communities will receive our special attention. In each, we will try to create a program that is new.

Janet has added a program of health education to the agendas of the meeting which *delegadas* hold with women. Until now, the women's clubs were making clothes and sewing most of the time. Every day of the week, Jan visits a different community and gives talks illustrated by pictures of babies with healthy faces, babies with runny noses, and nutritious foods served in attractive ways. She works in five communities, always with a *delegada*.

Jan has studied the principles of community development, and she feels that her most important role in a women's *centro* is to divert the women from their sewing to problems which do not ordinarily fit the narrow confines of a woman's world in rural Latin America. The women can organize garden clubs for profit. They can make their husbands think about sanitary conditions. They can provide a more hearty community spirit to the men's get-togethers by making sweet breads and cakes. Jan has had results already, and she has encountered difficulties too. Forming a community organization last month, the women elected as secretary a young girl who could neither read or write. Yet the women take very well to her; and this past Easter Sunday one women's club prepared so many goodies for a work meeting that the men returned to it willingly. Janet said it was the best Easter of her life.

Like Jan, I will work in five communities, each of them presenting special difficulties and challenges. Let me tell you a little about each of them: Nancuán, Hacienda Buenaventura, Hacienda Rupanco, San Juan de la Costa, and Catrihuala.

Sometimes a rural neighborhood has so little communication with other communities—never mind with the world at large—that it develops its own characteristics and traditions, its own distinct personality. Such a place is Nancuán, a little community not far from Río Negro. There are thirty-two houses in Nancuán, many of them belonging to families with the same last name. Its unique and troubled personality is nurtured through intermarriage within the community and within families themselves.

Almost everyone in Nancuán produces the same thing. Some have sizable plantings of sugar beets, a recent innovation, while dairy cattle have been the mainstay for many years and will remain so. The startling fact about Nancuán's dairy herds is that none of the thirty-two farmers owns a bull. Until last year, there was one; but it went on a rampage killing a small child, and it was shot. Now the people refuse to allow a bull in the community. This attitude is a luxury afforded only by Nancuán's location, which borders on a large dairy *fundo* containing numerous bulls, and the people know how to tear down fences at appropriate times. Besides being illegal, this practice hurts the small farmers because they have no control over the breed of the calves produced by these matings. The dairy cattle in Nancuán are a mongrel stock, and their breed is getting worse each year.

The *campesinos* of Nancuán are rough, cagey people, extremely individualistic and not given much to community life. There have been some bitter arguments within the community. For example, we were delayed for a week there when a man was severely wounded in a family feud. The year before there had been an incident at one of the *fiestas* staged by the Institute. The girl who was elected queen of the fiesta had unfortunately lived in wedlock for eight days with her husband when he was discovered to be already married. As the queen was being crowned, the families of her competitors began to mock and taunt her and the party ended with a beer fight!

Worse yet, politics complicated community life. The conservative mayor of Río Negro had begun a rural electrification project in Nancuán with private funds. When he left office, the new party in power found fault with the electrical transformer and made no attempt to help the people complete the installations. For two years people sat in their homes at night with light bulbs dangling from the ceiling but no juice. This experience hardly encouraged the people to think constructively about the future.

Our first meeting in Nancuán was held in the pitch dark. I asked about their need for a bull hoping that some suggestion, some new plan, would come from the floor. The idea of purchasing one bull to serve the entire community never occurred to them. When I talked of "artificial breeding," a practice recently introduced in the area, I met a blank wall of disbelief. (You should have heard me try to explain *that* in my elementary Spanish.) It became clear that only one subject interested the people: *"La luz, Don Tomás."* Even in getting the light, which concerned them so urgently, they were unorganized. The one accomplishment of the meeting was that a group of men was assigned to unravel the political mess surrounding the electric installations. I committed myself to this project as a means to an end. Once the political battles being raged at the people's expense are over, something can be done to better their lives.

Hacienda Buenaventura is the idyllic *fundo* owned by Roberto Urisar that I visited several times in December. In the past two months, I have worked a great deal here and founded a youth club. I teach the youngsters capture-the-flag and a variety of ping-pong games. When we set up the volleyball equipment there one Saturday, the entire community started to play.

However, the old problem of the *patrón* who is too good persists in Buenaventura. The people are well taken care of, yet their community organization lacks strong personalities and is disunited. The *inquilinos* and the *patrón* are all wonderful people. It is the system which is out of date. Symbolic of our difficulties there was what happened the day of our first meeting. The *patrón* unwittingly scheduled a trip to Osorno for polio shots, and everyone had to go, and so our meeting was called off. Eventually we hope to establish a consumer co-op in the *fundo* so that the people can transport their own goods and make some money in the bargain. However, everything depends on the disposition of the *patrón* and the feelings he makes known, directly or indirectly, to the workers.

Now that we live in Río Negro, Hacienda Rupanco is farthest away, yet I want to maintain contact with the people there so I have accepted the invitation of a small group of women to help them run a small cooperative store. These women live in a small section of the hacienda called Laguna Bonita. My efforts there are directed by the "ripple on the pond" school of Peace Corps philosophy; surely intensive and successful activity in this small area could have a long-range impact on the entire worker population of the hacienda. The women in Laguna Bonita acquired the ideals of the cooperative independently of me. Señora Alba Alquilar, the local schoolteacher, was the first to promote the idea. Señora Alba is the undisputed leader of this community, an ardent advocate of women's rights who was elected to the city council of Puerto Octay in the last election. A very likable but gruff person, Señora Alba allows a cigarette to hang from her mouth as she announces in the shrill voice she uses on the schoolchildren what the next project of the women's club will be. Señora Alba has the bad habit of thinking three months ahead with regard to the co-op and asking many questions that I find difficult to answer. Nonetheless, she and the other women seem delighted when I come and talk to them about groups like themselves who organized cooperatives in Denmark, England and Germany in the past century.

The president of this organization is a puppet if I ever saw one. This fifty-year-old woman (recently on leave to have a baby) always arrives late with a very purposeful walk. Then she sits all alone before the other women on a metal chair with her handbag on her lap and agrees with everything the schoolteacher says. It is terrible community development to run a meeting like this, but principles of community development are overridden by the confidence the people have in each other, the respect they have for Señora Alba and the way their respect is returned. The schoolteacher is very proud of the women in her club and is really one of them in her own special way.

The women's club in Laguna Bonita is a fascinating collection of widows, mothers and spinsters. When I pleaded with them to let the men into the cooperative, they replied, "The men don't do anything" relevant to community spirit. Yet these women can be exceedingly feminine. They allow me to finish explaining a detail of the co-op before they smugly inform me that they have taken care of that already. And when they show you their store, their pride is like that of a mother for her son.

Another place where we want to set "ripples on a pond" is San Juan de la Costa. The name refers to a broad area in the provincial coast, a small political district therein and a Capuchin Mission within the district. We hope to start a cooperative in the Mission to which many of the people in the coast could eventually belong.

This Mission has been the center of commercial, social and religious life in the coast for the past one hundred and fifty years. It sits on a hill and consists mainly of a large yellow church, a convent and a school for girls. Alongside these buildings are the warehouse for the self-sufficient four-hundred-acre farm, an office and living quarters for the one priest in attendance. These structures surround a churchyard where people cluster in small crowds and horses are lined up along hitching posts outside the Father's office. Seeing the traffic within this self-contained social and economic unit makes one lose the sense of isolation one feels while approaching San Juan from afar. In winter, the approach is never pleasant. It is usually raining, and getting there means taking an hour-long, soggy walk from the last gravel road.

Our first excursion to San Juan de la Costa began with a call at the Mission. We were welcomed there by Padre Auxencio, a Dutch missionary with a long beard who had been a professor of law in Amsterdam. He invited us into his dining room where we were served hot coffee, soup and bread after our long journey. Then he briefed us on his own experiences in the coast and said

our help was badly needed indeed. The picture Father painted of
life on the coast was even sadder than I had anticipated and we
found it was accurate in our visits to homes. The harvest was so
poor that many people could not obtain seeds for next year. One
man told me that he had sown five sacks of wheat and harvested
three. Being without income, the people cannot purchase food in
town and it is from the harvest that they expect their winter supply. "What will they do?" I asked the priest. "I don't know," he replied. "Perhaps they will have to rob." In a visit I made to one
home, an old man gave me his reaction to the poor harvest. "This
is just the way we live," he said, "until we die."

Father Auxencio says that the biggest problem in San Juan is
the people's suspicion of outsiders. This lack of confidence in others has been developed over a long period as the people progres-
sively lost their land and were pushed further and further inland
from the coast. Their fears are directed at any outsider, especially
at foreigners. (The Indians in San Juan refer to Chileans who live
on the coast as "foreigners.") Father Auxencio claims that he is just
beginning to win their confidence after two years. He said that
the *cacique*, or Indian leader, is so against change that he protests
even changes of personnel in the mission.

The *cacique* offered no encouragement to the original plans
to build the agricultural school in the Mission or to a redevelop-
ment program for the area. When Father planted pine trees in the
cemetery behind the Mission, they were torn up by the roots
because they were "foreign trees." Recently Communist infiltra-
tors have been telling coastal residents that the food sent by the
United States in this winter of need is a device to put them in our
debt and take away their land. This suspicion of the outside
world, probably justified by history, will be our most serious problem in the coast.

As we climbed through the hills and vales to visit homes in
San Juan de la Costa, our reception was often strange and
strained. When we said we came from Osorno, one woman said
she had never been there, only seventeen miles away. A man treated us very bluntly. "Why are you asking all these questions of us?"
was his only reply to our inquiries. An Indian woman would say
nothing at all, and another would talk only to Carmen and show

her her weaving. When Carmen spoke to her about weaving, the woman replied repeatedly: "These are done in the ancient way of doing things, these are done in the ancient way of doing things." While we talked to this Indian señora, her husband passed us by, entered the gate and started for the house. She muttered something quickly to him in a dialect I couldn't understand, yet I knew that what she said was about us and was not good.

The final place where I will work is Catrihuala, that mountain colony which lives in rebellion against the government and society. We are anxious to help the people there, especially to work out their problems with the government legally; and, in the past two months, we have made some overtures to them. In March, I traveled to Catrihuala with Father Eugene Stiker. The people had invited him up the mountain because they wanted to request U.S. surplus foods which AID sends down to Chile through the Catholic Church, because food is scarce and difficult to transport on the mountain in wintertime. I accompanied him, and while I was there I suggested to the leader of the community that they store up supplies in the summer and sell them through a cooperative during the winter months. This is all I have done. So far there has been no sign that the people of Catrihuala will accept our suggestion or our offer of help. But Catrihuala is a place I have reserved for special efforts if the people allow me to make them.

Love,
Tommy

Chapter 10

LETTER TO THE PRESIDENT: CATRIHUALA

After visiting Peace Corps sites in Chile, Father Hesburgh took back to Washington the story of my encounter with the Marxist Indian leader. When I hear that President Kennedy recounted the story, I proudly write to him about my experience and what I have learned about the warring ideologies, Communism and democracy.

July 14, 1962

Dear President Kennedy,

It was a great surprise to hear that you had singled me out for my "spirit of dedication." I am certain that in many parts of the ever-increasing sphere which the Peace Corps encompasses there are many who have their dedication tested more. I have yet to be seriously sick, whereas one-fourth of our group has had hepatitis or appendicitis. My living conditions are clean and comfortable, and I am sure that in other continents, such as Africa, the daily circumstances of life are much more difficult than they are in Chile.

Your mention was an undeserved honor involving a flash of kind fortune which brought my name to your attention from among the many who could have just as easily been cited. Nonetheless, I am deeply grateful for it. Now it is my duty to respond, and I can think of no better way than to tell you more about the people and place you spoke of on June 21. Forgive my presumption in assuming you might have time to glance through the story. The main reason, among others, for telling it to you is that it has taught me something about Communism and the role of my country in the world and because the conclusions I have drawn would be better stated by you than by me should I succeed in conveying them to you.

There is another reason for wanting to write you the story. I have been accused by the Socialist press in the most widely circulated newspaper in Chile of deluding you by inventing the existence of this village. Here is my translation of excerpts from the article.

BEATNIK YANKEE SCARES KENNEDY
WITH HIS STORIES OF INDIANS IN CHILE

Tom Scanlon is a Yankee youth of 23 years. He ought to have hair the color of carrots, freckled skin, drink a lot of milk, a shot of whiskey now and then and chew one *chicklet* after another. In his ranch of Dunmore,[1] Pennsylvania, he never missed a television program. He likes the ones with lots of Indians. In his sleep, he dreamed of the redskins.

Now Tom is in Chile. They sent him with the Peace Corps, telling him that they were modern Boy Scouts—young kids who had to act among the Indians and the Communists in Latin America.

Tom told President Kennedy about his adventures in Chile. They're the same as he saw in the television programs. The grave thing is that a President of one of the largest nations in the world has believed the story of Indians and villages buried in the snow.

Where is this village so picturesque? In what television program did Tom see all this?

You know that I was not your source of information for the story you told on June 21. I would now like to assure you that the vil-

---

[1] It puzzled me that this story accurately named Dunmore as my hometown because I usually told people I came from Scranton, a well known metropolitan area, rather than the borough of Dunmore. How did the Marxist press learn the precise truth? I'll never know.

lage and persons you mentioned are not products of my imagination. Catrihuala—the name means "lonely swan" in Mapuche—is
a very real place. It is situated in the coastal mountain range
of Chile southwest of Osorno. Like a lump on a camel's back, it
protrudes above a high, level plain where the last farm is located
before the land becomes virgin forest. A very bad road runs
steeply for twenty kilometers up the mountain. The people,
Chileans of both Spanish and Indian descent, live in shacks scattered through forests which are rich in some of the best timber in
Chile. *Alerce* [a kind of cypress] has been growing there for hundreds of thousands of years. Its wood is so fine and splits so even-
ly that an Indian can make five hundred shingles a day with only
an ax and a saw. It takes five hundred years before *alerce* reaches
harvestable size. The eighty families now living on some forty
thousand acres will probably exploit it all in this generation.

The people do not own this land although they think they
do. In the belief that they should be owners of the land they
staged the first successful takeover of a rural estate in Chile.
Armed and directed by members of the Communist and Socialist
parties, in 1957 a band of fifteen men marched up the slanted road
to the highest section of Catrihuala, occupied a home and began
preparing a campaign. Soon thirty and then fifty men arrived to
throw in their lot with the invaders. The real owners of the land,
a Spanish family by the name of Camero, responded by erecting
a barbed-wire fence to keep the rebel gang from descending the
mountain. Today they call this uppermost section of their colony
Alambrado, the "wired place."

Both sides engaged in a kind of guerrilla warfare—
sometimes in waist-high snow—and although the weapons of the
owners' forces were superior, the gang reached the bridge at the
bottom of the mountain in 1960. Don Gregorio Kintull, secre-
tary-general of the rebel community, took up residence in the
Spanish home where the administrators of the company's lumber
operation formerly lived. Don Pablino Melillanka, their strong-
willed, slow-thinking military leader, went to live in Alambrado
on top. Two Spaniards had been killed, fifteen workers' homes
razed and many rebels wounded. Don Pablino has a bullet lodged
near his spine to this day. He estimates that over fifteen hundred
rounds were fired during the three-year fray.

The national coalition of Socialists and Communists has had
its day. Catrihuala is supposedly one of their strongholds. The
people constantly refer to themselves as members of the "working
class" when they converse. Local authorities didn't approve the hir-
ing of a teacher for the vacant schoolhouse perched in Alambrado
because he would have made it a school in Marxism. When the
order was given in Santiago to remove the Indians from the mountain, news of the order reached Catrihuala before the police could
travel from Río Negro to the bridge. Roadblocks were established
and guarded with arms the people could never buy for themselves.
The police captain himself told me that he doesn't attempt the
occupation of the mountain because he can't afford to lose men.

Others tried unsuccessfully to enter. A government engi-
neer and his crew came to take some geological readings and
they were doing their business unobtrusively when they were
surrounded by armed men. They were so terribly menaced that
one fled into the forest. The others were made to drive their
truck down the mountain, with five armed Indians sitting on the
cabin. The one that ran away didn't find his way out of
Catrihuala until he had been presumed killed. Incidents like
these convinced the people of the province that Catrihuala,
though remote, was an ominous threat to their security. They
called it their Sierra Maestra, and whether the likeness was real
or not the people of Catrihuala would have welcomed the comparison to their Cuban heroes.

Catrihuala is a victory for the Communist-Socialist coalition
in only the political sense. Socially they have accomplished nothing. There is no education, no medical aid, and in the wintertime
very little food. The guerillas make money in the autumn when
the roads are good. In summer, trucks climb the mountain daily
buying the shingles and rough lumber which they leave lying
along the road. But no one has taught the people to save money
and buy their supplies in bulk in the fall for the long winter of
want. Nor do they know how to get the best price for their lumber. For a square inch of *alerce*, they receive thirty cents. In
Osorno, forty miles away, the price is eighty cents per square
inch. If it were milled, the price would be $1.80 per square inch.
Two sawmills remain on the mountain, left behind by former
occupants. They are broken. No one has taught the Indians to fix

them, nor loaned them the three hundred dollars necessary to have one fixed. The all-important question of reforestation is never even mentioned by their political leaders.

Perhaps the Marxists would respond that until they administer the government of Chile real social progress is impossible, and that political agitation is sufficient for the present. But they have less idealistic reasons for not teaching the Indians to get the best price for their lumber. The man in Río Negro who takes the greatest advantage of the people is Jorge Nur, the most prominent Socialist in Río Negro. In fact he was made a member of the city council in the last election. He is their local contact with their political patrons in Osorno and Santiago. He makes thousands of dollars a year in Catrihuala in barter exchanges of flour for lumber, and he encouraged them to revolt.

If you talk to the members or the community today, they will tell you that the years of armed struggle are over forever. There remains only a legal struggle for the government's recognition that according to the "law of the Indians" the land was theirs from the start. (By far the majority of the rebel community are Indians.) They speak of a Peace Treaty which Ambrosio O'Higgins—"father of Chile's George Washington," Bernardo O'Higgins—formulated in 1793, but never signed; and they insist that in the 1830s a similar land grant was actually made by the government. This legal decision is still pending, they believe, and so they have been told by their political leaders who actually did take the case of Catrihuala before the courts after the invasion was successfully completed. What their Marxist friends have not told them is that the case was lost and that the only legal gap in the case of Catrihuala is the removal by force of the Indians from the mountain. One could easily argue that they were morally justified in what they did after their race has been exploited for hundreds of years by the Spaniards and Germans. But legally they are without hope. These same papers deed the whole province of Osorno to the Indians. If they were deemed valid, half of the richest and most productive soil in the south of Chile would be proclaimed Indian property.

The present government no longer hopes to kick the Indians out. The Camero family has at least six other sites where they cut lumber. The solution is to expropriate the land from the family and sell it to the Indians on a long-term basis. There are many obstacles to this plan and the biggest is a lack of unity among the Indians themselves. After fighting together for three years, the community split into three groups, both geographically and ideologically. Don Gregorio Kintull, living below at the bridge, broke with fellow socialist Don Pablino who lived on top. In between were the Communists. The inability of the Communists and Socialists to trust each other is now the greatest barrier to future progress of any kind.

I made my first trip to Catrihuala the first Sunday in March. Father Eugene Stiker, a North American missionary, was making a trip to Alambrado to say Mass there for the first time in two years. He had been invited by Don Pablino. This trip involved passing through the lower sections of the mountain where roadblocks were established when unwelcome visitors were spotted from a house overlooking the bridge. We anticipated the worst, taking the precautions to bring none of the girls and to use Father's jeep because mine resembled those of the local police. Driving up the twenty-kilometer road was a torturous experience for it is more like a sheer, eroded cliff than a passage for automobiles. We passed the tiny shacks, the adjacent triangle-shaped huts which serve as kitchens for the Indians, stretches of burnt out, exploited or diseased forest, and an occasional oxcart or truck loaded with wooden shingles or crude lumber. The license plate on one truck indicated it had come from Valparaiso to take advantage of the bargain rates which the Indians are forced to offer for their lumber.

In Alambrado, we found a surprising but encouraging phenomenon; in the bright Sunday afternoon sun, the community was assembled to watch youngsters play soccer or throw quoits. The men and women were sitting in different groups. They had been waiting for us, but this was not the only reason for their gathering together. They already possess the community spirit that community development projects in Latin America try to produce.

We talked for a short while to Don Pablino until it became evident why he had invited Father Stiker to say Mass. Winter was coming on; the roads would soon close and the hungry months were about to begin. Could he oblige by distributing the wheat, corn, rice, oil and powdered milk which the U.S. Catholic Relief Service in the United States sends to Chile? Father Stiker said "Yes," and I offered them the services of the Institute of Rural Education as well. Then Father offered Mass, and we agreed to return the next day to talk about Food for Peace and the Institute with which the Peace Corps is working in Chile.

Father Stiker and I agree that it would be a much greater service to these people to teach them better economic practices than to give them part of their winter supply of food. So the next day, while he enrolled them in the plan for this winter, I talked to them about cooperative purchases of large quantities of food for the succeeding ones. Don Pablino was leery and asked me to put the recommendation in writing so he could present it to his companions in a formal meeting. I did this on the spot, handed him the paper and descended the mountain with little hope that the community would accept the idea. What I didn't realize was that I had mentioned the magic word "cooperative."

In early April we received a reply from the community of Alambrado that it would be interested in a co-op if it were offered a loan of money to get started. This justified another trip up the mountain—this time in my jeep—to explain that our assistance there was not intended to be financial but that they could secure loans from the national bank once they were a legalized cooperative. Then they took us to see what had prompted them to request a loan. On a side path off the main road was an old sawmill, badly in need of repair because it had not been used since the owners of the mountain fled in 1957. With an estimated three or four hundred dollars for its repair they could sell milled lumber for three times more than the rough lumber they sell now. Knowing this essential detail, we changed our tune when talking about the co-op.

We spoke of the possibilities of a cooperative for the production and marketing of their lumber which could at the same time buy and store winter supplies of food. Then we had our now famous interchange. Don Pablino wanted to be assured that we had no political intentions. He told us bluntly of their Socialist and Communist friends in Santiago and of how they were proud to be in their ranks. We answered that neither the Institute nor the

Peace Corps was interested in politics but only in helping the poor to find a better life. Then they suggested that we come and live with them in the heart of winter to explain the idea of a marketing cooperative when they were idled by the weather.

Their Socialist patron was there that day and he immediately began a polemic against the co-op by calling me a North American capitalist out to exploit them. He did this to protect his own capitalistic interests. To add to the irony of it all, he had been asked by the Indians to transport the sacks of *Caritas* food from Río Negro to Alambrado. Our jeep chugged ahead of his truck while he bore our gifts to the Indians. For obvious reasons, he carried only token amounts.

When I decided to work in Catrihuala, my goal was to help the small group in Alambrado hoping my work would have some meaning for all. This plan changed one day when we visited Don Gregorio Kintull, leader of the entire mountain community, in his home at the bridge to invite him to a fiesta we were staging on a neighboring farm. His son attended classes there and the party was for the parents of the students. Don Gregorio welcomed us warmly into his house where he told us the story of Catrihuala and the struggle they had waged there. He warned us that it was impossible to start a cooperative in Alambrado alone. It would have to be of the entire community. Then he manifested the dissension which was wrecking Catrihuala by advising us against working with Don Pablino and above all against associating with the *Comunistas* who "do not belong to the community" but live halfway up the mountain in a place they call the "crossroads." It was agreed that before our fiesta on Sunday we would chat with a community assembly which had already been scheduled for other purposes.

That Sunday we talked with a group of twenty-five or thirty men. I told them about the Peace Corps and your desire to help them. I said you had sent the Peace Corps in the same spirit that Ambrosio O'Higgins had formulated a Peace Treaty and that you and he were of the same Irish background. Above all, I insisted that we weren't interested in politics. A guest in a home cannot partake in family quarrels, I said, and the Peace Corps was a guest in Chile. It had to be a friend to all, but its work was with the poor—teaching the poor what economic strength they can have if they organize into cooperatives.

Kintull responded eloquently. He was in complete agreement with the formation of a co-op in Catrihuala. Nothing is gained, he said, with criticizing the present government or the United States. The Indians have to take advantage of all existing help—contrary to the opinion of those who live in the "crossroads." He claimed, "They do not belong to the community because they do not intend to settle there but only to exploit lumber while it remains in abundance."

The more Kintull talked about the Communism of this "out" group, the more I wanted to talk to them. I offered to come again the second Saturday in May to speak with anyone who might be interested in selling their lumber through a co-op. When I arrived that day no one was there but a friend of Kintull and a little man who called himself president of the community. We spent three hours talking and drinking bottle after bottle of *chicha*. It was discouraging to find few people and when they invited me to return the following Sunday, I told them it would be my last visit if more people didn't show an interest.

I decided that the coming Sunday meeting would be definitive as to whether we would continue in Catrihuala or not. Fortunately, Don Tito Steffens, a good friend of mine and an expert on cooperatives, was arriving in nearby Osorno that very day with the desire to visit Catrihuala with me. Don Tito has taught me all I know about Chilean cooperative law. He had designed the idea for the cooperative in Catrihuala. I went for him that Sunday at the home of Monseñor Francísco Valdés Subercaseau, the Bishop of Osorno, where he stays when he is in town. There I received the news that the Bishop himself was interested in Catrihuala. He was going with us. Although he has organized more co-ops in Osorno than any other man, he had discouraged my attempts on the mountain because of the dissension among the people and the land tenure problem. He was still skeptical and wanted to see for himself.

The Bishop of Osorno is a bearded, saintly man who drives like crazy in a pickup truck stopping for every *campesino* hitchhiker along the way. He speaks the Indian language and is one of the leading exponents in Chile of Pope John XXIII's encyclical *Mater et Magister*. He raced ahead of me in the long road to the coastal mountains and by the time we were approaching Catrihuala, the

back of his truck was filled with Indians. "Are the people expecting a meeting today?" he yelled back to them in their native
tongue. "Yes," they replied, "they are all waiting at the bridge."

. We arrived in the late afternoon and were met at the bridge
by small groups of men who led us to the house. "The priest you
came with looks like a bishop," they told me. "It is the *Monseñor*
himself," I replied, still about as surprised as they were. When I
entered the house I began the usual custom of shaking hands
with all those present but soon gave up because there were so
many. Kintull, astonished and moved, said he never hoped to see
a bishop in Catrihuala. He spoke for the eighty-five men who
were assembled.

Don Gregorio turned the meeting over to me and I began
talking about the cooperative step by step as Don Tito had taught
me. Then I read the results of a study I had made in Osorno of the
lumber market. When I read the Osorno prices, Kintull jumped
up and down in his seat like a little boy. Every few minutes I
paused and asked if they understood my Spanish. *"Se va entendien-
do, Don Tomás,"* they replied. "We understand."

I finished speaking and Kintull rose solemnly to his feet.
Then he gave us the good news. The day before the community
had reorganized itself in order to respond to our persistent visits
and to consider the idea of the co-op. He and Don Pablino were
now willing to work together and Don Pablino had been installed
as treasurer of the entire community. Kintull attacked those
"politicians" who had called me an imperialist set on exploiting
them and asked me to help him draft a letter to the Judge of
Indian Affairs requesting authorization for the co-op.

Kintull sat down and the Bishop burst into applause, making
his own eloquent speech in behalf of the cooperative and congratulating them heartily for the spirit of cooperativism which
they already possessed. He offered to send two members of the
community to a course in cooperatives which he is organizing.

But it took Don Tito Steffens and his twenty years of experience working with Indians to clinch the day. He explained that the
administration of the money would be completely in their hands,
anticipating the suspicions they had about my intentions. They
laughed and nodded to each other in recognition. He had hit the
nail on the head. Then he turned the meeting over to them know-

ing that the Indians wanted to make their own solemn speeches.

One by one they stated their agreement with the idea. "There is nothing in this but for our own good," they said. "Let us try it and if we fail we have lost nothing, but let us try it soon." Then they reminded me of my promise to come to live with them in the winter. We set the date for the last week of June and I promised to spend time that week with anyone who might be interested in the cooperative. The reorganization of the community had not included the group from the "crossroads." I feared that they were being excluded from these meetings. I know now that many of them were in the meeting that day.

In May of last year there was a meter of snow in Alambrado, so when we chose late June as the time for the journey we felt sure that nature would oblige. The day I was preparing to leave I heard that you had mentioned my proposed trip there, and I began to worry that only torrents of rain were falling. But rain served the same purpose as snow, and after arriving in Alambrado we had endless hours of discussion with the people who were kept indoors by the weather.

We left Río Negro on a Monday morning and were loaned horses in the farm where we had to leave the jeep. Our team was composed of René Bórquez and Carmen Carillo of the Institute, a Peace Corps nurse named Terry Atwood and myself. The trip on horseback took six hours and we arrived in Alambrado at nine that night dripping wet from the constant rain. The road had been difficult due to the early fog of the rainy night. Our horses stopped many times because they could not see, and we had to dismount and pull them forward. Luckily a tenant farmer overtook us on the trail and invited us to his home nearby. There we had fire, boiling water and a dry place to sleep. I never dreamt I'd have such a need for the common basics.

We arrived at the top the next morning and found the Indians waiting for us. Don Pablino gave us the vacant house which the community saves for guests and hopes some day to give to a schoolteacher. He brought us sacks of rice and flour which had been sent by Father Stiker. Finally he removed the stove from his own house and installed it in ours. Others cut firewood for us from the precious *alerce* and started a roaring fire on an open hearth in the adjacent kitchen shack. We talked with the people for a little while, arranged a meeting for the next day and set about preparing our program.

The next few days hummed with activity and people remarked that it was like summer again. René built a chair from *alerce* which needed only two screws. Carmen visited the *señoras* and invited them to a meeting to prepare for a party on Friday. Terry made the rounds like the public health nurse she is. In one home, all the children were covered with sores. By the end of the week, her treatments had them completely cured. She gave penicillin to a woman dying from pneumonia which had complicated chronic tuberculosis. When possible she tried to get across ideas about nutrition. (The babies' diet was bits of their family's main meal and milk from their mothers' breasts.) In general, health conditions were terrible. Don Pablino himself, I am very sad to say, lost three children in one day last winter. They died from "fever," he says, but who is to say which disease? There is no hope of any medical attention for these people in the winter, and very little in the summer.

Occasionally I accompanied Terry and talked to the men while she ministered to the sick in their homes. I remember sitting by the blazing fire in the oil-can stove of one partisan of the co-op watching Terry kneeling down and washing the dirty little arms of a child covered with sores. It is certain, I thought, that now we are living with the poor.

Our cooperative education sessions went well. They began with me fiddling a few Irish tunes on the violin and some tales about the people in the land where they were written: how they were *campesinos* too and had been treated very well in my country—to the point of being elected President. Then we got down to brass tacks explaining how their co-op would function. The co-op would be the middleman to buy their lumber at a fair price, send it to the market and sell at the highest profit possible. They would receive these profits in dividends at the end of the year in proportion to the amount of lumber each one had sold to the co-op. Never before had the basic principles of the cooperative movement had such applicability.

We had to preach an "open door" policy, and to insist on political neutrality. They wanted to exclude the "crossroads" group, on the grounds that they were Communists, and hoping to assure their exodus from the mountain. It was also necessary to insist on the principle of voluntary membership, as overenthusiastic partisans of the idea were threatening the foot-draggers with expulsion. Finally, we stressed the need for cooperative education as some of these people had no schooling at all. In these informal sessions, everything went well.

As enthusiasm grew, Don Pablino felt the need for a formal meeting of all interested parties. He asked me to invite Kintull to the top of the mountain for a community meeting. I complied and signed a written invitation, which they signed too. A few minutes later a loyal friend galloped down the mountain with the message. At midnight he arrived at our house with a reply from Kintull. "I am coming tomorrow and I'm bringing my men with me," he wrote. The new accord between Pablino and Kintull was still clicking.

The following night the meeting did not go well. I wanted to explain everything to Kintull's group and had overprepared. They remained quiet, asked few questions, and failed to understand my dictionary Spanish. Worse than that, I made the mistake of dominating the meeting, leaving them little time for their own solemn statements of opinion. Kintull diverted their attention with his polemic against the "out" group. Pablino tried to shove through a motion that only an Indian could be elected president, and very little progress was made. Another meeting was arranged for a week later, and I suggested the place. We had met at the bridge and at Alambrado. Now I wanted to meet at the "cross-roads" hopefully, I said, with the group that lives there.

Although the progress of the co-op lagged, the week's program continued rather well. René managed to persuade them to sow vegetables. He had located a tract of suitable land and listed those who would plant there and what they needed. The men from the bridge agreed to try the same experiment. Our informal conversations continued and soon they agreed to make an experiment in reforestation. The girls got the *señoras* making sweet breads, and René taught a skit and a few songs to some of the youths; and on Friday, the last night there, we had a party.

It was the Feast of Peter and Paul, a national holiday in Chile, and we made a big fuss over Don Pablino, serving him the only glass of wine in the house. He danced the *cueca* and then gave a speech. "Thanks to the Institute and our North American friends," he said, "for the many new ideas they have given us. We hope to have them with us again on the Eighteenth of September so they can share the abundance we have in the spring when the roads dry." The Eighteenth of September is their Fourth of July. Of course, we will accept the invitation.

We left Saturday morning heartened by the week's events and rested from the slow and relaxed pace of the week. More than anything, we were impressed by the community. They were organized, desiring a better life and ready to work to get it—three characteristics that community developers dream about. They needed only a teacher in whom they had confidence. Perhaps we had taught them something.

In the bright winter sun we could see clear across Chile. The ride was easy and pleasant and we chuckled about some of the ironic moments of the week as we rode along—how Don Pablino told me confidentially that the police had taken his gun from him in Río Negro and asked me to get him one of those neat North American revolvers; how one man, extremely impressed by the presence of gringos there, had said that everything we do gets back to *your* desk. Thinking of the city of Washington as your great big marble desk, and not wanting to correct the man in front of his friends, I nodded my assent.

A week later I arrived at noon at the "crossroads" with soap and antibiotics for the families afflicted by the rash and with enlarged photographs I had taken of the community. More than thirty interested parties arrived for the meeting. Based on my experience in the last session, I had resolved to talk in simple terms and converse with them patiently because even the interested ones still needed convincing. We talked informally until four o'clock, and you could see the interest growing. More important, the mistrust and dissension in their own ranks diminished. "The idea sows harmony," one said to me. "It is sowing harmony right now."

At four o'clock we were about to begin the formal meeting when a stuttering Indian arrived, greeted the others rather coldly and invited me to another meeting in the "crossroads." He represented the "out" group. I said there was no reason to have two meetings and that they could come to ours. The assembly agreed. To extend the invitation, I accompanied this man to where the other group was gathered. We arrived at an abandoned sawmill where another thirty or forty men were sheltering themselves from the rain. The first to greet me was the little man who called himself the president that day in Kintull's house. He asked me to give my explanations there, and I replied two meetings were unnecessary and impossible. They refused to meet with the other men and let it be known that they weren't really interested in the co-op anyway. Then a big, strapping man wearing a leather jacket began to question me.

"Why should we want a cooperative here anyway?"

"So you transport and mill your own lumber and save yourselves the profits which other people now gain by doing these services." Then I quoted the prices in Osorno.

"Are there cooperatives in the United States?"

"Yes. There are many."

"Then why is there so much unemployment if they are so great?"

"The cooperatives are partly responsible for the unemployment problem because as effective businesses they mechanize, and machines do the work that men used to do—just like the sawmill or a truck would do here. But unemployment there isn't like what it is here. There is government assistance to buy food with."

"That is not true. Six million people go to bed hungry every night."

"Six million people is a very small percentage of our total population and hunger there is different. There is always some food available."

"That is not true, they are hungry."

"If they are hungry, our government feels responsible for them. In fact it feels a responsibility towards all those who are hungry in the world. That's why we send sacks of flour and rice like these that arrived here."

"We received none of that."

"Our government can't be expected to help those who spent all their time criticizing us. We have our self-respect. We want to help but only when those who need it allow us to and respect what we stand for."

"You just want to make us dependent on you."

"Rather we want to make you independent economically. That's why we send people and loans to help in the formation of cooperatives."

"No. It is impossible. I will never believe it. I am another Fidel Castro."

"And I am convinced that my country can do more for the poor in Latin America than Fidel Castro."

At this point the small man politely broke off the conversation. Like the others, he had seemed to enjoy hearing the party line taken issue with. We ended up joking and I told them that if they became interested I would gladly work with them as I was working with the others, provided that they were willing to cooperate with the whole community. I informed them of our intentions to form a provisional directorate that day and invited them to elect an observer to all its meetings. With that we shook hands, made a few more joking remarks; and I headed back to the other meeting.

Kintull and Don Pablino were like teenagers talking to someone who had just talked to their girlfriend. What did [blank] say? And then, what did *you* say? And what did they say to that? Don Pablino said that when they became convinced, they were going to be the best members of the co-op. Kintull liked the idea of having an observer of theirs in the directorate. Then one Indian put me on the spot. "It's all right with me if they join," he said, "as long as they stop being Communists." I explained that such a political stipulation would be against the principle of political neutrality and would be very unwise but that they always had the power to exclude any individual from membership if his intention was to divert the co-op from its purpose.

In this formal meeting of July 7, the "cooperative in formation" of Catrihuala was founded. The provisional directorate was formed and a meeting of the directorate set for last Thursday. In that meeting, held in Osorno with Don Tito Steffens, the preliminary legal papers were prepared and a large stamp with the seal of the cooperative was purchased. The people are waiting for my next trip to Catrihuala in August with the trees which will be used in a reforestation experiment.

I have stopped explaining my presence in Catrihuala now. They accepted me and the cooperative for what we are supposed to be. The drama of the encounter between them and the Peace

Corps is more or less played out. What we need now is time and hard work to face the difficult task of teaching those who lack elementary education enough about the cooperative system to avoid a fiasco. Then there is the difficult question of land titles. We must try to solve that too.

Until the moment in which they began organizing themselves into the co-op, I always approached the mountain with the idea that the coming meeting might be my last. Perhaps they had received orders from Santiago to make themselves unreceptive to the idea because I presented it. Perhaps I would decide that the characters of certain leaders were too suspicious and unreliable. Perhaps some detail would be presented by the Chilean government which would make it useless to continue on. None of these things have happened and now I would consider tragic whatever might interrupt the regular, almost weekly, sessions in cooperative education which we hope to have on the mountain. Consequently I ask that this letter be given no publicity lest it becloud the important work at hand. If the story of Catrihuala is to be merely one of Marxist failure and not one of poor people's success based on American help, nothing will be gained. But the conclusions to the story should be made public because they have to do with the rivalry which now exists between the United States and Communism in these Latin American countries.

My experience tells me that Latin America has much more to gain by working with us than with International Communism. The Communist solution is a political one, and it must be presented as the political system to end all systems to a people whose natural propensity is to make one political experiment after another. Ours is more social and economic, going directly to the real problems of the people. Our solution is not a political theory which must wait to be applied, but a stimulus to processes which should begin without delay. We do not have to impose a foreign system of government on a strongly nationalistic mentality. We recommend that they find their own form of governing themselves, assisting all those that respect the freedom of the individual as the basis of the society and the economy.

I am jealous, Mr. President, of our country's right to be considered a leader in the world's struggle for development. Two hundred years ago, conditions of rural life in Chile were not considered "underdeveloped" at all. What made them "under-developed" was the fact that other nations eliminated similar circumstances and surged ahead. Our country was the first to surge ahead and to this day the definition of economic development is in terms of inventions and social welfare accomplishments which our nation has presented to the world as possibilities.

The great advantage of Communism is that it is committed to finding a better life for the world's poor. We can achieve that same reputation. This will not be simple for us because our government does not decide what the nation thinks. In our democracy, the people must be convinced that they have responsibilities to the poor of other nations.

Perhaps it is a youthful idealism to imagine that a whole nation would act in a humanitarian way even if the fear of Communism were not prompting it to do so. I believe it is no more impossible than democracy or human compassion themselves. It could be that this is our most important responsibility as Peace Corpsmen—the education of our people in their possibilities for doing great things in the world.

If this is our responsibility, we have not begun well in fulfilling it. The press reports about the Peace Corps have stressed our early successes rather than the problems that required our presence here. They make it seem we've already made a great contribution when, in fact, we are struggling towards a beginning. I fear the ballyhoo, Mr. President, the self-congratulation of the American people when they praise their own Peace Corps.

When I am working with the *campesinos* and Indians, I regard myself as the extension of the interest of the American people in their problems, and when I return to the United States, I hope to hear more questions about their health than my own. Then I will know that my country, of which I am overwhelmingly proud, is ready to take the place of leadership in the world which belongs to it.

                    Respectfully yours,
                    Tom Scanlon

Chapter 11

LIFE AND WORK IN LATIN AMERICA: A MATTER OF ATTITUDES

When a new Peace Corps group arrives in Chile, I am invited to discuss a personal discovery—one that has since become accepted as a fact of life in international business and development circles: Every person working abroad faces a critical test in recognizing cultural differences and adjusting to them.

November, 1962

W
hen Mr. Langford called me to Santiago to speak to new volunteers, he asked me to discuss with you the attitudes a volunteer should have toward the Chilean people.[1] The most fascinating aspect of my life here has been trying to understand the Chilean culture—what Chileans value, what they like and dislike, their habits. I still don't feel that I understand them fully, and the matter of attitudes is difficult.

The first thing you will notice about the people of Chile is their hospitality. They pride themselves on how they treat you in their homes. The time they spend asking you the way you like your tea may seem uncalled for, but it shows the attention they

---

[1] In the actual talk, I referred to Latin Americans, as if my year's experience had revealed the psyche of the entire continent. Having learned better over thirty years, in editing these remarks I have substituted the term Chileans to reflect more accurately the people I knew and what I was talking about.

give all guests. Entertaining guests and paying calls are their favorite ways of spending time.

Chileans frequently ask friends to spend the night in their homes, especially if these friends come from far away and can talk into the night about distant places. I have arrived unexpectedly at friends' homes many times after being stranded by a bus or a broken jeep. They expect us to come looking for shelter and usually prepare hot coffee and eggs because they know we have missed supper even though we refuse to admit it. Then sometimes that direct attention will stop. They cease offering things constantly and continue with family activities. This is not a sign that you have worn out your welcome. It usually means that they expect you to include yourself in. We worked with some university students in February; and, in the school that was our base of operations, we were received very well into the group. Afterwards some students complained that we did not participate fully in all their social activities. This was because we were not accustomed to being accepted so readily. At first we felt that although they were being kind, they would want some time to themselves.

There is nothing Chileans prefer to making friends. And they really appreciate the ones they have, making a fuss when they meet them on the street and asking them about their family and their activities. "How are you?" "What have you been doing?" "What's new in your life?" If you meet a friend four times in one day you pause and greet him four times. If you are too engaged in your work to say hello, they fear that you are upset with them.

There is an openness in their friendship which accepts all and asks very few questions. Chileans I know are not harshly selective in choosing friends. They are quick to detect human qualities in everyone and they accept new friends on the basis of the good they see in them. The rule of friendship is that everyone is welcome. Chileans going on a picnic or *paseo* in the country will frequently call out *"vamos juntos*—go with us and bring your friend," and if you do, they will consider their day more complete.

Their generosity seems unlimited and they seem to be unaware of time when they do you a favor. A volunteer told me of the time his jeep broke down one weekend in a remote village. A mechanic, whose future in-laws were visiting him for the first time, took an interest in his problem. Despite a home full of company, he worked on the jeep for an evening and a day, giving the Peace Corpsman a place to stay in the meanwhile. As payment, he asked only that the volunteer drive his girl friend's parents home at the end of the weekend.

Frankly I find it difficult to reciprocate in this; I am more stingy with my time and money. I count my *pesos* and minutes too carefully. Finding so many people who are so drastically different is an enriching experience.

The people of Chile are a gay people. They will sing at the drop of a hat and then dance around it. At the beginning, we North Americans are all a little embarrassed and unsure of the words; but in the end we all enjoy the conviviality. In Chile, you sing in the morning, afternoon or evening. It is a joy which Chileans are unable to do without for very long.

Humor is just as constantly a factor in their lives. Their wit is difficult to top, and they think up glib retorts that will catch you off guard. Many a *campesino* has left me speechless. Their brand of humor is not sophisticated. It is a water-throwing, sleeve-sewing, coffee-salting kind of humor which gives you the chuckles even though you thought you had stopped laughing at those things long ago. I finally caught on. One day they were complaining that *empanadas* (a national dish) were difficult to make from the enriched, surplus flour sent from the United States. "That's why we send it to Chile," I said. "It doesn't serve any of the really important purposes in the US." "Is that why they sent you?" they screamed in delight, pounding the table triumphantly.

Don't miss the Chilean *convivencia*—"living together," or social life. Chileans are not so fond of being alone as we are. They depend on each other for entertainment and intellectual stimulation. When someone withdraws to read or write alone, as we are wont to do, they wonder why and fear he is bored. I recommend you sacrifice a bit of your precious privacy and learn the joy of being together with good Chilean friends. The opportunity will probably occur when there is something more productive to do, but something so thoroughly good and enjoyable can be more important than the enterprise you were bent on.

I took off four full days recently to travel with the Osorno orchestra through the south of Chile. We played in the evenings and later disrupted staid restaurants by bringing our instruments to our seats and playing the nation's hit song, "May the Ugly Ones Die." When we were returning, I jumped off the bus in Río Negro and the orchestra played "The Star-Spangled Banner March" on the main street—at midnight. I returned to my duties with greater affection for the country in which I was working.

Chileans have an outstanding quality which is related casually to all the rest. It is their appreciation for life itself—the way they accept life's basic, tragic structure and love the good things it presents as it passes by. They are not afraid to express honest emotions. Affection, fear, passion and grief come to the surface immediately. When someone dies they dress in black for years, trying to remember rather than to forget.

Chileans are very frank about the ultimate outcome of life. This means that they are more fatalistic than we. Tomorrow is very much in doubt. "Si Dios quiere—God willing," we will be here a year from now, but nothing is so sure that it is worth planning for elaborately. Money that Americans spend on insurance policies and other investments in the future, they invest in the present moment; as for enjoying the moment, their appreciation of life prepares them very well. There is no end to a Latin's sensitivity to beauty, drama and other human beings.

Once I arrived in Santiago from Osorno and paid a visit to some friends at the university. "What's new," I asked conventionally enough. Their reply was typical. "The Andes," they replied, "they have filled with snow since you were here last. Have you seen them? They are beautiful." I had been thinking of a political development or some other news when I asked. For them the snow-capped mountains deserved mention first. The Chilean sense of beauty is so strong that it takes attention and time from other things. A Chilean becomes transfixed before a scene, an old building with a story behind it or a constellation of clouds or stars in the sky.

They have excellent taste in wine and food and they love to walk in the grass or sit in the sun. The most pleasant thing imaginable upon my return to the United States would be to view some familiar sights with friends from Chile and see the wonderful things our society has produced through their eyes. Chileans want more than just the comforts of life. Their spirit is free, inquisitive and adventuresome. They will undergo sacrifices and make great efforts to satisfy the urgings of an adventure-craving soul. Adventures of the soul are the sweetest and most pleasant. And so you have their love of poetry, their dramatic interpretation of ordinary events, their tendency to romanticize.

Mostly the Chilean's verve for life brings him to other human beings. Good conversation is the most important thing in his world and he is adept at making it. Tales of an interesting trip, expressing a new thought on life, discussions of politics and religion, and the ever-present humor mean there are few lulls in conversation.

Bonds of friendship, and especially family ties, are pre-eminent and Chileans are superb at analyzing human relationships and understanding other persons. Being a diplomat must be difficult here. Latins are experts on the complexities of human relationships. They mull, even brood, over the precise content of feelings between two countries and in interhemisphere relationships they bring to bear a subtle criterion which is distressing to us who want to establish new relationships quickly and start work on the problems at hand.

The outcome of this respect for others is written into the personality of every Latin. When they are with others they are gracious and polite. They serve you a glass of Coke on a plate, never leave you to wait alone, never yawn in your presence. Large groups gather for substantial lengths of time to send friends off or welcome them home. To pay these civilities, they deliberately lose time. Worth more to them than efficiency are their traditional manners which they have maintained as a heritage of the Old World. Good manners are the equivalent of good education.

I am not speaking about only the upper classes here. The aristocrats have a more polished style, but the *campesino* has the same gusto for life. These traits, perhaps unrefined, are developed to a high degree. *Campesinos* will spend hours discussing the best way to prepare a wild fruit jam. They love parties and dances. They have told me things about myself which impressed me with their perceptivity and understanding. When I say life among the Latins is enriching, I mean life among the *campesinos* as well.

I have enjoyed living here very much, but I find working here very difficult. It has been one of the most frustrating experiences of my

life. More than anything, North Americans like to keep on the
move. President Kennedy won a national campaign with the slo-
gan "Let's get this country moving again." We do not like to pro-
crastinate and let minutes slip by while we accomplish nothing.
For this reason the most general cause of frustrations in Chile for
volunteers has been the slow pace of life here. For example, if you
go shopping in the United States, you walk into the store, select
the item you want; a sales girl punches a cash register and in a few
minutes you are walking down the street again with your purchase
in hand. In Chile you never mention what you want to purchase
until you have greeted everybody in the store. Then you talk
about the weather for a while, and since you are a North
American, you answer questions about why you are in Chile and
whether you like it here. Only then can you mention what you
came in the store to buy.

Very often it is necessary to set an afternoon aside for business
in Osorno. Before evening, I compile a list of four or five "things to
do," and burst into town full of hustle and enthusiasm, anxious to
get everything done and be back home out in Río Negro the following morning. These afternoons usually go something like this:

Inevitably the first person I want to see is not there. Since he
is a good friend, I go to his home where I am told by the maid that
he has "just left" but that he will return "soon." The maid invites
me in to wait, but I have many things to do and so I ask the maid
how "soon" is "soon." "Will he be back in fifteen minutes or an
hour?" I ask. The maid gives me a deep, unknowing stare. "In a half
an hour," she replies, and that seems fine to me until she tacks on
a very ominous *"más o menos"*—more or less. This means my friend
may return anywhere from an hour to three hours from now. I
decide not to wait and I leave a message that I will pay another
call later in the afternoon. Then I rush off to see the second person on my list.

Arriving in this office I find, much to my surprise, that he is
in his office and unoccupied. It is good to see him, and he is glad
to see me and we talk a while, he shows me his office, tells me
about his trip to Europe, discusses politics and finally insists that
I join him for tea. Since I have not been able to mention the matter which brought me there in the first place, and since he is about
to have tea anyway, I must go with him. Finally we conduct our

business. It is given a small amount of attention during our tea-time talk, yet the result of our conversation is clear and satisfactory. I rush back to my first friend's house and find him waiting there as expected, but wounded to the core because he assumed my message meant that I would have tea with him, and he and his whole family have been waiting for the *gringo* to arrive. There is only one way to smooth over that blunder, and so I sit down and drink tea again. This takes an hour and as I wave good-by to him and his family it dawns on me that it is after six and all the stores and offices in town have closed.

Chileans do not have the same idea of time as we do. Delays in schedules are a matter of course for them; for us they constitute real setbacks. In general, they think of weeks when we think of days, of days when we think of hours and of hours when we think of minutes. They do not think of minutes at all. I am sure you could get along quite well in Latin America with a watch without a minute hand. The day has twenty-four units, not 1,440.

Even their hours are not clearly defined. In Chile they call them *"horas Chilenas"*—Chilean hours. These are rounded and vague. There is no difference between six and six fifteen. If you have a meeting at six and arrive at that time, you will be the only one there. "Six o'clock" means between six and seven. I tried looking for a pattern in their tardiness so that I could time myself accordingly. My conclusion was that there is none. This is not a deliberate setting back of the clock, just pure indefiniteness. I started arriving an hour late on purpose. That meant the people waited for me impatiently. So I tried being frank and pleaded with the *campesinos* that they be there at six o'clock sharp. Then they arrived at five.

I have never been able to convince them that being at a meeting on time means that something else could be done in the time ordinarily spent waiting. Their attitude is that time comes to them in large chunks and that wasting large portions of it does not end the constant stream available to them.

Our concepts of efficiency seem foreign to many of our Chilean friends. They seem to be without our desire—our drive—to improve an operation constantly, to do more in less time and with an ever-diminishing effort. Our home economists eliminated half the number of plates and kitchen utensils used to serve a meal at the schools, and they halved the time for many housekeeping chores.

Lack of concern for efficiency has been a source of many problems for the Peace Corps. More volunteers than needed for a project are requested and these volunteers find themselves without enough to do. In our work in Chile when local officials encounter us in one of our areas they assume we are spending all our time in this one place. Actually we are working in five. There are many times when our work in one area comes to a halt. The people can't spend all their time in community development activities and so we move on. (Actually with better organization and more resources, we could work in more than five.)

A volunteer's reaction to difficulties like these will be his most important test. Some volunteers have already failed, despaired and become bitter. They interpret their frustrations as indicating the Chileans' lack of interest in solving their own problems. The injustice in this is that it condemns the people on principles unknown to them. These volunteers have imported their own standards. Because the people here do not work as we do, but at a different pace and with less efficiency and different motivation, they are judged as being unwilling to work at all. Before this judgment, the Chilean stands mystified.

Another reaction to frustration is equally unacceptable in my opinion: to assume the attitude which some of our Chilean friends want us to have. They would have us become less concerned about the work at hand. "Your most important job here is to make friends everywhere, become one with us, win our hearts," they have said to me on many occasions. "The work is not that important." Certainly this is a better response than giving up and becoming bitter, but I recommend a different attitude to you: Along with winning their hearts, you should let them win yours. If you allow yourself to become good friends with the Latin American people and appreciate the way of life here, then your problems will appear in a new perspective.

Most difficulties which arise in the work situation can be traced back to the Chilean attitude toward life in general. A Chilean works hard at many things but not on the same matters we do. A Chilean does not stress his work as much as we do. He is more interested in matters which touch upon the heartstrings of life itself—with friendship or with beauty or with poetry. The result is that Latins excel in their ability to appreciate the real joys of life, while they fall short of our standards for working efficiently. The very thing which makes life in Latin America so pleasant also makes our work frustrating.

The United States offers a good point of comparison, and as far as what people value most, North Americans and Chileans live in two different worlds with two different centers. We have a work-centered society, and the human qualities we respect are the ones which get things done. We admire efficiency, organization, responsibility, dependability, speed, far-sightedness, industriousness, discipline, etc. Social niceties, leisure and even family relations are often slighted. Latins cherish civility, sociability, culture, self-respect, class, conversation, leisure, and human relations.

The fact that Chileans and North Americans live in worlds with different centers is evident in their two languages. There is no easy English translation for the Spanish word that expresses what a Latin American wants most in life. Similarly our concept of what makes life worthwhile is difficult to express in Spanish. *Pasarlo bien* has no translation in English. Literally it means "pass it well" and rough translations include "enjoy yourself," "have a good time," ad infinitum. However, *pasarlo bien* means much more than any of these. To *"pasarlo bien"* means to be in good company, to drink good wine, to have adventure—all these meanings are contained in the one phrase. How would you translate it into English?

More than anything, a North American wants a "challenge" in life. Deep down he tires of a job which doesn't demand his best energies. Many people accept a project because it is a challenge for them. This word justifies the greatest efforts. A North American wants accomplishment in the face of odds, success in performing the difficult, a project to which he can give an all-out effort. The word "challenge" literally translates into Spanish as *desafío* and I used that to explain to Chileans why I had come here. No one understood because *desafío* typically means the challenge you receive when someone provokes you to a duel. Whenever I used it, people thought I was running away from somebody at home; like a jealous husband, they suggested in jest. I finally decided that this concept of the utmost importance is rarely expressed in Spanish. If it is, I never heard it; and this alone indicates something. In the States you hear it everyday.

Chileans will choose a human consideration over a practical one every time. This has been brought home to me in a thousand ways. One day a Chilean co-worker and I were doing some business in Osorno. Since there were a number of items to be tended to, I suggested splitting the work between us and going off separately in order to wind up our business by the end of the day. My Chilean friend seemed startled—even somewhat offended. "No," he said, "*vamos juntos*—Let's go together." He preferred working together however slowly, conversing as we went, and not becoming excited about business left undone at day's end.

In Santiago I was trying to get a cab one noontime, when the streets are busiest because everyone is scurrying home for the main meal of the day. I saw ten people trying to flag down the many empty cabs that were passing. Very few of these cabs stopped. When I finally hailed one I asked the driver why so few drivers were working when everyone needed them and they could make a lot of money. "It is lunchtime," he replied in surprise. "They are going home to eat too!"

Our group had a Christmas meeting at one of the Institute's schools in the north where the school building's quaint old Spanish courtyard taught me an important lesson: Spanish courtyards are highly inefficient. To go from one side to the other, you must go completely around the square. There is no cutting across. The most logical thing in the world, in my opinion, was to cut a path from one side of the courtyard to the other. I mentioned this to a school official. She thought it over briefly and said, "Oh, but it would be very ugly and ruin the whole effect."

What could be more impractical than *onces?* The afternoon tea often takes an hour and interrupts your day just as you are beginning to rally after the two-hour layover for lunch. Yet a Chilean without his *onces* is like a North American without a job; his life ceases to make sense. And *onces* is only the third meal of the day. There is still one more to go. In fact the daily schedule of meals in Chile illustrates a major difference between a Latin American country and the United States. The Chilean meal schedule is designed to give the maximum possible time to the essentially human act of breaking bread together. Our meal schedules, on the other hand, are meant to be quick and nutritious and allow the greatest possible time for accomplishing things.

The Chilean's preference for the romantic over the practical is evident in planning work. For a Chilean, the creative element in any project is the planning, having the idea. The meaning, the grace, the substance of any work lies in its conception as an idea. Once discussed and decided upon, a project seems to lose its interest for them. Implementation is a lesser concern. The idea is what really counts. In fact, a Latin will hesitate to embark on even a small project unless its rationale is well in order.

This attitude has caused serious problems for the Peace Corps. Chileans are very excited about the idea of the Peace Corps. They ascribe great importance to our decision to come here but give little thought to how they will use us when we arrive. At the early stages of our experience, we had great difficulty in getting to work. However, none of our Chilean friends ever complained. In fact very few of them understood why we were so concerned.

Understanding differing attitudes toward life and work helps explain some of the problems we encountered in our community development work. I expected a strong community spirit, thinking of plazas and town squares, symbols of community life. These expectations, however, were surely bruised. *Campesinos* are so individualistic in the way they work that I decided they have little community spirit at all. Then I learned the contrary. The people in rural villages of Chile express their highest values communally. The plazas and squares create opportunities for living together, not working together. They worship, sing, mourn and rejoice together even more than we do. We work through associations, community chests, corporations and clubs more than they. If you schedule a community meeting to discuss crop improvement or road building, few persons will appear. If you announce that the meeting is to arrange a fiesta, all will attend gladly.

Understanding the Latin people can help explain the problems of paternalism also. We have always felt that our most important task was to make poor people more independent. We have been against landowners, Communists and even the government when we felt they were nurturing people's dependence on themselves rather than helping people get along on their own. The problem has been, however, that the people seem to prefer a father-son relationship to a business relationship. The people are easily patronized. *"El es un padre a nosotros,"* they say, "He is a father to us." It is one of the highest compliments they can pay. They even say it of us at times, and we then know that we have failed to undo the web of dependence for which the Latin culture is partly responsible.

That the Chileans feel that our attitudes are one-sided and that our society needs more contact with theirs was made clear to us last year in El Quisco. Our co-workers staged a skit about the adventures of the Chilean "Tranquillity Corps" sent to the United States. There the Chilean volunteers worked in large corporations, went to the lowest men on the organization charts and introduced new attitudes. Longer coffee breaks and more leisurely lunches were among their goals. They replaced the custom of bringing work home with regulations to frequent the opera and theater and to walk in the country at least three times a week.

I would like to project further the doings of this imaginary Tranquillity Corps. At the end of their two years in the States I am sure they would feel defeated. They would find themselves enjoying what we enjoy and overworking themselves. Then it would be time for a new group to arrive and for the others to go home and learn to live again. One of those tired veterans might be asked to speak to the new group. The first thing he would say is that it is great to work with the *gringos.* Then he would follow with another theme, probably longer than the first, that it is frustrating to live there. His concession would be, I hope, that in the final analysis we are very interesting friends who really need their help right now.

Your experience here can provide a critical test. By your example, you can show that we can understand each other despite the differences in our cultures, that our two worlds with different centers can overlap so that the dark areas of one can be brightened by the light of the other, that the two poles around which life revolves in Latin America and North America will attract rather than repel each other. There is no one in a better position than you to demonstrate that North Americans and Latin Americans can establish genuine and productive friendships and learn from each other.

If you can maintain the perspective of a good friend toward the Chilean people, you can help give the Alliance for Progress what it really needs, a soul. As it stands, the Alliance is a practical solution to the economic and social problems of the hemisphere, and many North Americans wonder why this is not enough. But the Latin people want more than pragmatic solutions in this hour of national decision. They want an ideal. We cannot decide which development ideology they will accept; they must decide that for themselves. But we can give them something that has a spiritual value, a strong friend who understands them and is challenged by their need for help. If real friendship were the basis for the Alliance for Progress, I think it could begin to unleash its potential.

Thirty years ago a wise President stressed the human side of Inter-American relationships and articulated a "good neighbor policy" toward Latin America. Although the concept was distinctly North American, they responded to it with appreciation. Now we need a concept equally meaningful to North and South alike, one even more expressive of our need to come together. You can maintain your own "good friend" policy toward the Chilean people and show that the real spirit of the Alliance for Progress can prevail in Chile and throughout Latin America.

Chapter 12

A VICTORY IN
VEGETABLES:
THE CO-OP IN RUPANCO

*Reviewing our work and disappointments, I can report to Father
Hesburgh wonderful success in one community along with problems in four others. Often the thorniest problems arise because of
influences from outside the community itself.*

December 14, 1962

Dear Father Ted,

When you visited us in Río Negro, you asked us to keep
you up-to-date on our community development efforts.
I'm sorry to say I can't report success in all five of the
communities that we showed you on the map. But we made
progress in some and our experience with the people of Rupanco
really makes me feel that I have one important accomplishment to
relate—not my accomplishment, but a signal achievement by the
people of Rupanco themselves.

In another area, San Juan de la Costa, we have encountered the
problem of slow-moving government bureaucracies. In this case, the
government is actually placing obstacles in our way. Helmut Seeger,
the head of the local Ministry of Agriculture office, has refused to
approve the people's plans to form a cooperative. Chilean law
requires that this permission be granted before the formal organization takes place. All I can do is continue to meet with twelve local

leaders who are preparing for the day when the government's permission arrives.

Government permissions of this sort are given rather freely in other provinces of Chile. The delay here is caused by a rivalry between the government and the institutions sponsoring the co-op. When a local government office really wants to cooperate, no paperwork stands in the way, but when the contrary is true, it becomes well nigh impossible. In one city where we had a friend in the government, the Peace Corps took out forty driver's licenses in one day. In another less friendly area, we were told we had to reside in the city for three months before we could apply for a license.

A few weeks ago, the people from San Juan made a simple request. They asked the local judge for Indian affairs to advise them of their rights to form a cooperative. They wanted to be assured that an Indian group could form a cooperative the same as any other Chileans. I knew that legally they could and told them so. Still, they wanted it in writing from their own judge. I traveled to La Union twice to request a letter to this effect. Both times the judge promised it. It never has come and it never will, because the Ministry of Agriculture and other local government offices around here are controlled by the Radical Party which has an old antipathy to the Catholic Church, and the co-op is being organized out of the mission in San Juan, a church organization.

A similar political problem has emerged in Nancuán, a very small community just outside of Río Negro that I also told you about last April. The neighborhood of about two hundred people has many needs—for better livestock, tools and techniques for milk production. Their community spirit had been dampened, however, by the failure of a project to provide electricity. The project was begun by the municipality of Río Negro and soon got bogged down in politics. The political party which began the project was defeated in a town election and the new mayor saw this rural electrification project as closely associated with his political rivals. All work stopped. The people sat for two years with light bulbs dangling from the ceiling but without electricity. When it became clear to us that nothing could be accomplished in the community until the electrical problem was solved, we began pestering everyone involved. The Rural Electric Cooperative in Osorno finally saved the day by helping the people purchase the missing equipment in installments. Today there is light in Nancuán.

It sounds simple, but it took six months of meetings and nego-
tiations with local authorities. The knottiest problem was that while
the political issue remained undecided, the Communists made a play
for the allegiance of the community. During one of our meetings, a
stranger arrived and tried to incite the community to steal the power
from the municipal power lines. Great discussion followed, and the
people turned him down.

Even after that issue was settled, however, politics may have the
last word in Nancuán. This same mayor of Río Negro is now accus-
ing me of working for the Christian Democrats in Nancuán. Our
motives have been so completely distorted that we may not attempt
any more community development there lest the people's community projects get stymied by politics again.

In another area, Buenaventura, we have been held back for a different reason: paternalism. This *fundo* is where we made one of our
first stops a year ago, and we were welcomed warmly both by the
people and the *patrón*. Buenaventura is probably my favorite place
among all the areas we worked. It is a beautiful dairy ranch. The
buildings, land, cattle and the people themselves are very well cared
for by the owner. If every *patrón* were as good a person as Don
Roberto Urisar, a social problem might not even exist in Chile. The
people had a fine community center (built by the *patrón*) and share a
happy community life. Their greatest need was for a little more independence of the *patrón* who, because of his concern for the people and
his good nature, had snuffed out their initiative. Consequently we
invited the *inquilinos* in Buenaventura to join the vegetable marketing
co-op we were organizing in Rupanco. This would give them the
chance to work with others outside their area and to have a small
independent income. The people liked the idea but Don Roberto dis-
approved and so it never went beyond the preliminary stages. We
decided to stay in touch with the people of Buenaventura but not pursue community development projects there, because their material
needs were well taken care of and there was little we could do about
their greatest need—for greater self-reliance and independence.

But forces within the community itself created our greatest setback of all. In Catrihuala the people were ready to file papers for the
legal establishment of their cooperative. The roads were hardening

on the mountain after the winter rains, meaning that the first trucks would climb the steep roads and the first cooperative sales could be made. We had met with the people of Catrihuala again and again until the idea of a cooperative was clear in their minds. We had made so many trips up the mountain to plant trees for reforestation projects and to talk to them about other plans for the area that they had begun calling us their friends and teachers. But the last trip had a sad ending.

We went there to discuss a plan for studying the shingle market in Puerto Montt, a city about ninety kilometers away. It had been surprising to us that the leaders of the cooperative-in-formation had not passed by our houses in Río Negro to discuss the plan as they usually did, and we worried that something was wrong. About five miles back in the woods at the very top of the mountain we found the president of the cooperative, Pablino Melillanka, making shingles. He sat on a stump and told us the bad news. A temporary alliance we had made among different forces of the community had been destroyed. He had made a sale of shingles to a local *fundo* owner who promised to come to the top of the mountain for them with his tractor. Other elements in the community, living farther down the mountain, had offered the buyer the same price—less the trip to the top. A price war broke out. Three different factions in the community now want to form their own co-ops, but they will not unite to form one.

Despite our previous differences, I had introduced Helmut Seeger and the local Ministry of Agriculture program to this community hoping it could work there too. But the government effort met the same fate as we did. The people wanted to form three different community organizations on the mountain. The Ministry also refused to work under these conditions. Janet finds that even the ladies' sewing circle is split. Thus the people of Catrihuala now remain without our assistance, or the government's, because of their own inability to get along with each other.

One other experience in Catrihuala put something of a damper on my enthusiasm for going there—although we have continued to go. Perhaps I am exaggerating but I sense a certain danger there.

In October, precisely during the days when the United States and the Soviet Union were at the brink of nuclear war over the Russian missiles in

Cuba, Janet and I made a visit to Catribuala. In retrospect this may not have been a prudent time to go as the Indian people there are a fiercely pro-Castro group that had illegally seized and occupied the mountain in the first place.

Our meeting was in the home of Gregorio Kintull and his family. This was a large, roomy structure which previously housed the general manager of the Spanish lumber company that the Indians had driven from the mountain. After meeting with the men, and while Janet continued her session with the ladies, Don Gregorio invited me to accompany him on a walk into the woods where, he said, he had something to show me.

As we walked through the woods I noticed Kintull was carrying a large wooden stick, almost a cudgel, but I made little of it. Soon however we came upon something that gave me the willies. Off the path a short distance someone had strung an ox skin on a wire between two trees, almost like a curtain. On the other side of it a man was busy cutting the fresh carcass into large pieces.

Before arriving in Catribuala that day, Janet and I stopped in a small community consisting of a store and a school, both run by the same family. We heard from that family that a neighbor's ox was missing—this was big news that traveled fast—and it presumably had been taken by someone in Catribuala.

Now to steal an ox—worse, to kill someone's ox— is a very serious crime in a poor rural place. An ox or team of oxen is a sign of prosperity; it might cost a year's wages. It is a means of transportation as well as a beast of burden. I remembered once seeing four carabineros (national police officers) escorting a man on horseback to jail with the head of an ox on his lap, publicly demonstrating that he had been arrested for this crime.

So out in the woods I wondered, was this what Don Gregorio wanted me to see? Apparently not, for he kept on going, large stick in hand. Instinctively, I picked up a large stick of my own and now the two of us just ambled along through the woods without speaking.

We came to a clearing and turned and looked at each other. I was totally confused about what the purpose of this meeting in the woods was, but I feared that Kintull had allowed me to witness the criminal slaughter of the ox because he didn't expect me to come back. Maybe he was confused too. Maybe it was because he saw me with a stick in my hands as well (though not a terribly frightening sight), but Don Gregorio abruptly turned and suggested we return to his house.

Jan and I have gone back to Catribuala several times, and I continue to meet with Don Gregorio and his crew. Still, I do believe that my life *may have been in some danger that day in October. I spoke with Janet about it and she feels I may be exaggerating the risk. However, in Santiago, my co-worker René Bórquez shared with me reports that he had heard since then that Kintull had been bragging in Catribuala that he was going to do me mortal harm.[1]*

Though four other efforts in nearby areas stalled or ground to a halt, in Rupanco after months of organizing work and plain agrarian toil we have succeeded in organizing a vegetable marketing co-op on the hacienda. This is an attempt to teach the people to grow large quantities of vegetables and market them cooperatively. From the beginning it has been a lesson in how difficult it is to get things done. The first day I started on this project, I learned an important lesson: never try to work when the people want to play.

On May 21, Jan Boegli and I had a full day's activity planned—near the coast in the morning and at Rupanco in the afternoon. We were going to work. But the 21st of May is one of Chile's biggest holidays, and the Chileans were going to play. Jan and I both stuck doggedly to our intentions—to each other's despair. The jeep, as if it were siding with the Chileans, began the day with a flat tire. There was no one in town to fix it. I borrowed the parish priest's spare and set out, gas needle on E, to do my day's work. No gas station was open. One gas attendant who lived nearby was usually an obliging soul on Sundays and I found him helmeted, decorated and plumed for the parade, obviously not in the mood to dispense gasoline. We decided to make our first destination with what we had, and buy gas after this man had made his appearance in the parade. Determined by the courage of our decision, I swung the jeep around and headed out of town, but the parade beat me to the bridge and we sat for an hour as it passed, smiling, friendly-like to the good-natured souls who thought we were there of our own accord and asked if we were enjoying the holidays. I met all our commitments that day, but we were two hours late for everything; and I vowed I would never try to work on a holiday again.

In Rupanco, another thing I learned in our "vegetable plan" is

---

[1] The section in italics, while describing the actual event, was not included in letters to anyone at the time for fear of causing alarm at home.

that the *campesinos* become discouraged easily. We used a very novel
approach and we were not sure it would succeed; there were at least
five occasions already when people wanted to quit. "The people say
the plants will never grow," was one objection. They grew. "The cut-
worm has ruined the cabbage plants and defeated the project" was
another. The cabbage plants were replenished. The words *"no se puede
—it's not possible"* signify a fatalistic attitude that is holding the people back. Whenever I hear the phrase I become very stubborn and
set about proving the person wrong.

Rupanco is the site of the huge Hacienda Rupanco, one of the
largest *fundos* in Chile, which covers 150,000 acres. The families of
two of the *delegados* who live with us in Río Negro work there as farm
laborers. The *central* of the Institute there was an old dilapidated
building loaned to us by the Hacienda. Around an old wooden table
in the kitchen of this rural school we discussed the project as it progressed through its various stages. The workers on the Hacienda live
in seven sections, little clusters of houses and small workshops,
spaced three or five miles apart. The co-op was formed with laborers
from six of the seven sections, and as we raced from one section to
another we headed directly toward the Andes with three volcanoes
sometimes in open view until the road veered right and skirted along
Lake Rupanco near the snow-capped mountains themselves.

My role in the formation of the cooperative in Rupanco was
very small. Among the 750 farm laborers there, many people had
spoken of cooperatives before. Two had been formed but they were
small, only slightly effective, and lacked legal structure. I had been
invited by a local schoolteacher to talk to the consumer co-op she
was forming among thirty members of the mothers' club in the
school. There we encountered a problem of numbers. Legally
speaking, a hundred people are needed to start a consumer co-op in
Chile. I took the problem to Don Tito Steffens in Valdivia, a leading authority on cooperatives in the south of Chile. The solution he
offered was logical but too sweeping for me to have dared imagine.
He advised me to form one large cooperative for the whole
Hacienda, and he offered to travel to Rupanco to plant the idea
among the local leaders.

One of the reasons we were so intent on getting to Rupanco on
the holiday was that Don Tito Steffens could go then and the people were free to have meetings. We assembled those interested in the

co-op. There were schoolteachers, bosses, workers and ourselves. Don Tito conversed for two hours with these community leaders, congratulating them on what they had accomplished so far and pointing out some of the defects of their former efforts. He convinced them that a co-op made up of all the workers on the *fundo* was perfectly possible. The advantages were unquestionable but there had been doubts as to the people's capacity to control democratically such a large business enterprise. For the sake of the laborers and of the movement itself, Don Tito encouraged us to try.

The type of co-op under discussion was a multi-activity one, a *cooperativa campesina*, as defined by Chilean law. This can develop any kind of cooperative activity—distribution of consumer goods, savings, credit, housing construction, etc.—by simply stating it in its constitution. The two main interests in Rupanco were the purchase of groceries and the possibility of marketing produce in Osorno.

A co-op that develops two different activities at the same time can become very complicated, and one schoolteacher suggested that they start teaching about co-ops immediately. Don Tito agreed but offered another suggestion as well: start with an experience in working together. This was my cue for the presentation of our project, *Plan Hortaliza* or "the vegetable plan."

By this time the plan was not exclusively my idea. Christian Valdivieso, director of the Rupanco *central* and a university graduate in agriculture, had taken an interest. He supplied all the technical information while I studied the market and organized the details. It called for the participation of twenty members of the co-op to plant five acres of vegetables among them, each person planting one-fourth of an acre in his backyard. Although many details had already been worked out, we wanted to discuss the project with this committee of local leaders, especially with regard to the vegetables which should be planted. To facilitate marketing, a limited number was necessary. Carrots, lettuce and cabbage were finally chosen.

Plan Hortaliza was an instrument to teach the people to work together in a cooperative way. It was separate from the co-op because as yet the co-op had no legal right to buy or sell. Between May and December, these two ideas went their separate ways. The initial group of community leaders, aided by a teacher from the Institute *central* and the local parish priest, began the campaign of explaining the co-op to the workers on the Hacienda, who chose its name and elected a provisional directorate which began inscribing members. *Plan Hortaliza* followed a systematic schedule. By the end of June, Christian and I had found the twenty people whose fencing and soil were good enough to carry on the project. Then we began working together with the people in planting the gardens.

The plan involved many agricultural techniques to which the people were not accustomed. It called for the use of nitrate and superphosphate fertilizers which they had hardly ever used before. The seeds were certified and procured from a reliable source. Weedkillers were used, and a spray chosen to blot out a disease which had ruined almost everybody's cabbage crop the year before. Simple things like planting in rows and thinning crops were new to many of the participants.

In almost mid-winter (July) we planted the seedbeds of cabbage and lettuce at the school and distributed the fertilizer and carrot seeds to the people. We gave our explanations to groups of five or six and in addition made countless visits to each garden during the spring to check the seedlings, review difficulties and spray. In general the cooperation of the people was fantastic. They followed religiously the norms we set down. Only occasionally did they hesitate. The carrots came up so beautifully that they thought it was a shame to thin them and throw all those lovely plants away. One lady wouldn't let me near her carrots with weedkiller. Another set aside the lettuce plants until she felt the moon was in the right stage for planting. But in the main they captured the idea of the experiment, worked very hard to prove it successful, and supplied information about the land and climate which was indispensable.

Working with the women was pleasant and our best tactic was to get the plump *señoras* giggling like schoolgirls before giving them the news that they had to plant their lettuce farther apart than they wanted. Because the men had only Sunday free to work in their gardens, we had to work on Sundays. This meant we'd hand out plants for transplanting when they hoped to rest. One man, Guillermo Casas, standing with a bag of cabbage plants in his hand, put me in my place by asking me if I were a Christian. But two weeks later, after rabbits raided his cabbage patch, this same gentleman journeyed to Osorno to buy new plants so that Don Tomás wouldn't see his garden looking so miserable.

This was the kind of cooperation we received from the people.

Mother Nature cooperated less. In one section, frost wiped out the carrot crop. We planted again. The lettuce seedbeds under our charge in the *central* produced much less than we needed. Uncle Sam saved the day with $20 to buy lettuce plants. In almost every garden the cutworm arrived and destroyed more than half the cabbage before we got there with DDT mixed with bran to tempt and then annihilate this monster. Fortunately, our cabbage seedbeds produced so well that we replaced every destroyed plant at no extra cost.

These events made for some very bad days in September, but the people placed their trust in us and never complained of the difficulties. They were experienced enough farmers to know what had not been our fault.

❄

Our hopes rose with the new plants. Soon in twenty different places around Rupanco, the region grew a sizable, lush garden of vegetables unmatched by anything seen before. The project quickly had a pedagogical effect on neighbors as they asked questions about the orderly rows of crops in three different shades of green. As everyone grew quite satisfied, I began to worry. I remembered how the mayor of Río Negro had reacted when I informed him of our plan. He told me of a fellow *patrón* who had produced thousands of vegetables and had been unable to sell them because of the tight grip which the large, year-round producers near Santiago have on local markets. We had 20,000 cabbages, hundreds of thousands of carrots and 40,000 heads of lettuce developing beautifully in the ground. I began to wonder how hungry the people of Osorno were feeling those days.

From the very beginning we had explained that the project was an experiment, and with regard to the anti-blight sprays, certified seeds and fertilizers, it was successful. Now came the crucial moment in the whole experience: Was it possible for the *campesino* to compete in local markets with the large producers in Santiago? They needed our help now more than at any other moment, and almost all the members of the Institute team rallied to spend some days in December helping them locate the market and devise marketing procedures.

Our first sale was on December 1. We packed 1,500 head of lettuce in the Peace Corps jeep and Institute station wagon at six that morning. If we rose early, the people rose earlier and did all the harvesting in the early morning dew so that the lettuce would arrive as fresh as possible. One person from each section went with us to help make the sale.

Two o'clock that afternoon found us standing in the rain in the farmer's market in Osorno with very low spirits. Large quantities had been delivered to grocery stores at a good price; some had been sold at the farmer's market, but at least half of the lettuce was still sitting in the station wagon. Nobody bought in the afternoon so there was nothing to do but send the discouraged people back to Rupanco. We took the lettuce to the Jesuits' home and went to a restaurant for a four o'clock brunch.

We learned a great deal that day. Although our lettuce was better and fresher than what was shipped down from the north, it was still too young and needed to form a better head. Also we discovered that it was easy to undersell the big producers. Their lettuce sold at 100 pesos a head in the local market. Because we paid little freight and no intermediary commissions, we could sell at 50 pesos and still make a sizable profit. Also, we learned that the farmer's market in Osorno was not a producer-to-consumer market; its vendors were intermediaries who bought *campesinos'* crops at a pittance and sold them at more than double the price. Consequently the public saw no more reason to buy there than anywhere else.

While the rest of our group took in a movie in Osorno, a new volunteer named Ken Buckstrup and I set out to deliver the lettuce to charitable organizations. Before we did, we made one final try at selling. Earlier in the day I had grabbed a basket of lettuce and walked through a shantytown. The reply from inside these cardboard-box-like windowless houses had been cordial but discouraging. "Sorry," they all said, using the exact same expressions, *"no hay plata*—there's no money here." After hearing this for the tenth time, I asked when there was money. "Tonight," they said, "the boss arrives with his paycheck." Perhaps the boss might want to buy some vegetables, we thought as we pulled up to the same little settlement that evening. Ken sold from the jeep and warded off the flocks of children who clamored around the curious sight of a gringo selling lettuce. I took one basket and started peddling through the streets. In five minutes the basket was empty. Two hours and two poor settlements later, we had sold all the lettuce we had been about to give away.

For those of you who might think that selling lettuce in the streets of shantytowns is carrying the Peace Corps idea a little too far, I would point out that the most common role played by active Communist propagandists in Chile is precisely that of a street peddler. After doing it myself, I now know why; I have never felt so close to the people as on that late summer evening in December. Peddlers are perhaps the only people that the poor can give a hard time. We got doors slammed in our faces and some real curt "no's," but the price was worth the opportunity to see the people and talk to them as they really are.

This experience constituted the most important lesson of the day. We sold cheaply—three heads for 100 pesos. At this price we not only made a substantial profit for the *campesinos*, but we also made vegetables available to a poorer class of people who don't buy sufficient quantities of them at the market price. A whole new dimension was added to our work and we saw that it had a secondary but extremely satisfying side effect. When *campesinos* learn to produce for the local market, the poor people in town get better and less expensive food.

The other December sales went more smoothly as we put into practice what had been learned. Radio and press advertisements helped tell the people in Osorno of our presence in the farmer's market. We learned the arrival day and hour of the train which brought produce from the north and we timed our own sales accordingly to occur a day or two earlier. Every trip meant the discovery of new possibilities for sales, and the vegetable growers became more and more adept at taking advantage of the established ones. When we arrived a week before Christmas with the first carrots of the season, our vehicles were so swamped by clamoring housewives that we couldn't even unload. With this, sales ceased to be a problem.

By the time half the vegetables had been sold, the plan was already a financial success. Between them, twenty *campesinos* had made 600,000 pesos, or 30,000 pesos each on average. Their original investment had been 7,500 pesos apiece.[2] When compared to the minimum daily wage for farm workers of 700 pesos, these profits represented a substantial increase in their yearly income. One women told me she had paid her yearly taxes on her small farm from the sale of her lettuce alone.

---

[2] At this time $1 was worth about 1,000 pesos.

The people had depended on our help constantly until our work with them settled into a routine—a trip to Rupanco the evening before a sale, a short sleep on the floor in sleeping bags, waking wearily to the hum of milking machines at dawn, greeting the *inquilinos* in the morning fog, a long day in the farmer's markets, brunch in the mid-afternoon with the people in a dingy restaurant where we analyzed the sales we had made, and a trip back to Río Negro. Sometimes it was a seventeen-hour day.

The question we began asking ourselves was whether our project had been a success in community development. Were the capacities of the people to organize themselves economically and progress strengthened in any way, or were they dependent on our assistance? Their participation in the plan had been constant. The fact that we worked side by side made them work harder, not less. Making plans, however, was another thing, and when we called a meeting of all the participants, we knew we were approaching a crucial moment. Would they take the idea as their own or would they thank us very much and say it was a shame we wouldn't be around next year to do the same thing?

The first meeting, right after the initial sales, gave us cause for concern. Naturally shy and in strange surroundings, the participants responded very little, accepted their first dividends and went home. I returned for a second meeting with them. Now came the moment of truth. By this time, everyone knew each other well from working together in the market and had been enthused by the way they were making money. At this meeting, the people bested each other with anecdotes about their experiences selling and compared notes on what vegetables were sought in the markets. They made suggestions for bettering the plan in the coming year.

During the meeting I had a hard time getting a word in edgewise. Finally I managed to present two pressing problems. The next sale had to be without jeep or station wagon. The sale after that had to be executed completely by the participants and their representatives, as I was returning to Santiago. Three days later they rented a truck for 15,000 pesos to carry the vegetables, loaded it one evening, and cleared 150,000 pesos the following day in the Osorno market. What remained unsold they carried to a friend's house near the market, and two *campesinos* stayed over to sell the following day. As they rushed about their business, I began to feel like an extra thumb; and when one *señora* picked up a huge bag of cabbage and walked by me as I struggled with a smaller one, I decided I wasn't needed anymore.

When I arrived in Santiago, I bought 27,000 pesos worth of seeds—some for vegetables I had never heard of before—for late summer seeding. Next July we'll help them expand the project to more members of the co-op, but basically the idea now belongs to them and will be taken over and supported by their cooperative. The evening before our last meeting, the directors of the *cooperativa campesina* in Rupanco met to discuss *Plan Hortaliza*. In February they will establish a Sales Committee with its own funds and its own directors within the structure of the organization. These directors will be chosen from among those participating in joint sales and will be a part of the co-op's administrative council.

Unfortunately, the cooperative itself and the cooperative store are now in a precarious position. It aroused widespread enthusiasm at first and over two hundred fifty *hacienda* workers bought a total of one thousand shares of stock in the enterprise. This amounted to about $750 before a galloping inflation. Then it ran into trouble with the Chilean bureaucracy. A prerequisite to purchasing groceries and selling them to members is the Ministry of Agriculture's approval of their plans to form a *cooperativa campesina*. The Ministry has delayed giving that approval for four months. Another necessary permission is that of the owners of the *fundo*, without which it is virtually impossible to form a cooperative. So far the corporation formed by the Santiago owners of the *hacienda* is still unwilling to allow its laborers to establish their consumer cooperative alongside the *pulpería*, or company store. While suffering these delays, the money lay dormant, uninvested, and lost over 30 percent of its value in the inflation.

Meanwhile, the mothers' club of the school where this whole story started continued to run a cooperative store informally. Last May they had a working capital of 180,000 pesos. In January, their capital had increased to 350,000 pesos because selling at current prices brought them a 27 percent profit on their merchandise. At the end of the year, the ladies had the right to these savings but elected to leave the capital intact and increase the services of their tiny store in the attic of the school. Their example, and that of those who sold vegetables, lit the lamp of hope for the other two hundred farm laborers still interested in a cooperative in Rupanco.

Although it will be years before we can be sure, I think some community development work was accomplished in Rupanco. Our methods diverged sharply from the standard but resembled those which other Institute teams used effectively in other parts of Chile. This resemblance became very clear to us during the Peace Corps Christmas reunion in Santiago where we recommended it as one of the best methods for achieving community development in a Latin American country. We call it result-demonstration; it consists not only of demonstration of new grasses or better seeds but of projects which show that the *campesinos* can do things they never dreamed of doing before with new techniques, a spirit of cooperation and a little extra work.

Sincerely,
Tom S.

Chapter 13

WINDING DOWN FOR ANOTHER YEAR

During the holiday break, I write another general letter to friends describing the extraordinary nature of the Peace Corps experience—both for some communities in Chile and most especially for a few young Americans.

Malloco, January 1963

Hello Again,

I am in the *central* or rural school of the Institute of Rural Education in Malloco, a town just outside of Santiago. Here the Institute teams from the Chiloé, Valdivia and Osorno areas have come together to plan their programs for the coming year. In similar summer sessions in other *centrales* all Institute staff members are meeting to plan the year's community development activities.

The Institute witnessed phenomenal growth in 1962, increasing its activities by more than 100 percent and, with help of Alliance for Progress funds, building six new *centrales* down the skinny length of Chile. These changes will influence us heavily in Osorno next year. The number of *delegados* who will work in rural communities has been increased substantially and in March our whole team will operate out of a brand new *central* in Osorno.

The Peace Corps has also grown. Last year we were forty-five. Now there are one hundred volunteers in Chile: sixty with the Institute, twenty with an organization called TECHO which works in urban development, and the remaining twenty with a YWCA project in a new housing development near Santiago. In the Osorno area the number of volunteers sent to work with the Institute is being doubled from four to eight.

It is not my intention in this letter to report the gamut of activities of these volunteers and their organizations, but rather to sketch broadly our life and work in Río Negro last year. Even this is not an easy task. We are so engrossed in our work that it is hard to recall what would interest someone in the States. Our lives are so different that it makes accurate description difficult; and to top it off, all the words on the tips of our tongues are Spanish not English. Yet in six months we will have the responsibility of recounting our experiences to you. Perhaps this letter might reduce the problem of communication I am bound to have next July.

For many Chileans in Santiago, our region is extremely remote. So it seemed to me when I first went there more than a year ago. Now it seems the center of things, and I feel much more at home there than I do in Santiago. It could be bias, but we believe we work in the most beautiful part of Chile. The south of Chile, especially the area around Osorno and Valdivia, is a region of rivers and small wooden bridges, of sprawling lakes with deep blue waters and dark rising edges of forest. It is rich in lumber and there are any number of local craftsmen who make carvings which remind one of the region itself.

German immigrants settled there and developed a very productive dairy industry; they frequently compare the region to Switzerland. Some help to complete the resemblance by building chalets on top of the green hills which rise into mountains. We are never out of sight of the snow-capped Andes and the volcano Osorno pops into view continually, even when you least expect it.

Osorno is a lovely town where horses and wagons mingle with automobiles in traffic and horse-drawn coaches still compete with taxis. The *plaza*, or town square, is the prettiest I have seen in Chile, with a rotund concrete bandstand, large pool and walkways that trace harmonious figures when you look down on it from above. Osorno has just about everything: hotels, restaurants, movies and fancy shops. It was there that we came occasionally in the past year to revive our drooping spirits.

Osorno is progressive as well as picturesque. In both these aspects it contrasts with Río Negro, where there is still some damage from the 1960 earthquake and serious danger of unemployment for the workers who live in the shantytown beside our headquarters. The town's only industry, a flax mill, was destroyed in the earthquake. Río Negro is a place you can return to after a month's absence, ask "what's new?" and get stared at as if you were crazy. If you can't afford the time to travel to Osorno and want to let off steam, there is really no place to go.

We've had many such unforgettable moments with Chilean friends, be they fellow workers on the Institute staff, country folk or people in Osorno. Perhaps the most enjoyable experience of the past year was playing the violin with the Osorno symphony orchestra and touring with it one extended weekend through the south.

Life in the two houses of the Institute in Río Negro was a bit of a strain. Without maids, refrigeration or supplies of canned goods, eating was a problem. The morning cup of coffee and slice of bread was the fruit of an hour's work; that's what it took to chop the wood and get a fire started in the stove. A meal was a real production and since we ate all our meals in the girls' house, they ended up with extra burdens. The average day saw one meal in addition to breakfast in Río Negro and the other—if there was one—in the country or at a restaurant depending on where we were working that day.

Our homes had comfortable and uncomfortable aspects. In July when hot water was installed, cold-water shaves and showers became a thing of the past. We had electricity from the start. Since our team was small, I had the luxury of a private room where I could warm up by a small heater and try to reacquaint myself with my more philosophic past. Because of limited space and facilities, one room in the girls' house was kitchen, dining room and living room in one. This was the only really warm room during the cold, damp winter.

We traveled from one region to another in a little green jeep that hardly ever rested. If I had a meeting in the evening, Jan would schedule one in the afternoon, and we would study bus and train schedules until we had elaborate systems of uniting person and jeep in one spot when it was most needed. As our community grew, we relied heavily on trains and buses; and male members of the team hitchhiked on the backs of trucks not knowing when we climbed aboard if our travel companions would be people, animals, or sacks of fertilizer. Going by horseback, while most romantic and "peacecorsey," is the slow, sore way and was used only when all other possibilities were exhausted.

Without doubt the most tiring aspect of our work was jeep travel over gravel roads for long periods of time. I could gauge during the day the hour when sleep would overtake me in the evening by the number of kilometers I traveled in the jeep. Dust in summer, mud in winter and flat tires year-round all complicated matters still more. There were many times when we had two or more punctured tires in a day. Only once did we have serious motor trouble, but it came at eleven o'clock the night of the hardest day of the year and left Jan and me seventeen miles from home with no way to get there but walk. So we walked, and arrived at dawn.

I used to worry that our guests—especially those fresh from the States—would find our days wanting in activity and producing less than they had imagined possible. We have had to learn to function at the pace of the Chilean people themselves, to think in terms of days instead of minutes. Poor communication, bureaucracy and the lack of IBM-style organizations mean that some details require a whole morning when they could be taken care of by a telephone call in the United States. Chileans regard the North American *hurry* as insensitive and senseless. This adjustment of learning to work in a Latin society—of forming an integral part of a social mechanism so very different from our own—was the most difficult of all.

A plan completed as scheduled or a deadline met is what would make our work click and make interest in our work mount and engross us. Few things happened on schedule, and staying interested in the work required continuous willpower. Added to this difficulty was the great challenge of the work itself. The roles of a Peace Corpsman in the Institute, of a North American working on Chilean social problems, and of a community development worker in the areas we chose were still relatively undefined and there was little experience to depend on. Each step involved creation; and norms of action—our criteria of success or failure, even our daily schedules— had to be invented as we went along. Our team was sent to Río Negro with the commission to select certain communities and raise their standard of living. The rest was up to us. We were without local supervision or material resources such as machinery or loans to entice the people to come to our meetings.

Last March two Peace Corpsmen starting their work in another area were getting to know a community for the first time. They asked one lady what was the biggest problem they would find there, and she responded dourly, "explaining to the people what you're doing here." They, like us, gave their explanations during the year. But the constant pressure to create—to find a way to move forward with nothing but the resources of the people themselves—was exhausting. I returned to Santiago in December mentally tired and psychologically stale, inert.

The months rushed by, but our projects moved slowly. Nevertheless, we did accomplish something. The countless trips that Jan made in the jeep and on foot with a large awkward posterboard and briefcase full of visual aids had the most intangible but perhaps most important effect of all. She concentrated on a certain number of *centros* and visited them almost weekly with cooking, health or nutrition advice. The products made in these sewing-circle type meetings under the direction of the *delegadas* were exhibited in Riachuelo, a small town west of Río Negro, and they were the talk of the town.

Our promotion of cooperatives went well, and in three different areas we were able to get three or four committees to join together in plans for a regional co-op. In all of these areas the people made the preliminary legal transactions, had enthusiastic education sessions and began purchasing items collectively. In Rupanco, we initiated a project designed to teach the people the possibility of producing and marketing on a cooperative basis.

This letter would not be complete if I failed to tell you something about our lives when we're not in the south. During the past year I was called to Santiago three times—in July for a physical exam, in November to help with the training of new volunteers, and at the end of the year for reports and reassignment. The first time I journeyed away from Río Negro, the bright lights and busy traffic of Santiago were a shock to me. Conditions in the hotel were unbelievably glorious. One of the girl volunteers, without hot water for five months, reports that she took a nice hot bath, stood up and showered, and then took a hot bath again.

During an excursion to a local nightclub, the shocks continued. The band started playing fast music and we decided we'd show them a real rock 'n roll. As we started, everyone gathered around two Chilean university students twisting like I had never seen it done before; the twist was not yet respectable when I entered the Peace Corps. Soon there was no room on the floor and we had to sit down. In December we began making our comeback. A new group of twenty twisting volunteers were with us in our Christmas meeting and by New Year's Eve we were able to twist, proudly, most ecstatically, until dawn.

Santiago provides a chance to visit with other members of the Institute who aren't from the south and to renew acquaintances with other Chilean friends there. In July a group of six University of Chile students and I had a reunion dinner where we reminisced about the month we spent together in the south working with the *campesinos* in a University summer project. The following weekend we went to the mountains to a ski resort for the day.

I took advantage of the July break by taking a week's vacation in Buenos Aires. In December neither time nor money allowed such a luxury so I rested in the way that practically all Peace Corps volunteers have done in the past year. I went to the Langfords' house. Walter Langford, our director, and his wife deserve credit for service way beyond the call of duty. They rented an apartment bigger than they needed with the explicit purpose of making it a home for volunteers. It has been much more than that—home, hospital and central station for all forty-five of us. Mrs. Langford served home-cooked meals to hordes of people each week. When someone is sick or just tired, she yanks them out of service for a day or two and tries to fatten them up. When there are operations or diseases, all recuperations are made with her care and surveillance.

A year ago she had never heard of hepatitis. Within three months she had six cases on her hands—and it was necessary to rent another apartment just to house sick volunteers. Even then her apartment was so full that one patient held court from his bed in the dining room. Rest periods for hepatitis last as long as three months, all of which are spent on a special diet. As one jaundiced patient put it, "She's one woman who will never wonder where the yellow went."[1] The Langfords were called upon to give away two brides in

---

[1] A reference to a ubiquitous advertising jingle of the time, "You'll wonder where the yellow went when you brush your teeth with Pepsodent."

less than two months and to help three other volunteers arrange their weddings. One of these is in a small village called Chol-Chol, 400 miles south and toward the coast. Mrs. Langford is bringing her own silver punch bowl because she doesn't expect to find one there.

Answering my university friends' questions about our work and lounging in the comfort of the Langfords' home give me a perspective which is difficult to maintain when I re-involve myself in Río Negro life. Perhaps some of the conclusions I draw there are worth recording here:

What makes the Peace Corps a valuable experience for me is not only the satisfaction that it brings. I'm afraid I must say, perhaps to the delight of Peace Corps critics, that the most important thing is the adventure. Many of our experiences surprise us as we're having them. We call them "who'd-ever-think" experiences because that's what we said to ourselves when we hitched an old gray mare to a milk cart and rode through Rupanco spraying DDT on vegetables... When we came south in the stylish express train with 500 seedlings carefully hidden under the seat... When we chased a fox through a field with the jeep... When we pleaded with a cantankerous old cow to get out of the middle of the road and let us pass.

In rural areas of southern Chile, we can relive some of the good old days of our own country. This in itself is an adventure. We sit around wood stoves on winter evenings and rise the following morning in a house where there is no thermostat. We crank wall phones and scream into them as if we didn't believe that the wire could carry our voice. We travel in trains tugged by puffing steam locomotives and hitchhike on trucks made in the 1920s.

The work is an adventure too. I suspect that to a certain extent every Peace Corpsman ends up doing something different than he planned—accepting challenges for which his previous experiences had not prepared him. My job has been the adventure of a philosophy student in the countryside. I've enjoyed riding horses through herds of cattle and eating jams made on the farm from wild fruits with novel tastes, delicious on hot bread. I like working with hogs, cows and vegetables. Conversations and books about poultry raising, hog shelters and pastures fascinate me, perhaps because these topics are so new to me, perhaps because they are so applicable to our work and perhaps because plain old Mother Nature is confronted there. When

I leave Chile I won't remember it as Santiago or Osorno, but by picturing large meadows clear and pale in the light of the far south, with livestock scattered among the mountain beeches and straight dirt roads passing along the split-rail fences.

If adventure means going somewhere few have gone before and unearthing unappreciated beauty, our adventure is deeper still than the events of our daily life or our work. It consists in discovering more each day about the human resources of the *campesinos*. It is a truism to say that they are human but it's an experience of another dimension to see their humanity in all its richness regardless of the superficial aspects of poverty or limited learning.

Our adventure has been to accompany a few of them in deed and all of them in spirit in the initial steps they are taking toward a better life. In this we have had the privilege to work with Chileans who believe in these people and sacrifice themselves to wake them up to their possibilities as human beings. Of all my experiences in Chile, none is so inspiring as listening to an educated Chilean who understands the underprivileged poor in his own country as he reads to us the sad music which he sees in their lives.

Perhaps our adventure serves not only ourselves and the *campesinos*, but our country as well. I believe that it does.

                    See you all in North America soon,
                    Tom Scanlon

Chapter 14

OUR WORK IN RURAL DEVELOPMENT: SAN JUAN DE LA COSTA

Over the course of three days, I help train a successor Peace Corps group that will serve in Chile. This provides the opportunity to talk shop—to tell the story of our most successful cooperative project—and to describe my last six months of service as a volunteer. [Note: These talks were given at Notre Dame after my return to the United States.]

When an ex-volunteer meets new volunteers in training, he has a variety of feelings: sympathy for the frustrations that lie ahead, understanding of their enthusiasm to enroll in the Peace Corps, even a little envy. Not that he is tempted to go with them. The idea has little appeal to him now because he has had the experience and knows it can't be repeated. Rather he envies them the way a person leaving a restaurant envies those just sitting down.

The Peace Corps is not as pleasurable as eating out. When someone asks me if I "enjoyed" the two years, I don't answer with an unqualified "yes." There were moments that I enjoyed very much and others that were discouraging. It's better to say that I "appreciated" the experience and all that it meant to me. I am grateful to the Peace Corps for giving me the opportunity of a lifetime, and I would recommend it to anyone. The Peace Corps is certainly one of the great organizations in the history of our government, and I am happy to have been a part of it.

This course is rather a sad event for me. Having finished my tour as a Peace Corps volunteer, this may be the last time I will "talk shop." But if it is to be my swan song, it will not be about the organization as such. After a volunteer has been in the field for two years, he thinks less about the Peace Corps itself and more about issues related to his work.

I presume that a volunteer who taught school in Ghana or a nurse who served in the Philippines, for example, would be filled with ideas relating to their work and would be anxious to discuss them with someone who is about to take their place. I think it is important to capture these ideas before settling back into our routine in the United States. In this way we can establish a dialogue within the Peace Corps, even a tradition of ideas, on the topics of development with which we have some experience.

Over the next three days I want to share some of my ideas with you on how best to achieve rural development. By "rural development" I mean reaching the rural communities of very poor farmers—the kind you will work with in Chile—and helping them move themselves forward toward a more prosperous, healthy, and happy life. To do this, I want to first tell you the story of San Juan de la Costa and a cooperative that we started there that I believe will become our most important "rural development" project in Chile. But San Juan represents more than a possible Peace Corps success story to me. It illustrates also the problems that arise when different institutions dedicated to promoting "rural development" are uncoordinated, work at cross-purposes, start fighting with each other, and allow politics to enter into their efforts to help the rural poor.

San Juan de la Costa covers an area of 400 square miles in the coastal region of the province of Osorno. Though there are no exact figures, some 30,000 inhabitants now live there, more than half of them Huiliche Indians and the rest of Spanish descent. The coastal inhabitants live on poor lands in overcrowded conditions. The huge area is made up of one tiny farm after another. Nowhere is the repetitious landscape broken with villages. This is a place without a main street. The only centers of civilization are three religious missions which have been there since the eighteenth century.

Until five years ago, San Juan was a forgotten place. The people lived in abject misery without thought of a change for the better; and each year more children were born, and more and more families struggled to earn their meager living off the impoverished land. Perhaps San Juan would still be abandoned today had the Minister of Lands and Colonization, Julio Philippi, not requested the sociologist Julio Sierens to make a study of the area. His two-volume report was so shocking that a special program of government assistance became a clear necessity.

The study revealed one of the most depressing social situations in Chile, and many people became challenged by the need to help San Juan advance. San Juan is atypical for Chile, and therefore held a great fascination for a country that considered itself free of the problems of large, impoverished Indian populations such as those in Bolivia or Peru. San Juan, with its backwardness and poverty, caught the nation by surprise.

Professor Sierens began his work with a group of students from the Universidad Católica in the summer of 1958. He had to complete the work alone in the fall. For obvious reasons, he was not able to apply comprehensive scientific methods. Instead, he worked with samples, taking a kind of Gallup Poll among the coastal people. His findings showed that in terms of public services, agriculture and living standards, San Juan was among the most poorly developed places in the country.

Schools, roads, medical facilities, and even police protection were crying needs. Agricultural diversification was a prime necessity. The lands were producing so little wheat that the only solution was to turn eroded fields to pasture or plant trees. These lands had once been productive, but poor use and erosion had emaciated them. The people were making the situation worse by sowing the same crops year after year without rotation or fertilizers. Another local practice needed curtailing, *roces a fuego*, clearing the land by fire. When someone wanted to clear a forest, he set it afire, which saved having to work it with the ax but lost precious lumber. On one day Professor Sierens noted twelve forest stretches being burned.

With little education or resources, the people could hardly be blamed for what they were doing to the land. Only a very small

percentage of the children could go to school. Seventy-two percent
of the farmers did not even have land titles indicating clearly which
fields were theirs and which were their neighbors'. The cost of a
fence for two and a half acres was estimated at $90. Most people did
not make that much in a year.

Neither could they be blamed for the way they lived—miserably, according to the Sierens report. Here are some of his findings:
Sixty percent slept on floors. Forty percent lived in homes without
windows. Seventy percent had homes with dirt floors, and thirty-five
percent had one-room shanties housing eight or ten family members.
In 1958, among the 233 deaths recorded in one part of the Costa, 60
percent were babies under three, and all but four of the 233 were
buried without a death certificate.

Their poverty meant that the cost of dress clothes was prohibi-
tive. What underclothes they had were usually made from flour sacks.
Their food was what they could produce. When times were bad, a hot
pepper in hot water substituted for many main meals. In some cases,
the people were not even accustomed to distinguish between breakfast, lunch and supper; they were all called *comidas*, "meals."

Isolation and scant communication with other parts of the country meant that the Indians in San Juan maintained their own culture.
They had *machis* or *curanderos*, doctor-exorcists who made themselves
prosperous by treating diseases. Ancient beliefs harked back to a
bisexual god of the Huiliches, and death cults still mingled with their
Christianity. A *cacique* (chief) named Naipan exercised a conservative
influence and expressed the mistrust which the coastal people felt
toward outsiders; Naipan had no power under the law but Professor
Sierens surmised that without him the coast would be in a state of
anarchy. In this, the sociologist was mistaken.

The *cacique* soon found himself a forgotten power in the face
of a new social movement in San Juan because the Chilean government acted soon after Minister Philippi received the report. All local
government agencies were instructed to render as many services as
possible to the poor people of the coast, while the Ministry of Lands
and Colonization began the slow process of solving the problem of
land tenure. Wisely, the program was initiated on a community
development basis; help was channeled to communities of farmers
who were willing to work together on their own behalf. Helmut

Seeger, the representative in Osorno of the Ministry of Agriculture, was assigned to run the program. As of last spring, it had begun working with twenty communities.

The first year was one of great accomplishment, and it soon became Chile's most famous experiment in rural community development. Señor Seeger coordinated efforts of the Ministry of Roads, the Ministry of Education, the Corporation for National Development. Schools were built, and roads were opened to places unknown to automobiles. Tractors loaned by the government helped many people begin partial mechanization of their farms.

The most important aspect of this program was supposed to be that the people were responsible for the progress made. They were to work on every project and help in the planning. These plans ranged from building social centers and roads to running raffles. Once organized in groups, the people requested technical aid and material resources from both government and non-government sources. They also used their community organizations to express group needs. For example, they complained to the government about a lazy judge and a faulty bridge. Finally the communities in San Juan joined with communities in other parts of the province to form a provincial association of small farmers, called the *APPAO*. All this was done under the tutelage and at the direct suggestion of Señor Seeger and the Ministry of Agriculture.

While the Ministry program was in its initial stages, another effort to help the people began under quite different auspices. Don Tito Steffens, a cooperatives expert from Valdivia who did co-op development work for the local bishop, and I visited the Mission in San Juan de la Costa. By this time, I was Don Tito's regular work partner in Osorno. That day Don Tito and I spoke to a group of leaders assembled in the meeting room of the old mission. Hearing this expert on cooperatives caused the people to resurrect plans they had made two years earlier. Don Tito agreed to help them and asked me to be his contact with the people. Quite happily, I complied.

My tutor in cooperatives and I had by that time established a routine. The first step was to organize a small-scale store which could give the people experience in running a small business and educate them to the kind of services a co-op can provide. A legal

prerequisite to this step was the approval by the Ministry of
Agriculture of the people's plan to form a co-op. That approval was
not forthcoming in San Juan de la Costa.

Although the number of residents involved was small, although
only a few belonged to communities organized by the Ministry, and
although the purpose of the co-op was to perform consumer and marketing activities not conducted under the government program, these
plans were delayed for a year. The Ministry maintained that the cooperative would parallel the communities and duplicate their work.
Meanwhile conversations about the cooperative continued. When a
number of people expressed interest in joining, Señor Seeger made a
rule that no one could belong to a community and a co-op at the same
time. In effect, he decreed that by belonging to the cooperative, a resident of San Juan would forgo his right to government services.

Helmut Seeger and Tito Steffens were the two men I had
grown to admire most in Chile for their work among the poor. I had
dreamed of being able to devise a program that would combine the
technical skills and energies of these two men. I could not understand why the Ministry opposed the cooperative so vigorously. We
were not competition for their large program in any way. We were
operating without any external resources. We had only one technician on our staff. We simply wanted to help sixty farmers follow
through on their desire to form a co-op.

However, since members of the cooperative were cut off from
technical services and credits normally provided by the government,
we organized a program of credits and technical assistance similar to
"the vegetable plan" we had carried out in Rupanco—only with hogs
instead of vegetables. Ten members of the future cooperative agreed
to sow an acre of winter oats and clover for pasture, to fence this small
area off, and to build a small hog house in the newly seeded field.
After they had made the necessary preparations, we provided the
farmers with a recently bred sow. The farmers were to care for the sow
and its litter, castrating, vaccinating, and feeding the animals according to methods we recommended. At the proper time, the cooperative would arrange a joint livestock sale in Osorno.

Our idea was small in scale, but we think it was farsighted. We
hoped to convert some of the eroded land to pasture and to transform
part of the farm production of co-op members from wheat to live-

stock. We wanted to put a cooperative into business selling products the area was suited to produce. The Ministry, on the other hand, was extending credit for seeds and fertilizers to plant wheat, a crop not suited to the area, and its efforts did not contribute to the development of any permanent economic institution.

During the summer (January and February) my IER counterpart and I wandered by foot, horseback, and jeep through the most remote sections of the coast and selected participants for the hog plan. In those months, I heard some disturbing things about the relations between the Ministry of Agriculture and the San Juan communities. Stories of high-handed dealings with the people were legion. One group of small farmers was cut off from government assistance because it delayed in joining a Ministry-sponsored federation. When other communities were accused of having "inconvenient attitudes," technical and economic assistance was cut off. Although the "community development" program in San Juan was accomplishing a great deal materially, the people were not learning to speak for themselves and were not being allowed to act independently. This was exactly opposite to the community development approach we were taught in the Peace Corps. The worst part was that the Ministry program was sponsored by grants and loans from the United States government. In fact, Señor Seeger was the apple of many AID officials' eyes and had been sent by AID to the United States to study community development. This conflict between the Ministry program and the San Juan cooperative was an example of very poor coordination between the AID program and the Peace Corps.

Gradually, I was to learn that there were deeper reasons for the conflict; these were political. The Ministry of Agriculture in Osorno was controlled by members of the Radical Party, one of the blocs in President Alessandri's conservative coalition government. This party had a traditional hostility toward the Catholic Church. Señor Seeger began to accuse the Mission in San Juan and me of working in behalf of the Christian Democrat party and its nominee for president in the 1964 elections, Eduardo Frei. I saw no sign of Mission involvement in politics in all the months I worked in San Juan, and I certainly wasn't. Nonetheless, the accusations went all the way to Santiago. I was asked by the president of the Institute, Jaime Serrano, to meet with

Minister Philippi himself and explain that these accusations were really nothing but unfair charges leveled by someone who wanted no rival development effort in the coastal area.

The experience in San Juan de la Costa brought home some troubling and challenging issues for me. I found myself thinking about how efforts aimed at helping the rural poor in Latin America should be organized and carried out. In order to help formulate some answers, I used my vacation time last April to travel to Colombia, Ecuador and Peru and to visit other Peace Corps volunteers working in the rural areas.

What is the best role for Peace Corps volunteers in rural development? I believe the potential of this role has frequently been overlooked by the Peace Corps itself. Frequently volunteers and Peace Corps officials talk as if their work had little to do with the long-range development of the host country. However, due to the ever increasing numbers of volunteers, the Peace Corps is rapidly becoming one of the most frequently seen and heavily counted-on forces for constructive social change in rural areas of Latin America. Plans are for the number of Peace Corps volunteers in Chile to jump to five hundred. These volunteers are valuable and strategically placed development personnel, well-trained and well-motivated. They have a unique contribution to make which should be taken seriously.

In failing to understand the volunteer's true potential, the Peace Corps has often been confused by its own image. The image of the Peace Corps volunteer, toiling side by side with groups of Latin men and living in rugged circumstances, has become so embedded in the minds of volunteers and staff that they think the volunteers' most important work is to go out and do manual labor. This image of the Peace Corps is photogenic, and it really does depict an essential part of the Peace Corps idea. But it should not obscure a more important side of the contribution which volunteers can make to improve the operations of host country institutions.

Because of the background and training of most volunteers, this is the work for which they are best suited. Most volunteers assigned to rural areas today are low on technical skills. Generally, they are graduates of liberal arts colleges with little practical experience in farming.

Peace Corps volunteers are best at being organizers, innovators, coordinators, and communicators. They really can't compete with the *campesinos* in doing manual labor, but if they are made responsible for implementing an idea on schedule or devising a new project, they will burn the candle at both ends and leave valuable precedents behind.

Our most important contribution in Chile was in this area. The Institute itself said that what it valued most about the Peace Corps volunteers were the new ideas and methods which we brought. The home economists started special courses for school dietitians. The nurses gave health training to the women community development workers. The men in the Chilean group helped the Institute to do pioneering work in the formation of small farm cooperatives.

In my view, this is the real meaning of the counterpart idea which was so central in Peace Corps thinking at the beginning. Volunteers were told that they had to train someone to carry on for them after they left. This idea has its value but it can be hard to implement because counterparts change and there can be a chasm of cultural and educational differences between a volunteer and his counterpart. But there is another level at which the counterpart idea makes even more sense, and that is the institutional level. I think the Peace Corps as an institution has an enormous impact on the institutions to which it is assigned. An entire Peace Corps group can leave their methods, habits and ideas behind and know that something of themselves will carry on. When we arrived in Chile we learned that the IER had a very different idea of organization than we did and we had to work hard to adjust to their way of doing things. But I believe we changed them a little as well.

Some of the institutions to which volunteers have been assigned are so scattered, uncoordinated and weak that it is hard to work with them. In Ecuador, over twenty-five institutions work in the general area of rural development in a very uncoordinated way. In Peru, I visited a home construction project where the Peace Corps volunteers could do nothing because their host institution was unable to procure land titles for the people whose homes they were going to help build. Under these circumstances, volunteers often just start working on their own; they have to create their own projects. Some are more successful than others. No one creates a project as productive as he would like it to be. The resultant efforts are too personal, too undirected and too unrelated to the development of the institutions which those countries need.

What does AID have to do with this? A great deal. Working in the national capitals with host governments, AID personnel are constantly making decisions that have a great impact on the institutions created to help rural people. The job of creating institutions, giving them funds and training and other resources, is AID's job, not the Peace Corps' task. In this sense, the Peace Corps cannot solve its own most serious problem. It falls to AID, working with the host government, to create the kinds of programs with which volunteers can do their best work.

This leads me to conclude that the most important roles of the Peace Corps and AID complement each other perfectly. AID can create the institutions and supply the framework in which volunteers can work in rural development. The Peace Corps can provide important rural development institutions with essential grassroots support. To accomplish this, AID and the Peace Corps have to plan together—something they don't do today.

There should be joint planning in the use of senior technicians, junior technicians, Peace Corps volunteers and other resources which the United States can provide to support rural development institutions. Our experiences indicate that the support of AID or the Peace Corps has a great influence on an institution. That influence must be exerted for the good. If our help is given indiscriminately, or if we are uncoordinated among ourselves, we are partly responsible for the ineffectiveness of the resultant programs.

There are many examples of good cooperation between AID and the Peace Corps. In Colombia, AID made a grant of $38,000 to the community development program to which volunteers were assigned for school construction. Three times the number of schools normally budgeted by AID for that sum were built. In Ecuador, the Peace Corps and AID are working together to create credit unions.

There are also examples of very poor coordination. In our case in San Juan de la Costa, AID and the Peace Corps were working with two rival and competing rural development efforts. Also in Chile, AID had boatloads of grain with which it hoped to encourage a livestock plan. We had such a plan, the people were prepared to pursue it, and the hogs needed grain. But we had to get the grain from other sources because our project was too small for AID to consider including in its plan.

To balance matters out, however, AID and the Peace Corps are coordinated in their support of the IER. AID has provided funds for a substantial number of new "schools" for the Institute and our contingent of volunteers has been helping to get the schools open, train the staffs and serve as teachers.

For AID to work more closely with the Peace Corps in helping rural people, it would need additional personnel outside the capitals. At the present time, there may be one or two persons in the AID missions who are concerned with the institutions that work with local people. These AID officials, of necessity, live in the capital city and advise the government at high levels. They are not familiar with the conduct of programs at local levels or of the administrative lags which occur. When they do venture into the provinces, it is for too short a time to get a good grasp of the situation. An AID program which stressed rural development institutions would require many junior level officers to fill the gaps between the operating personnel of these programs and the national capital. These junior advisors would live in the provinces and be expected to involve themselves in the administration of the program. They can do this without taking the final decision-making authority away from host country administrators. These AID representatives could easily be recruited from the ranks of former Peace Corps volunteers.

These thoughts add up to a vision of a national program of rural development that would be worthy of the poor farmers with whom we worked for two years. I believe that a national rural development effort could be very successful and effective if it were based on the following key ingredients:

- a national community development program that has the backing of the highest authority in Chile;
- private federations of cooperatives ready to help poor farmers go into business as co-ops;
- technical assistance to these co-ops provided in ways that help them grow products for which there is a demand in local markets.

I believe that AID and the Peace Corps could make important contributions to these development efforts, but to do that they need to sit down together and deploy their resources in a coordinated fashion.

My vision skips over the problem of politics because there is little in my experience that teaches me how to control the disruptions caused by political antagonisms. However, I think that political parties in Chile, and AID and the Peace Corps as well, need to be aware that unless we come up with comprehensive approaches to the problems of the poor farmers in Chile, another movement is standing by that promises a better life for all at a price that none of us would want to see our friends in Chile pay.

Now I want to talk with you about how we functioned during our last six months in Chile with incomplete resources and imperfect institutions and how we were able to get something done regardless of those limitations.

You will recall that AID and the Peace Corps are working together to expand the number of IER schools. In March, our Institute team was sent to a brand-new school in Osorno to begin the new school year's work. (March, being the fall in Chile, is the beginning of the academic year). Jan Boegli, Amos Roos, Ken Buckstrup and I moved out of our quarters in Río Negro. This move marked the beginning of new responsibilities for us. In addition to helping out at the school in Osorno, we were to serve as advisors to the Institute's entire community development effort in the Osorno province. We were anxious to experiment with this new role since it gave us the opportunity to phase ourselves out of projects which were too closely identified with the *gringos*. But our plans ended in frustration. This was due to the fact that the Institute had neither the resources, organization, nor official backing required to mount an effective community development program.

One difficulty which arose was that the Institute did not have enough money to pay room and board for the *delegados* they sent into the field. The Institute insisted that the local communities support them. Consequently, we could accomplish nothing in March while the *delegados* looked for places to stay. Unfortunately, there are many places where such a frequent visitor is not welcome, and we could not be certain where we would be working until April.

Another problem with the program was the lack of clear lines of authority within the Institute. The *delegados* enjoyed a great deal of autonomy and would answer only to the central powers in Santiago, certainly not to us and not even to the director of IER operations in the province.

However, the most serious problem was that the *delegados* would find, upon entering a community, that it had already been organized as a committee of small farmers by the Ministry of Agriculture. In contrast to all the resources of the Ministry, and the quick credit, fertilizers, seeds and other benefits gathered through its program, the *delegados* had very little to offer. They could help the communities to organize and to request help from other sources but the Institute was not very successful at obtaining the cooperation of other agencies either.

The Institute did have some important successes in the brief period of time it had been working in Osorno province. An experiment with a vaccine against hog cholera proved dramatically successful when all the hogs in a given community died except those given the vaccine by the *delegados*. One *delegado* taught the members of the community to apply disinfectants to their trees with branches and then helped them raise the money to purchase a mechanical sprayer. Another *delegado* took unemployed teenagers off the street and taught them how to make furniture. The girls on our team conducted very popular sessions with the ladies and gave advice on sanitation, diet and health which raised the level of understanding of these matters throughout the province.

However, such outstanding personnel could have been used in programs which had a far more dramatic impact on the problems of the people. The ideal would have been for the *delegados* to serve as community development workers for the Ministry program (something which it really needed), but this was unacceptable both to the Ministry of Agriculture and to the Institute.

Contrary to other Peace Corps volunteers in our group who found their work progressing smoothly in their final months of service, my frustrations were at an all-time high due to the problems with my new assignment. Luckily for me, April was to be a vacation. When I returned to Chile, I decided to spend most of my time continuing my work with the cooperatives in San Juan de la Costa and Rupanco.

Two developments seriously affecting our work took place while I was on vacation. First, President Alessandri issued an executive order revising the law on cooperatives and removing the requirement that the Ministry of Agriculture approve the formation of each *campesino* cooperative. That cleared the way in San Juan de la Costa. Secondly, the company that owned the Hacienda Rupanco decided that it would not permit its workers to organize into a cooperative. This gave us a lot of talking to do about cooperatives in Rupanco.

The issue in Rupanco was a delicate one that required many hours of soul-searching in Santiago and Osorno. Legal organization was impossible without the good graces of the company, and since the owners of the Hacienda would not let us respond to the peoples' needs, the Institute felt we should not work there at all.

On the other hand, we did not want to abandon the people in Rupanco. Janet and the *delegadas* had organized five cooperative shirt-making shops during March and had sent three girls to a special IER course to learn about making and marketing shirts. Buying clubs (small consumer co-ops) had been started in three places, and the vegetable plan was just at the take-off stage. We decided to take these issues to the people. If they wanted to continue these projects on their own initiative, we would help them. Officially, however, we had to abandon the *zona*.

The reaction of the people in Rupanco was heart-warming. Gustavo Torres, the director of the IER team in Osorno, first spoke at a community in Rupanco called La Junta. He mentioned our need to take orders only from the *campesinos* and not from the owners of the company. "We order you to stay," they interrupted, before he could finish his statement. Without further ado the people proceeded to a series of unanimous votes in favor of continuing the work with shirts, vegetables, and buying clubs.

The buying club had been functioning a little over a month, and it already brought benefits. Its organizer made me dizzy as he quoted every price on peas and nuts from every store in Osorno showing how much the members of the buying club were saving. We told the residents of La Junta that all these projects had to spring from their own initiative because we would not be there to promote them. In my case, I added, I was leaving the country. "You can go," they said, "because you have organized us, and we can continue on our own."

In Maitenis, another settlement of laborers within the *hacienda*, the people came in hordes to hear what they feared would be our swan song. A few asked for their money back from the buying club. But a strong nucleus remained—more than thirty. The shirt project was not only continued but another young girl was sent to take the course. Maitenes had only one vegetable grower the year before and he had been fired, so the plan did not continue there.

In Laguna Bonita, where the buying club idea started, the only setback was that this industrious group of ladies became impatient with us for letting the *patrón's* whim delay the shirt project. They threatened to drop us, not the project. I had to accompany Jan and the *delegados* to explain that the *patron's* decision had given us need for pause. The ladies, appeased, accepted us back into their good graces.

Only in one section of the entire Hacienda did the workers decide to sever ties completely with the cooperative idea. Even there, the group that had sold vegetables decided to continue doing so.

We continued to work with the people in Rupanco informally until I completed my service. I worked especially hard planting vegetables, and I noticed that the technical assistance we provided the year before was really paying off. This year everything was much easier. There were always a few more people willing to give it a try. There were fewer suspicions. The participants in the program understood more quickly the practical advantages of the suggestions we made. They saw much more quickly the practical applications of every suggestion we made. They took more initiative getting the fertilizers and making cold frames and hotbeds, and they decided to pay cash for the seeds and fertilizers we acquired for them. They asked the Institute to help them make experiments with winter crops. It occurred to me that with continued technical assistance and some gentle pushing, this group could double its production.

In San Juan de la Costa, the people decided to proceed directly to the constitution of their cooperative and they set the date for the charter meeting. We immediately began an intense education campaign. With the committee of organizers we reviewed the co-op's statutes article by article, and their relation to national cooperative law. Two general assemblies were held prior to the official constitutional meeting—one for extensive discussions with the manager of a consumer co-op in Osorno, and the other to advance the tedious procedure of nominations for directors. In addition, an Education Committee composed of representatives from seven geographic divisions of San Juan met with us weekly as we explained the theory and practice of cooperativism, using as texts little two-page pamphlets which we wrote the week before. Whenever possible, we accompanied these representatives to their areas and participated in the study circles they arranged with their neighbors.

Until the final moment, new members continued to enroll in the co-op. The Ministry's continual polemic against it made a great advertisement, and the people mistakenly thought that we were an alternative to its program. Quite a number welcomed the alternative. About two weeks before the charter meeting, an entire community walked into the meeting hall led by its president carrying their official records. He asked for the floor and solemnly enrolled the entire community in the co-op, depositing immediately all the necessary dues into the coffers of the organization.

The Institute gave us great support from Santiago. The meeting date coincided perfectly with the beginning of a special course for managers of *campesino* co-ops. The San Juan de la Costa manager would be chosen and sent the following day to this course. When the day for the charter meeting finally arrived, a team of special legal advisors came from the central offices of the Institute to help conduct it. The seventy-two people there that day gave their patient and undivided attention to all the discussions, elected their officers and enrolled themselves as charter members. This took over an hour because it involved signing their names three times, and they were out of practice at this. Although the meeting lasted five hours, the spirit toward the end was one of great enthusiasm. I was so tired that I felt little sentiment one way or the other besides a strong sense of the importance of the event and a confidence that the people knew well what they were doing.

Another feeling was gratitude for the stroke of luck which delivered the disheveled figure and ingenious mind of Amos Roos to Río Negro the year before. Amos had learned a great deal about managing co-ops. In the final months, he put this knowledge to good use. He invented and taught the people the system of accounting used in the consumer co-op. He worked with the people in their homes and even helped them with their arithmetic. The cooperative education program in San Juan and the preparation for the charter meeting were all directed by Amos. He stayed for a few weeks after his tour of service with the Peace Corps to make sure that all his projects had been completed or left in good hands.

The cooperative development work in San Juan could really have benefited from some assistance from the Ministry of Agriculture but, of course, it never received it. We had to handle not only the cooperative education program but technical assistance as well, and we were ill-equipped for that. We had to inspect the individual parcels of land set aside for hog foraging, see to it that shelters were built, and teach the people to plant oats and pasture land. Even the responsibility for the daily care of the hogs fell to us. I spent two solid weeks feeding and caring for the hogs after they contracted hoof-and-mouth disease. When a heavy rain made the boar's shelter inadequate, we had to build him a new shelter in the rain. When food for the hogs ran out, we had to beg grain from local charitable sources. Our day usually included feeding the hogs in the morning, afternoon meetings with the elite in Osorno, and then cooperative education sessions in the *zona* in the evenings.

The last months were the most difficult of all, given the strain of administering such a broad plan without adequate resources or organization. We were under constant pressure to create, observe, and judge our work all at the same time; and to deal with the inclement conditions of steady downpours, cold and mud. Distances were our greatest problem. Racing from one area to another was very trying, and the meetings we neglected due to a missed bus or a jeep that wouldn't start discouraged us terribly. But we have found that the only way to accomplish anything is through tremendous effort, not that the work requires long hours or hard work so much as patience, endless imagination, and hope.

There were three principles which we respected rigorously in the final months, and I recommend them to you. We allowed no projects to be developed on the basis of exclusively North American efforts. Even though we may have had the idea originally, it remained a project of the Institute. In some of these projects, the *delegados* worked harder than we did. One day, I missed a bus to a study circle in San Juan and gave up on getting there. My Chilean colleague missed his too, but he walked twenty miles getting to the meeting and returning.

Secondly, our projects were all developed through discussion with the people themselves. Wooden hog houses struck us as essential in San Juan and would have cost only $6 to build. The people made it clear that they could afford only straw hog houses this year. In Rupanco, I was sure that the people should sell strawberries and couldn't understand their reluctance to produce them commercially. Later, I discovered why. The flock of children in each home devours the strawberry crop before it can turn red. Each time, the people foresaw obstacles or opportunities which never occurred to us.

Thirdly, we insisted that every decision about the co-op or agricultural extension work be made democratically. Two persons we hoped would be elected to the cooperative's financial oversight committee were turned down by the people. When we were undecided about which kind of co-op to create, the people made the decision.

There is need for a democratic approach from the very beginning. You must listen patiently to the people, wait for them to make their own judgments and respect these judgments even if you feel they're about to make a mistake. If this mistake would be from ignorance, you can try to educate. If from stubbornness, you can try to demonstrate results. But if their decision is in full view of the facts and in good faith, there is only one thing to do and that is to let them go ahead and do it their own way. You shouldn't interfere by dictating. Perhaps they will prove you wrong.

For a Peace Corps volunteer, democracy is more than an ideal or a political system. You can have both without real democracy. For you, democracy must be an approach to development. It must be an attitude you maintain when dealing with the people which assures them that the problem is theirs to solve. For the people, democracy is their ability to determine their own future. It is a fragile plant which can grow steadily if it's cultivated, or be damaged dangerously by a major act of impatience.

I suppose you could say that our work in the Peace Corps ended on July 7 in San Juan de la Costa. This was the day the cooperative was inaugurated and I took my last trip over bouncy roads to tend a project in the *zona*. Around seven that night, after having been with the people all day, Amos and I took our leave. We had avoided all talk about farewells for me during the meeting so that the day would contain no other emotion than the joy of beginning. The members of the cooperative's board were electing its president as we left, and I thought they were beginning the period when I would have most liked to be with them—when their cooperative was beginning to function and bear the desired fruits. The same was true in Rupanco where they were waiting for the rains to quit so they could begin planting their seedbeds. This had been a time of great satisfaction for us last year. Yet thinking twice about it all, it was a good time to leave the *campesinos*, too—remembering them with worthwhile plans and a spirit of progress waiting for the spring.

Chapter 15
GOOD-BY TO CHILE

Looking back on two years as a Peace Corps volunteer, I tell my friends at home about the admiration and affection I have for the Chilean people, especially those with whom I worked most closely and productively, the campesinos.

September 1963

¡Estimados Amigos Gringos!

Toward the end of my two years in Chile, I spent a month of vacation days traveling through other countries and seeing the work of other Peace Corps volunteers in South America. I flew as far north as Colombia, which is really halfway to Scranton, yet as my vacation time expired and I hopped south again through Ecuador and Peru, I had the sensation of returning home, not of going farther away. Arriving in Chile had the flavor of coming home. Seeing friends and familiar places again, watching the parade of finely-styled women along the avenues of Santiago and returning to my world of work made me realize that I had arrived somewhere I belonged.

Like all Peace Corps volunteers I am partial to the country in which I lived for two years, yet Chile is *different* from other South American countries. It is not a poor country but belongs to the middle class among nations; and, like all middle classes, it has a respect and a propensity for democracy. Also, the Chileans have a

friendly spirit and spontaneous hospitality unparalleled by anything I encountered in my brief experiences in other places.

As a Peace Corps volunteer, I came to Chile to make sacrifices
for the small subsistence farmers, the *campesinos*, and my two years
here certainly presented opportunities to work on their behalf.
Nonetheless, it is difficult to live sacrificially in Chile; the people
won't stand for it. The day I returned at the end of my vacation I
received a familiar invitation more times than I could accept, *"Vamos
a comer a nuestra casa*—let's have dinner tonight at our place."

The doors of a Chilean home are open not only to foreigners.
I remember the very handsome woman with a quick smile who
flagged down our jeep one day and who, we discovered, could not
hear or speak. We wanted to assist her to her destination but were
unable to communicate with her and find out where she was going.
So we drove her to the schoolhouse where we were working that day.
At the school, she was fed and classes were interrupted while all the
children flurried off to find someone who might know where she
lived. Finally, one returned with the answer, and I drove the woman
home. But our curiosity did not end there. Wherever we went that
day we asked about the deaf and mute woman who had been traveling all alone on remote roads. Others had heard of her, and the story
emerged that her journey had been a difficult one. She had begun a
fifty-mile trip on Saturday; we had encountered her on Monday, only
halfway along—because wherever she stopped for a bite to eat or to
gesticulate a request for directions, she had been taken in and given
food and lodging for the night.

As the time approaches to leave Chile, Peace Corps volunteers
in the city of Osorno have experienced Chilean hospitality to the
fullest. Bidding farewell to Chilean friends has became an extremely
arduous and time-consuming task. Our final month in the country
has been filled with those social events which Chileans call *despedidas*,
"send-offs." It has been a month of lumps in our throats as we were
sent-off more than a dozen times. Our students staged skits for hours
at a time. There have been intimate dinners, raucous gatherings and
touching ceremonies in which little gifts were bestowed on us by
groups of *campesinos*. During our last weekend in Osorno, four parties
began at noon on Saturday and went continuously until 7 A.M.
Monday. They were interrupted only by the time needed to travel
from one to the other.

Another explanation for the number of send-offs would be that Chileans love a party and find any excuse to have one. Yet I have the impression that they like send-offs least of all. "Even at a funeral," the director of our school said to me, "there is something to rejoice about because the person who is lost is with God, but at a send-off we are aware of nothing except that we are being deprived of a friend."

Our Chilean friends realized that our nostalgia in leaving is tempered by the thought of returning home. "Although we do not know them, give our regards to your family," they called to us as we pulled away. As the two years end, I am anxious to go home again, to cease being a foreigner, to speak my native tongue and to live in surroundings I have known all my life. Yet I know, even while in Chile, that I will miss many things from my second homeland—the avocados, seafood, wines, delightful local customs and especially Chile's glorious natural landscape highlighted by the precious *copihue*, her national flower whose red blossoms are scattered wildly through the mountains and found in all the marketplaces at this time of year.

I will miss speaking Spanish, too. My Spanish is not elaborate or polished, but it is a second language which I use without a moment's hesitation. Spanish is like a long and complicated song which has taken a long time to learn and which gradually has become an accompaniment to the actions of every day until I take it for granted, accustomed to singing it and hearing it sung in the Chileans' own special way. It is like background music which fades out so suddenly that you wonder why and when you will hear it again.

More than anything, I think of people as I prepare to leave. A Peace Corps volunteer's foremost interest is in people. People are his reason for going to a distant country, the substance of his life there and his reason for staying when the winds of frustration blow hard. His relationships with citizens of his host country and the extent to which he developed their human resources are the final criteria upon which his success or failure is judged. The memories of friendships made in two years and the personalities encountered along the way are a volunteer's best souvenirs when he returns to the United States.

I have lived with the Chilean people in three different contexts: within the Institute of Rural Education, in the rural communities and in the city of Osorno.

My closest friends in Chile were staff members of the Institute. In my last five months, I lived in a school recently constructed by the Institute along the two-lane highway which connects Valdivia and Osorno, the two largest cities in the south. The school site is only four miles from Osorno, a city of over 80,000 residents, and thus it combines the advantages of rural living with those of being near the city. Basically, however, we were in a rustic setting. Across the narrow highway was a large *fundo*. The small home of a *campesino* stood at the corner made by the highway and the dirt road leading from the inner reaches of the *fundo*. Each day we see the truck of the *patrón* with large silver milk cans speed down the dirt road and turn into the traffic of the highway. Many times in the evening or during the day I would walk down that road and watch a steer graze by the fence or huddle near the sparse, slanting mountain beeches in the center of the pasture.

On our side of the highway, the Institute owns ten acres of land chipped out of a *hacienda* belonging to the governor of the province. He had donated the land just two years ago and the Institute already had managed to place a school there. As the winter grew colder, I woke up each morning to a misty, bucolic scene. The ground, disfigured by the mud of the day before, would be hardened and frost-coated, and I would not be able to see our benefactor's fence just two hundred yards away because the fog was so thick and low. I would go out to the kitchen of the school and warm my hands over the stove before taking the students to feed the animals in pens so white with frost that they appeared to be topped with snow.

The school building itself was of concrete painted green and white. It was divided into four sections connected by long corridors. Inside the school, Chilean professors and Peace Corps volunteers shepherded seventy *campesino* youngsters through classrooms, workshops, dormitories and common rooms—all of which were still incompletely furnished. Directly in front of the school was a square block building where the director Gustavo Torres lived with his wife and child. This small addition also contained a dormitory for the girls on the Institute staff and a conference room where we kept the maps and files for our work in the rural villages surrounding Osorno.

Above the school on a slanting green knoll sat two tiny houses which also belonged to the Institute. One was a Peace Corps house of plain unfinished wood in which Elden and Judy Stang, a recently married Peace Corps couple, made their first home. The other small house, of concrete to match the school, was originally meant for the caretaker, but three of us who worked in the rural villages lived there. We were very satisfied with our living quarters, although they certainly were not plush. Judy and Elden's house—with the stovepipe on one side and an outhouse in the back—looked like something out of Appalachia. One afternoon the Stangs were entertaining when the house began to shake on its foundation. An earth tremor, everyone surmised, since we've become accustomed to sudden land movements. Elden stepped outside and found that this tremor was caused by a burly hog scratching himself on one of the posts of his home.

For the seventy students and fifteen members of the Institute staff who lived on our tiny campus, there was one spigot with hot water—sometimes. Elden and Judy's house had a stove but no plumbing; ours had plumbing but no heat. There was usually one warm room in the main building where we could all come and work on especially cold evenings. Our food at the Institute was nourishing and tasty—if you like lentils and beans.

Classes were taught by five Chilean teachers and four Peace Corps volunteers. The horticulture and animal husbandry classes were taught by Chilean *profesores*, while Fred Morgner and Elden Stang prepared the course in rural carpentry, the school's specialty. Between March and July, Fred and Elden were able to conduct one course and train two apprentice carpenters to continue their work when they left. Judy was the school dietitian, and she was incredibly effective in imparting her methods to a very dynamic counterpart.

The Institute refers to its schools as *centrales* because they are centers for activities which extend way beyond the walls of the classroom to thousands of *campesinos* in the nearby provinces. The *central* in Osorno was the base of operations for ten Chilean men and women and four Peace Corps volunteers who worked in rural communities and neighborhoods. These Chilean village workers, or *delegados*, lived in the remote areas and used the *central* only as a stopping-off point or for monthly meetings. We preferred to live outside the *central* also, but as we concluded our work with the Institute, the Peace Corps volunteers were asked to form a roving community development team to assist the *delegados* with their work in cooperatives and in health projects. Amos Roos, Kenneth Buckstrup, Janet Boegli and I functioned in this capacity, and so we lived at the school too.

The more we worked with the *delegados*, the greater our respect for them grew. For many reasons, they had a very difficult assignment. They were trying to bring the gospel of progress to people much older than themselves. Being of the same class as the poor farmers and a lot younger, their reception was often cool. To win the confidence of the people, the young men *delegados* would work in the harvest or construct a loom side-by-side with them. The problems faced by female *delegadas* were even more complicated. They taught ideas about health and nutrition which would have been new to their own mothers, and silently the women questioned their authority. Then they faced the possibility of misunderstanding or even physical danger as they traveled from one rural community to the next.

Certainly one of the Institute's greatest accomplishments in its ten-year history has been the selection and training of its *delegados*. Their perceptivity and intelligence made them indispensable to its work. Their judgments about personalities and communities were very sound; and once these judgments had been made, the *delegados* were a long time changing them.

One day, in a monthly meeting at the central, René Bórquez, the *delegado* with whom I worked throughout my time here, explained his experiences to some eager neophytes about to go into the rural communities for the first time. He spoke of Institute policy, of group dynamics, of the do's and don'ts to follow in founding a community organization. These were all practical techniques which he had analyzed out of his own experiences. Although this talk was given spontaneously, and although René has only four years of formal education, it was a brilliant discourse by any standard.

The functions of those who worked in the school were vastly different than those of us who continually visited the *zona*, yet all of us in the Institute lived and worked as a team. Sometimes the *profesores* visited our communities and even the students knew which projects were being developed in the outlying areas. In our turn, we taught some classes. Janet was responsible for the health of the students and taught them hygiene. Amos and Ken handled the morning gym period and taught a weekly course in math. I taught classes in cooperatives and community development; though I felt my attempts were not very successful at communicating the notion of community strength or cooperative endeavor to *campesino* youngsters in a classroom. One of the more seasoned teachers in the Institute told me that he was content just to make the students communicate with each other during this first experience away from the isolation of a typical *campesino* home.

The Institute intended that the work in the *zona* should complement that of the school. Many of the students for each six-month course in the school were drawn from the communities where we worked; on the other hand, the school's farm served the local people, and seeds and livestock were raised there for distribution in the *zona*. Caring for the animals and plants involved in these projects was good practical experience for the students. One lesson which the students received while I was there, however, was neither anticipated nor hoped for.

When the students and I went out one morning to feed the hogs, which we were raising for a rural cooperative, we found the animals hobbling around with very little appetite and with high fever. Immediately, we summoned the veterinarian and he pronounced a verdict of *fiebre afstosa*—hoof-and-mouth disease. From that day, we practically lived in the hog house, giving injections, and hauling clean food and water to the hogs. We had to bathe them in a copper sulfate solution, which from all indications stung like bees. Three of us were required to hold the animals down and in the end we were wetter than they were. If ever I felt like the prodigal son for joining the Peace Corps, it was the week I tended swine.

One gilt [a young, unbred female pig] became so sick that we had to isolate her in the warehouse. Then our hundred-dollar boar was stricken and we had to isolate him also. He was at one end of the warehouse and the gilt at the other. The boar recovered unexpectedly and we discovered that he had burst out of his pen, crashed through to the sick gilt and was chasing her all through the warehouse, under unused beds, over sacks of flour, toppling farm tools and anything else in the neatly arranged warehouse. The boar, we decided, was cured. As for the gilt, the only change in her condition was that perhaps she wasn't a gilt anymore. When all the hogs were healthy again I suffered a twist of irony. I sprained an ankle in a basketball game and this gave grounds for everyone in the school to claim that I had contracted the dreaded disease myself.

Usually our experiences combining the resources of the school and *zona* have been more felicitous, thanks in part to the talents of the director, the slim, neat man named Gustavo Torres. Besides being an extraordinarily gifted administrator and having a very winning way with the students, Gustavo is an excellent artist. One evening we needed illustrations for a pamphlet which we were preparing on cooperatives and asked him to provide them. Gustavo obliged us immediately. The next day, the *campesinos* were so appreciative of our *folleto* [pamphlet] that they presented us with a two-year-old turkey. They wrapped it in a burlap bag and threw the bundle, kicking, cackling and snapping, in the back of the jeep. When we arrived at the school that evening, we dropped the bird in Gustavo's quarters. The next morning he was confronted by the irate bird in his bathroom before he was even awake, and that evening we all joined in a turkey feast.

Even though we were seldom at the school together, our community life was a source of great strength for all of us. A bond developed within the team which transcended national differences. We were one effort in behalf of the *campesinos*. Whether at a routine meal, eating the livers of recently butchered sheep in the kitchen on a rainy afternoon, or at a fancy dinner prepared to celebrate someone's engagement or to mark our own departure from Chile, we have enjoyed being together. On Sunday evenings, the students would stage an entertainment or we would show a movie. When a national holiday arrived there was little need to go outside the *central* to celebrate because it could be done within the close circle of friends we had there.

The members of our team came to understand each other better than I thought Latin Americans and North Americans could. We made jokes which assumed that they understood a subtle, even abusive North American sense of humor; and they entertained us with their guffaw. The language problem has not been a delicate one. The Chilean girl who supervised the institution's kitchen could make a throaty "r" just like a North American, and she loved to mock us with it.

For the community developers on our team, life at the school had a secondary importance. In the early part of each day, we would leave the *central* for the rural communities in the jeep or in the blue *furgón* [minibus] of the Institute. Out there we would meet the *delegados* or tend to one of the projects which we had begun the year before. Late that evening, usually after midnight, we would fight sleep as we returned over long, dark roads to the *central*. "How they make sacrifices," Judy's counterpart would exclaim, convinced that our routine involved many hardships. But our work was not so rugged as it seemed. We had to work nights and Sundays because these were the times when the people were free to discuss community projects. But they were also the occasions for meals and *fiestas*. Chileans love to do business around a table, and we ate many of our meals out with the people. If we tried to rush away, we would be warned gently, "You cannot go now, something is being prepared."

In the rural neighborhoods we served, we had more in common with the school teachers than anyone else. Once when we were completing our day's work early, around six, we discovered that it was one schoolteacher's Saint's Day. Saint's Days are like birthdays in the United States, and some of this schoolteacher's friends had prepared a party. "Could we stay an extra half hour?" we were asked. Of course we stayed, but we knew better than to believe the half-hour estimate, and it was eleven o'clock before we stopped dancing and began the long journey home.

My mind is crowded with memories of life among the *campesinos*—of coming upon a family in the dusky hours before the evening meal when the children were doing their lessons at the table, the men were warming themselves near the stove and the women making bread. I remember meetings with the people, and one which was typical of the pace and mood of them all. We arrived at a schoolhouse where a crowd of *campesinos* was waiting in the blinking light of candles, enjoying a general conversation. They were in no hurry that evening because it had rained during the day and there had been no work on the *hacienda* where they lived. They heated the classroom with an antiquated wood-burner, and we discussed community topics for hours. It was hard to tell when this meeting began or where it left off because it had the nature of a conversation. Afterward we drank a glass of wine at a community leader's house and then we were informed that further down the road a meal had been prepared for us.

There were numberless occasions when the *campesinos* shared their hearth or their table with us. Sometimes it was just a cookie or a plate from the stew boiling in the fireplace. But they always served something and this provided time for us to talk with them and it gave them the opportunity to place our friendship on the desired basis. They received from us and we from them. We were their friends.

The philosophy of both the Peace Corps and the Institute was that we should establish more than a working relationship with the *campesinos*. The Peace Corps always stressed the need to live with the people. The Institute went further than that. The Institute believed in the education of the *campesino* by the *campesino*; and all members of our team, either by birth or association, belonged to that class. The *delegados* came from homes of small farmers. Two of them had families on a *hacienda* where we worked. I was happy to be considered a *campesino* and welcomed the easy access I had to the homes of the people through our co-workers. I felt most at home in a *campesino's* home when it was the home of one of the *delegados*.

Because the Institute existed for the *campesinos* and belonged to them, the *campesinos* treated it in the same casual manner in which they treated each other, and did not always respond to the urgings for a better life. We were to discover, however, that their affection for the Institute was deep and far-reaching. There have been many indications that our work had had its effect on them. One such indication was to find communities continuing projects which were instigated by *delegados*. Another came when a *campesina* woman told me, almost defiantly, that I should go home because I had organized her community and its members now knew how to work on their own.

The supreme satisfaction of the two years has been to hear people reminisce about successful projects in the past, not only because this meant they had met new challenges successfully and were capable of formulating plans, but because of the enthusiasm which these experiences bred—the facelift it gave to the usually somber, fatalistic farmers as they saw a whole new hope, a whole new world open up before them and greeted it with confidence and a smile. And on those days I would take a new hope into my own heart that we had, indeed, created new leaders.

The reception which I received from the campesinos was always friendly because I represented the Institute and because the arrival of a gringo talking about progress in their community was a unique experience for them. Whether they regarded me as a celebrity or a novelty, I was never ignored. Frankly, it made me proud to be important to these people—and gaining their confidence was an honor and something of an accomplishment. It was not difficult to reciprocate their respect. The quiet dignity of the old folks reminded me that not long ago my ancestors were *campesinos* also. The younger *campesinos* taught me things which few of us know in the United States but which are common knowledge in rural Chile. I learned to skate down a muddy slope on horseback and to carve shingles out of the trunk of a tree with an ax.

On one occasion, they assumed I learned more quickly than I really did. A man was guiding me on horseback toward a huddle of houses called Huitrapulli on the coast. He was leading two oxen fastened to a yoke and teaching me how to steer the beasts and keep them on the road. When it started to rain, he headed home for a poncho and asked me to keep the animals moving in a straight line. I did fine until we approached a barn with a poorly constructed fence around it. The oxen saw the barn and headed through a hole in the fence. I whoa-ed and hollered to no avail. So I dismounted and ran after the oxen; but before I overtook these generally slow-moving creatures, they had entered the barn, bedded down, yoke and all, and were eating the owner of the barn's hay. I was not familiar with this farmer or his dogs, and I knew I was in trouble should either find me in their barn trying to remove a team of oxen. I chased the team around the barn until they finally went outside just to get away from me. After twenty minutes the disgruntled beasts were back on the trail. Luckily for my pride and the reputation of the United States, no one witnessed this episode, except the animals and me. However, my guide did seem surprised when he returned an hour later and we were only a mile beyond the point where he had left us on the road.

There were moments during these days spent with the *campesinos*— when exchanging civilities from horseback with strangers along the road, while smoking black tobacco with the men or dancing with elderly widows to a wind-up Victrola, that I compared my life to theirs. And thinking of the problems facing the people of our nation, I was unsure whether it was better or worse to have been born among the poor.

It was not always that way. When I first saw the *campesinos* from a distance, their life seemed strange and very unattractive. Democratic adages had taught me that we were all created alike, yet modern society had so transformed our lives with education, comforts and other facilities that the masses of people without these benefits seemed to exist across a gulf. I found it difficult to see that their lives could be anything like mine—that they would not be a vacuum of meaning. This initial impression, part of the culture shock which we all experienced, lasted until I made my first trip to live among the small farmers. From then on, the Peace Corps experience was a daily lesson that basically the *campesinos* are the same as we and that whatever differences exist are really only relative.

Occasionally the *campesinos* share our interests exactly. For instance, it was a *campesino* who told Peggy Ahern about our country's famous astronaut. She had been working for days in a remote area, where Glen Trebour had driven her in his jeep. After being out of contact for quite some time, Peggy encountered a man who had a transistor radio. When he discovered she was an American, he started screaming, "*Glenn se dió tres vueltas*—Glenn spun around three times," over and over again.

"That's awful," she replied, thinking of the mangling Glen and the jeep would have received as they rolled over and over. "When did it happen?"

"I think it's wonderful," he said. "He returned to earth this morning." The farmer was talking about America's first space traveler, the astronaut John Glenn.

On another occasion I traveled for hours on horseback into the most isolated area of the Chilean coast, and I was congratulating myself for penetrating that far into the wilderness as I reached the home that was my destination. The first thing my *campesino* host told me was that the evening before President Kennedy had celebrated his birthday quietly with his family, and that the President had been working very hard in the previous two days and needed the rest.

The *campesinos* did not know all we know about the modern world. When I showed them 35-mm slides of themselves raising vegetables, one drunken fellow chatted gaily with the projected image on the wall. "Pure progress, pure progress is what these gentlemen teach," he said to his friend in the picture as if he were expecting a reply.

The feelings, activities, and moods of the *campesinos* are only relatively different from our own. The same mood prevails before a holiday. The students in the school become as excited about their graduation dance to the strumming of two guitars as our high school seniors about their gala proms. A family excursion in the third-class coach of a train to the city for the day is not that different from our outings in the car. The women waiting for their heavily illustrated magazines each month, and the young leaders we trained until they were running around their community like big men on campus, proved to me that there is one psychology for all of us.

Campesinos have the same faults as we do. I remember the day I learned that women everywhere are victims of vanity. An elderly woman who was a regular participant in the sewing circles which Janet arranged was seen one wintry day walking in the rain and mud toward the meeting house. Janet noticed she did not have shoes on and thought how unfortunate it was that her friend had to travel barefoot in wintertime. At that moment the woman arrived at the wooden flight of stairs which led into the meeting house, cleaned her feet in a puddle, slipped into a brand-new pair of shoes and pranced gracefully into the meeting.

Even in their failings, however, the humanity of the *campesinos* shines through. They are deceived by superstitions, the products of wild and misguided imaginations. But superstitions can also be regarded as the mind's first inkling toward science—toward finding the causes for things. The dreams of the *campesinos* far outreach realities, but who among us is different? Their judgments could be mistaken, yet contain a grain of poetry and truth. "To kill an ox," one sage said to me, "is the same as to kill a man because an ox is a companion to man's labor." The *campesinos* often tried to interpret the law in their own favor—usually incorrectly, yet in some attempts it was obvious that a latent legal mind was at work. One insisted in all seriousness that the government should build a new road for his community from a fund designated for calamities because "our road is a calamity if I ever saw one."

Young *campesinos* have the same reactions as young people in the United States when placed in parallel situations. Occasionally, we held dances for the Institute's schools for girls and boys. These affairs reminded me of the bittersweet mixers which we used to organize for freshmen when I was a senior at Notre Dame. The week before these affairs, the excitement would build up to a terrible pitch. The girls would be as nervous as brides, and the fellows would groom themselves by giving each other the first haircut of the season. On the weekend of the dance, all classes would stop and preparations would consume the entire time. Then would come the magic hour.

The boys would file into the vacated dining room of the girls' school, and the two groups would form impenetrable lines at opposite ends of the room. For an hour the two groups would stare at each other while Peace Corps volunteers, directors, teachers and visitors would all dance, hoping to break the ice. After a great deal of time and music was wasted, the dance would begin, and at five o'clock in the afternoon we would be trying vainly to end the event so that the boys could jump aboard the back of our truck and head home. Our problems would not end there. Soon the letters would begin flowing between the two schools. Judy Grant Stang, the home economist for both, became a free postal service until she learned that such correspondence was frowned on by the Institute.

The personalities I encountered in rural Chile were the same as those in the United States. One widow was strong-willed and simple, a hard worker who made me want to laugh because she was so intent and serious. Some men were quiet and sensitive; others bawdy and devilish. There were grandmothers who spoiled their grandchildren, and henpecked husbands, young farm youths searching for their place in life, very poor men with great dignity and self-possession.

The most important insight we were given into the minds of the *campesinos* revealed the immense promise of these individuals who comprise the lowest stratum of Chilean society and impressed upon us the sad fact that their potential for contributing to their country's progress has yet to be developed and has, in most instances, been wasted.

Among our *campesino* friends, we noted some outstanding talent. There were song writers, moralists and men of great political acumen. Some would amaze me by their participation in meetings, their grasp of the issues, their cautious sagacity and their ability to express a point of view. There were women with exuberant personalities, great strength in the face of adversity and with sensitive and very understanding souls.

Some days more than others we could see through the ever-present signs of poverty to the person there. There were moments of insight more powerful than the rest when the potential of the people opened before our eyes. One happened on the day I encountered a political leader among them trying very cleverly to preserve his power against the forces of change. It was late afternoon in a mission courtyard, and I saw an old man tucking a crop of long hair under his hat and leaning on his staff as he prepared to make the journey home. It was the *cacique*, an outmoded political and social leader of the Huiliche Indians in the coastal region of the province. Whether he approached me or I approached him, I do not recall; but he was the first to speak.

"What are these strangers doing here?" he said in his own dialect through an interpreter to the padre. "They have come to talk about a cooperative," the priest replied. For five minutes we discussed the idea of the cooperative with the *cacique*; and after he decided that he did not favor it, he abruptly though cordially took his leave. Our whole conversation had been through an interpreter who solemnly prefaced the cacique's remarks with the words: *"Así dice el señor cacique*—thus speaks the lord chief." When he had left, I learned the most amazing thing about this man. *El señor cacique* speaks perfect Spanish and does not need an interpreter, yet he conducts all official conversation in Huiliche to maintain his image and status in the community.

One final episode exemplified what should be told about the human resources of the *campesinos*. On a Sunday afternoon I was explaining to a community why they should form a cooperative enterprise which would sell their lumber on the larger markets and at a better price. Until then, they had sold individually to whoever was willing to haul their wood away. I was having difficulty in communicating the notion of a cooperative, and I noticed that the leader of the community was impatient to say something. When I finished, this man, who had been to school one year in his life, rose solemnly to his feet. "Friends," he said, "what Don Tomás is trying to say can be put in another way. I have been acting like the owner of an orchard who let all his apples lie beneath his trees so that anyone could come and take them and pay whatever he liked. That man should build a fence around his orchard and make a gate so that he knows who enters and how much he pays. Now, in our case, that gate and that fence would be our cooperative."

Not all our associations in Chile were with the *campesinos* or the Institute. When we moved to the school, from which we could see the flickering lights of the city, I felt a strong desire to participate in the life of Osorno. The year before Osorno was a city which we loved to visit. Then it became a place where we lived, and we met people of all ages and from all social strata there because, although the Peace Corps is meant primarily as a help to the poor, we certainly never believed that our mission precluded being friends with anyone who was a friend of the United States.

Osorno is fifty miles from an ocean, a ski resort and a chain of mountain lakes. As our departure neared we realized that many of us had never been to these places, so we spent a day taking them all in, in one frantic sweep. At the end of the day we arrived at a wondrous lake called Todos Los Santos, its emerald green waters fluorescent in the faint light of evening. We had dinner at a lodge at the edge of the lake and ate steaks so delicious that they must have been smuggled across the lake from Argentina.

In town we participated in activities which appealed to all classes in the society. Ken Buckstrup taught English in the Chilean-North American Binational Center. Four of the male volunteers played basketball for one of the local teams. (One overenthusiastic basketball coach sought out Janet for his team because of her relative height next to the average Chilean. But Jan made her contribution by singing a strong soprano in the city chorus.) I played a weak violin in the Osono Symphony Orchestra, and for their final concerts the chorus and orchestra merged in the choir loft of the very beautiful Lutheran church in Osorno and performed the Hallelujah Chorus from Handel's *Messiah*.

Our social contacts with *Osorninos* were limited because our work with the *campesinos* left us little free time, but I think it would have been impossible to maintain the pace of the urban Chileans' social whirl anyway. We consequently limited ourselves to a few close friends whom we visited frequently—a labor leader, an accountant, some landowners, our doctor.

As for dating, my experiences were meager. I had only one date with a Chilean girl and it was a disaster. Chileans will tell you that the Spanish tradition of keeping their daughters behind barred windows has no hold on them now, but still I found their attitudes to be very different than ours. At 7:30 one evening I told a girl I would drop by *luego*, thinking that the word meant "later" when idiomatically it meant "soon." I arrived at 9:30 and was met at the door by her big brother who informed me that she had retired for the evening.

Perhaps things are different in Santiago, but wherever you go in Chile, there is more protectionism than in the United States; however, some volunteers fared well. Four bachelors out of twenty-seven in our contingent came back with Chilean brides.[1] I can only admire the stamina of these men, who passed through the intricate labyrinth of near and distant relatives to pay the tedious series of little attentions which lead up to the first date and to endure the carefully chaperoned calls which they had to make before getting a few minutes alone with their girl.

Even appearing as a bachelor, it wasn't easy to participate in social life. Three things make me drowsy and unsociable, even when I am with friends. One is to be out after eleven o'clock the night before a work day. Another is to drink wine. A third is to eat a heavy meal late at night. Chilean banquets, the most common form of social gathering I attended, were usually held in the middle of the week and began at 10 P.M. with cocktails. Around eleven, a full course dinner was served along with red and white wine. By midnight, I would be immobile with exhaustion and a desire for sleep; however, the worst was yet to come, because for the Chilean metabolism all this food and drink is fuel for the party which is only beginning.

One evening I enjoyed my revenge. Sitting at a long, elegant table with some aristocratic friends, I was full of sleep after the normal portion of wine served at a Chilean meal. They were lost in their conversation and not noticing my heavy eyelids, while I longed to leave that gracious place and return to my little shack for a night's rest. Suddenly, someone recently returned from the United States arrived with a bottle of one of our finest bourbons. He poured skimpily— making sure there was some for all and then some left for another occasion. We toasted the country that could produce such a brew and sipped slowly. Shortly afterward, the bourbon had done me a great service. I was revived; and as I looked up to speak to my companions, they had their heads bowed, heavy with the sleep engendered by the strange potion. From then on, I knew the weapon to use at Chilean banquets, even though I never had the means to acquire it.

Except for dating and banquets, however, we were very well adjusted to Chile by the time we departed. The days of culture shock had passed and I had learned not only to recognize cultural differences but also to work with Chileans and finally adopt some of their

---

[1] Of forty-five in our group, fourteen volunteers married one another.

mannerisms. I began to enjoy the very relaxed and human Chilean ways of devoting much time to a minor detail and to care less about efficiency than grace, friendship and style. I began to approximate the Chilean sense of time and knew just how late I should be for a particular occasion. Once I was late even for the Chileans and that is quite an accomplishment for an Anglo-Saxon. When a dinner was served without wine, I would complain about it to myself privately. When new arrivals from the United States came to Osorno, I would scrutinize their conduct and notice the difference between their way of looking at things and mine.

There were many reasons to be apprehensive about returning to the United States. After two years of coffee and bread in the morning, a North American breakfast seems impossible. North American lunches promise to be a shock. Judy Stang was browsing through her old American cookbooks and complained that her lunch recipes omitted all the main courses. The Peace Corps officials and psychologists who flew down from Washington to conduct a final conference with us warned about the potential difficulties of "re-entry." Our conclusion was that a Peace Corps training program for returning to the United States was necessary—to recall our English a little, to train us not to shake hands every time we met someone in the street lest they all think we returned to run for office, and above all, to eat the native food.

But it really won't be that difficult, and as I enjoy the pleasure of sliding back into old forms, my thoughts will return frequently to the row of pine trees which our Peace Corps team planted at the entrance of our school. We put them there so that we could grow symbolically with the school and advance as the *campesinos* themselves advance, because after two years in Chile and the way we spent them there, we can say in a very real way: "*Somos campesinos nosotros*—we are *campesinos*. We are *Chilenos*."

Su Amigo,
Tom

Afterword
LOOKING BACK

More than three decades after leaving Chile, the world is a very different place. My life has been shaped and changed by my youthful years as a volunteer and everything that the Peace Corps led to...

The world knows that Chile turned topsy-turvy after my Peace Corps tour ended in 1963. It went Marxist through free elections, then became a military dictatorship through a coup, then voted out the *junta* and became democratic once more. My life went through about as many sea changes—in ways and for reasons that would become common among later Peace Corps volunteers. First, I found myself seriously adrift, like so many PCVs, yet when I got my bearings it was by using some of the skills—and the mindset—which I had learned in Chile. Bottom line: the Peace Corps changed my life and showed me the way to find my life's work.

In my last letter to friends back home, I predicted that "sliding back into old forms" would not be difficult. Older and wiser today, I wonder if I ever really did fit the old mold again. As most of the 140,000 returned volunteers have learned in the past thirty-five years, re-entry is not easy. A Peace Corps volunteer returns a different person. On the plus side, the volunteer gains a much broader sense of self and real pragmatic knowledge of what he or she can accomplish; a volunteer also has the ability to see people and events from very different cultural perspectives, and to appreciate national differences. On the minus side, life at home seems narrower; few professions or "niches" offer the breadth of action, the dramatic exposure, the challenge, or the latitude to make one's own decisions that the Peace Corps gives. Furthermore, few returning volunteers found many friends or family at home who had the patience and attention span to hear about the whole new world that opened up to us in the Peace Corps.

At first I was one of the lucky ones; I could talk at length about my experiences—and be heard—as I accepted dozens of invitations through the Peace Corps Speakers Bureau to make speeches at civic gatherings and on radio and television. But the lecture circuit hardly had career potential for me, and in the fall of 1963 I found myself back in graduate school—in the Latin American Studies program at Columbia University thanks to a Ford Foundation grant designed for returning Peace Corps volunteers. My direction seemed clear: I wanted to work in international development and help focus the attention and resources of the United States on the needs of developing countries; I meant to convince my fellow citizens that it was in the best interests of the United States to nurture prosperity and democracy in the poorest parts of the world. Tom Dooley was my role model (though we didn't use that term); John Kennedy was my leader. My plan was to earn academic credentials and go to work for the Kennedy administration carrying out assistance programs in the developing world.

Then came November 22, 1963. I was studying in Columbia's Butler Library that noon when the news flashed from Dallas. First I went to church and then I went home to Scranton, because for us, as for so many Americans, President Kennedy's loss felt like a death in the family. The day after the assassination I received a call from Padraic Kennedy at Peace Corps headquarters. The agency had decided, he said, that two former Peace Corps volunteers—rather than officials—should represent the Peace Corps at the

President's funeral. I and Brenda Brown, an African-American woman who served with the first group in the Philippines, were chosen for this sad honor.

Brenda and I sat in the nave of St. Matthew's Cathedral with Col. John Glenn and his wife, Annie, who were representing the space program. We rode and walked with them to the hill in Arlington Cemetery where the eternal flame burns now. My most vivid memory of this day is standing on the steps of the Cathedral after the funeral Mass, a callow member of one of the most distinguished gatherings of individuals in history—including a score of heads and chiefs of state—and feeling in no way honored or impressed. Rather, I was afraid: that the foundation of the Peace Corps and of our country's commitment to a new kind of world leadership had fallen tragically and inexplicably from beneath us. I realized how much of my own new commitment in life had been forged in response to the personality and leadership of John Kennedy.

The following May I finished my course work at Columbia and was accepted to study for a doctorate in international politics at the London School of Economics. But the old disquiet and lack of enthusiasm for academic life returned and I put off going. Instead, I moved back to Scranton and wrote my thesis for the Latin American Studies degree at Columbia (on the foreign policy of Chile's Christian Democrats), then returned to the thesis for the philosophy degree at Toronto (on Hegel's "Lectures on the Proofs for the Existence of God"). In 1965, I received two master's degrees. While living in Scranton, I took a job helping President Johnson's anti-poverty program get started there, and I taught a philosophy course at Marywood College—the only college teaching I would ever do.

In the fall of 1965, I moved to Washington. I had offers from the Peace Corps but decided to work for AID (now USAID) because it had a stronger development agenda and more technical and financial resources. I started out in the Bureau for Inter-American Affairs and was soon promoted to the office of the Coordinator of the Alliance for Progress. I helped arrange President Johnson's trip to the Punta del Este Summit in 1967 and worked with him during a stop in Surinam on his return. But before two years were up, I realized that a life in government was not for me and I retired after one of the shortest federal careers in history.

Moving on, I accepted an offer from a group of western agri-businessmen to manage a ranch and run an agricultural school in Zacatecas, Mexico. The idea was solid and I subscribe to it still: that private investment in agri-business could help eliminate rural poverty in Latin America. The problem was that my cowboy investors never came up with the investment capital to develop the school or the ranch—or even to pay my salary. I spent over a year in Monterrey "waiting for the dough" and living on what little "retirement" fund I had accumulated. My first experience in the private sector made Peace Corps service seem like working in a well-protected cocoon.

I returned to Washington in January, 1969; I was thirty years old, I had no job or recognized professional skills, and no apparent future. Mom, Dad and Jim were beginning to really worry about me—and I to worry about myself. I took the LSAT exam and considered applying for law school. Father Ted talked to me about going to work at Notre Dame, but admonished me that this would require resuming my doctoral studies. I was lost, except for one thing: I knew I wanted to be involved in international development work.

Back in Washington I learned that I could pay the rent by taking "consulting assignments" for government agencies and private companies working for federal agencies. My first experience in this kind of work had come while I was living in Mexico and took a commission from an American university to arrange a short training program for Peace Corps trainees in rural areas around Monterrey. I secured government approvals, designed the course, arranged for site visits, and managed a training program that was a great success. This consulting work required ingenuity and creativity; it was rewarding and it was fun!

In Washington I took assignments to evaluate VISTA projects on Indian reservations; to set up community action agencies for the War on Poverty; to train Peace Corps volunteers; and to write proposals for consulting firms. I earned $50 and more a day. In the process I learned how the companies that employed me worked—how they got business, recruited staff and got a job done. By the end of the year I decided to form my own consulting company, and with my brother Jim's help it was incorporated on March 1, 1970. It has been my career ever since.

An assignment the previous fall had involved the Overseas Education Fund, when AID asked me to perform an "evaluation" of OEF efforts to stimulate the involvement of women in civic life and development projects in Latin America. The word "evaluation" seemed too scientific and judgmental for this task. I suggested a gentler approach: to establish "benchmarks" to gauge what had been accomplished and make creative suggestions for improvements. To avoid confusion with a more rigorous study, I called this a "benchmarks study." The government bought the idea and the result was a paper more useful to both OEF and AID. The term "benchmarks" had a positive, creative ring, and so aptly described my approach to consulting that I called my company Benchmarks, Inc. (In those days the word "benchmarks" was not over-used; it was a land surveyor's term for fixed points used to measure the location of other points. The only other use I knew was as a brand name for bourbon!)

For twenty-five years, Benchmarks has provided the niche that I could not find anywhere else. It has been the vehicle for me to be involved in social development work both abroad and in the United States. I never tried to build Benchmarks into a large organization. Rather, I modeled it along the lines of a medical or legal practice. I sell my time—and that of a few associates—to clients and apply our energies to the projects they entrust to me. Working intensively with a small client base, I have developed trusting relationships. All the clients I have today have been with me for over five years; some for over ten. Another unusual aspect is that we haven't really specialized in any one field. While we have experience in managing nonprofit organizations and getting things done in Washington, Benchmarks remains a kind of "AB" generalist, to use the Peace Corps term for a volunteer who is willing-and-able but has no technical specialty.

Running Benchmarks resembles my Peace Corps experience in that "consulting" for an evolving group of clients can be precarious. It is often stressful, even financially insecure. Nonetheless, consulting has worked for me (as in these days of corporate down-sizing more executives and managers make it work for them). I found that consulting gave me the same kinds of freedom and required the same kinds of ingenuity as the Peace Corps! It was a form of work that allowed me to prosper—even to marry (as I did in 1984) and raise a family. For twenty-five years, Benchmarks has enabled me to participate in many exciting and worthwhile projects at home and abroad. Yes, it even allowed me to continue the Peace Corps ideal of helping others and doing good work around the world! A few projects enable me to carry on the Peace Corps agenda directly.

• For almost a decade I worked directly on an issue that I identified as a Peace Corps volunteer. In 1983, AID Administrator Peter McPherson and Peace Corps Director Loret Miller Ruppe asked Benchmarks to identify ways in which the Peace Corps and AID could work together more closely. Thus we began to manage an interagency effort that sparked AID-Peace Corps cooperative initiatives in sixty countries where both organizations had a presence. These programs combined the technical and material resources of AID with the good will, enthusiasm and community-level efforts of Peace Corps volunteers.

• A current contract has brought me full circle vis à vis the Peace Corps. Benchmarks has signed on for a second five-year stint at helping USAID administer Food for Peace, the program that sent the food which Father Stiker and I brought to Catrihuala! My role is to convene regular meetings of the two government agencies most involved (USAID and Department of Agriculture) and private voluntary agencies (such as CARE) to discuss how to make better use of surplus food commodities overseas.

• Another project has enabled me to pursue the Peace Corps' "second goal"— to teach the people of other countries about the United States. This project has also been the most challenging and has required the most travel—twenty-three trips to Asia. In 1988, the Fudan Foundation, a small, private, American organization, asked me to take over its programs in the People's Republic of China. The foundation had received several million dollars from a USAID adjunct to build a Center for American Studies at Fudan University in Shanghai. I directed the design and construction of the building and the development of the academic program. Teaching about the United States in an open and objective way in China is not easy, especially after Tienanmen Square. Despite government crackdowns and the open hostility in U.S.-China relations, we completed the project. The foundation now has a magnificent building on the Fudan campus where experts teach about American politics and society.

Looking back, so many paths of my life that once seemed so winding now appear to be gentle meanders which began with the Peace Corps. For instance, my longest volunteer involvement arose from the course that the Peace Corps propelled me to pursue. In 1972, a small family foundation in Washington had a vacancy on its board of directors and wanted to bring on a younger hand who had experience abroad. After a series of long conversations with the president, Claudia Marsh, I became the youngest director of the Public Welfare Foundation.

PWF was the brainchild of Claudia's late husband. Charles Marsh made millions as the owner and publisher of many newspapers, and he practiced a unique form of philanthropy. He helped individuals facing hardships all over the world through a network of trusted individuals. (In Calcutta, Mother Teresa was one of them in the 1950s.) Thanks to the rising value of the assets Mr. Marsh bequeathed, and thanks to excellent work by the staff and directors, PWF's resources grew from $20 million in 1973 to over $300 million, and annual grant totals have reached $17.5 million. We have helped efforts as diverse as launching "Sesame Street" on public television and preventing AIDS in Haiti. For twenty-three years, PWF has taken as much of my time as a major Benchmarks client—and given me as much satisfaction. Last July my fellow directors elected me chairman.

As for Chile, it has remained the same and changed entirely—like me. To telescope history, in 1964 Eduardo Frei Montalvo, a Christian Democrat, won the presidency with the first clear majority in decades. He promised a "revolution in liberty" and instituted some agrarian reforms but did not get far. In 1970, Salvador Allende Gossens led a Socialist-Communist coalition to win the

Marxist victory we had feared. Allende pursued a radical program
of political and social change, and nationalized industries until
chaos ensued as workers seized farms and factories. In September
1973 the military staged a coup and Allende committed suicide;
the Marxist movement had come and gone! General Augusto
Pinochet Ugarte seized dictatorial powers and directed a ruthless
campaign against Marxists; thousands were tortured, killed or
exiled. In 1980 he imposed a constitution which promised a "grad-
ual" return to democracy, starting with a 1988 plebiscite in which
there would be only one candidate—the junta's—and citizens
could vote "yes" or "no."

As the country prepared for the plebiscite, Patricio Aylwin
Azócar, new head of the Christian Democrats, convinced his
party not to reject the constitution or boycott the upcoming election but rather to campaign for a "no" vote against Pinochet.
Other parties followed suit, the election was conducted fairly, and
the "no's" won a clear majority. The success of pro-democracy
forces led to dramatic changes, and a set of constitutional reforms
was approved in 1989. Patricio Aylwin was elected to a four-year
term as president, and Eduardo Frei Ruiz-Tagle, son of the earlier
president, is now serving a six-year term. Both Aylwin and Frei
represented a broad coalition of parties, the Concert of Parties for
Democracy. There are serious flaws in the new system, but the
radicalization of Chilean politics seems a thing of the past.

Pinochet's economic policies were hard on the poor and
brought a fierce recession. Nonetheless, they led to heavy foreign
investment in Chile, diversification of exports and domestic prosperity. By 1990 Chile had the healthiest economy in Latin
America and today it is one of the most prosperous countries in
the hemisphere.

Though I have been back to Chile several times. I have never had
the time to reach southern Chile. So while working on this book,
I contacted my fellow volunteers Elden and Judy Stang who I
knew had returned in Chile. They not only had interesting news,
they put me in touch with a young man, Javier Navarro, whom I
commissioned to travel to many of the places in which we
worked in the early 1960s.

How have the rural communities I knew fared in southern Chile? Some have shared in the new prosperity, but not many and not much apparently. Navarro reports the kind of hunger we saw in San Juan de la Costa and other places is rare today, and sanitary conditions have improved in all but the very poorest homes. But there are still two Chiles, one prosperous and the other very poor, as 40 percent of the rural population lives at or below the poverty level. Today there is a growing national commitment—both within the government and in the opposition parties—to address the very difficult problems of poverty and inequality.

The Stangs' experience reflects a very relevant "Peace Corps success story" and illustrates a crucial aspect of international development: When Judy and Elden Stang went back to southern Chile thirty years later, they went with private investment and new technologies, and they have helped give a powerful stimulus to local agriculture and the nation's economy. Their story belongs in any update on the long-term impact of our Peace Corps group.

Elden, one of the youngest volunteers, had entered the Peace Corps after only one year of college. He set up a carpentry shop and taught carpentry at the school in Osorno, where Judy was the dietitian. Theirs was one of the first Peace Corps romances. They met during the training program at Notre Dame, married in Santiago in 1963, and after their marriage lived in the school grounds. (Their home was the little shack which shook as if by an earthquake whenever a hog used it as an itching post.) Returning to the United States, Elden went on to complete his bachelor's degree and earn a doctorate, while Judy took a master's in food science. They then moved to the University of Wisconsin at Madison, where Elden taught fruit crop science and became an expert on the genus *vaccinium*—cranberries, blueberries and lingonberries.

In 1992 the Stangs went back to live in Chile, where cranberries were virtually unknown. Working for a California investor, they helped create a new company, Cran Chile, Ltda. They imported 600 Wisconsin cranberry plants, and using high-tech methods produced 40 million plants to stock over 700 acres. Cran Chile's annual exports are expected to reach $100 million in five years—a remarkable boost to Southern Chile's economy. (PS: Visiting the Osorno *central* last spring, Elden and Judy found that the original equipment he had installed—and the recipes she wrote—are still in use!)

The young man they recommended to me learned that life at Hacienda Rupanco barely changed under President Frei. Real changes came under Allende when the entire hacienda was expropriated, but the land was never distributed to the *inquilinos* who lived there. Rather, the government took ownership, formed a cooperative and distributed cash to co-op members with the idea that they would use it to develop the land. No technical assistance was offered, nor help in organizing communities or cooperatives. Rather than invest the money in crops and animals, many Rupanco residents spent it on consumer items in Osorno. When Allende was overthrown, the military government restored the hacienda to the original owners, who later sold out to an Arab sheik and some Chilean investors who still own the land today. The hacienda, an example of agrarian reform in reverse, is larger now than it was in 1960! While the standard of living in Rupanco has improved (largely due to an increase in the minimum wage), Rupanco workers still live in poverty.

In San Juan de la Costa, the *campesino* cooperative that Amos Roos and I nursed into existence still functions. Moreover, the hardy and prolific breed of pig we introduced was still in evidence. The *cooperativa* serves principally as a cooperative store today, having passed through good times and bad. Father Auxencio, who only retired from the mission in 1996, says the co-op died and came back to life several times in thirty years. The most consistent problem has been poor management in lean times and embezzlement of funds in fat. During the Allende years this co-op, like many across the country, went communist. While this brought hostility during the early Pinochet years, the co-op in San Juan implemented several worthwhile projects.

The greatest improvements in agricultural practices and use of land in the San Juan area have come from a source that none of us could have foreseen in 1963. Under the open economic policies of Pinochet's military government, Japanese, Austrian and Chilean wood pulp companies purchased much of the land from the Indians and reforested the area. They provided jobs and built schools, hospitals and roads. Living conditions are considerably better, yet San Juan remains today the fifth poorest area in all of Chile. Many young people leave the area (the women to become domestic workers in Osorno) while the older ones stay in San Juan on land that is no longer their own.

In Catrihuala, nothing has improved; quite the contrary. The Indians are still pressing their land claims. The *alerce* is all gone, felled and split into shingles; no reforestation has occurred. The Marxist leader, Gregorio Kintull, continued to fight with Pablino Melillanka until Don Pablino finally moved to a neighboring town where he died eight years ago. Don Gregorio remains the leader of Catrihuala though he went to jail for violating national forest laws. Released in 1996, he moved in with a daughter down the mountain—below the snow line.

When we 'Chile I' *Piscorinos* came together for our thirty-fifth anniversary celebration at Notre Dame, our group was linked by speakerphone to the present Peace Corps staff in Chile for a conversation that lasted an hour. We asked about a lot of things pertinent to Chile today, and we asked about the Institute for Rural Education. IER, we learned, has flourished to the point that it is the premier private organization doing rural development work in Chile. It is, Peace Corps staff reported, "way beyond anything the Peace Corps could help now."

The IER celebrated its fortieth anniversary in 1994, so the wave of Peace Corps contingents assisting it in the 1960s came at an important, early moment in its life. Today the Institute boasts of training students from forty-two provinces in over thirty educational centers, twelve of which are technical schools that trained nearly 2300 country youths in 1995. Most important among the accomplishments which IER cites today are the hundreds of thousands of *campesinos* who have belonged to community organizations, cooperatives, mothers clubs, neighborhood associations and even unions that were started with the help of Institute *delegados*, young leaders recruited from the ranks of *campesinos* themselves—our old *compadres*.

❊

Several years ago National Public Radio interviewed me for a retrospective on the assassination of John Kennedy. The reporter asked what impact Kennedy had on my professional life. I could only answer that the Peace Corps changed my life.

The Peace Corps did more than provide an outlet for my youthful idealism. It brought me out of academe into a world of action where I more rightfully belong. It opened my eyes to personal and professional challenges that have lasted a lifetime and that continue to increase in complexity and importance. And it gave me the tools to address these challenges. I use Spanish every day in my work for Mexican and other Latin American clients. I understand that people in other countries and other cultures think in ways that are very different from our own—and that our ways can seem very strange to them! My experience in Chile forced me to be creative, indeed to create my own job, as I wrote then "to find my work, at last!" Similarly, after I left the Peace Corps, I decided to create my own company, my own professional niche in life. To find my rightful work in the real world—my life after the Peace Corps—I had to get creative and invent it!

❅

Two prized possessions adorn my office. One is a letter from John Kennedy that was handed to me by Father Ted when he arrived in Rio Negro. It is a "keep up the good work" message that the President sent to all 'Chile I' volunteers, but it is especially important to me because it was the beginning of an indirect dialogue I had with the President. When I look at that letter, I think of the fears I had for the Peace Corps and for John Kennedy's vision of America's leadership among Third World nations as I stood on the steps of St. Matthew's Cathedral after his funeral. Those fears for the work of the Peace Corps proved false: 140,000 Americans have served in the Peace Corps in 130 countries since then. Further, the Peace Corps has become a kind of graduate school for people who intend careers in international development. Virtually half of today's employees of USAID are former Peace Corps volunteers. Peace Corps alumni are also heavily represented in agencies such as the World Bank and the Asian, African and Inter-American Development Banks. Many staffers in private voluntary organizations such as Save The Children and World Vision are former volunteers. Calling together this band of volunteers and sending them forth to do good work in the world now appears to be one of John F. Kennedy's most important, inspiring and lasting achievements.

The second prized item that hangs on my office wall is a photograph of Tom Dooley. It is inscribed, "To my philosopher friend, Tom, from a more Socra*tian* kind of guy"—"Socr-Asian" is how he would have pronounced it. This inscription sums up what Dooley was always saying to me. "Get involved in the world, especially the developing world. Look to the needs of other people. Look to Asia!" What a wonderful exhortation that was! And it was the same challenge that John Kennedy offered to the American people when he created the Peace Corps in 1961.

It is my hope—and I think it would be the hope of the 140,000 Americans who followed 'Chile I' into the field—that if Tom Dooley and John Kennedy were alive today, they would feel that—so far—we are doing pretty well.

ACKNOWLEDGMENTS

The debt that I owe to two very distinguished Americans for making this book possible is evident from the text. I received more attention than I deserved as one of the 'charter' volunteers, and this was due in large part to the kindness of Father Ted Hesburgh and Sargent Shriver. My profound thanks to them for making my Peace Corps experience possible and for the personal support and encouragement they have given me—then and later. I am also grateful to Notre Dame University, to our director Walter Langford, and to my fellow Chile I volunteers for a magnificent, unforgettable experience.

As noted, this book has survived an extended hibernation and unique metamorphosis, having been born in letters from Chile thirty-five years ago. Mary Kiesel, my dad's legal secretary, received the letters, retyped them, mimeographed them, and sent them out. She read every word I ever wrote from Chile. My repeated thanks and fond respect to her memory. My thanks also to Mom and Dad for their understanding of my decision to join the Peace Corps.

When I returned home in 1963, Celia Lynett Haggerty, a life-long friend, neighbor and a talented writer for the Scranton Times, helped me put the manuscript into its original form. I hope she will be pleased that it is now seeing the light of day, and I want to express my appreciation for her help so long ago. I am also grateful to Nancy Kohl who typed the first manuscript.

A more recent family friend, Mary Finch Hoyt, reviewed the manuscript several years ago, made suggestions and urged me to find a publisher. Without her encouragement these Peace Corps papers would have stayed in the drawer.

Distant friends Cristián Valdivieso and Javier Navarro provided important information for the Afterword from Chile. Closer to home, designer Tom Suzuki and his colleague Connie Dillman contributed their great talents and good humor to make this book a visual pleasure. Very special thanks to Kathy Murray who has played a central role in the book's publication and marketing.

I am indebted to my college roommate and dear friend Terence Smith who put me in touch with Philip Kopper and Posterity Press. The final editor and publisher of this collection, Phil has given much more to the project than he bargained for. His sound editorial judgment and guidance in transforming the manuscript into a book, and his perfectionist's approach to the details of publishing, make me confident that this volume will take its place proudly in the library of works about the Peace Corps and the Kennedy epoch, and from there will enter people's lives.

T.J.S.

The Peace Corps' 1961 community development *zona* in southern Chile has Osorno at its hub surrounded by a web of roads. Solid lines show thoroughfares by local standards—gravel roads at best. Dotted lines are rougher routes, often tracks worn by trucks and oxcarts across the coun-

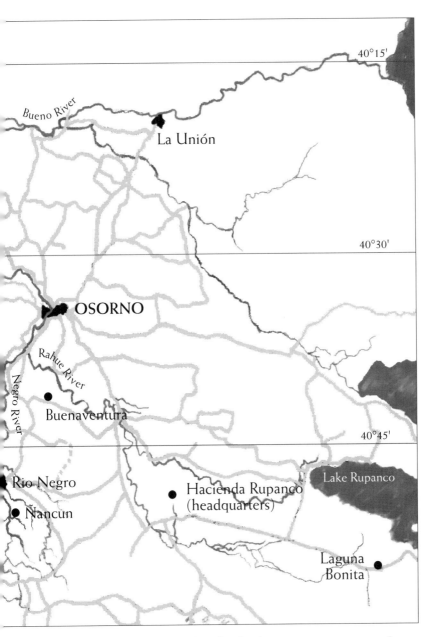

40°15'

Bueno River

La Unión

40°30'

OSORNO

Rahue River

Negro River

Buenaventura

40°45'

Lake Rupanco

Río Negro

Hacienda Rupanco
(headquarters)

Ñancun

Laguna
Bonita

tryside. The mountain road to Catrihuala does not even appear here, though the author took it many times. The large-scale plan (left) shows Osorno near the southernmost named place at a latitude where Chile is barely 100 miles wide.

Colophon

Waiting for the Snow was designed by Tom Suzuki,
Tom Suzuki, Inc. of Falls Church, Virginia, with the
assistance of Constance D. Dillman. Cover design
by Kristin Bernhart. The book was printed by
BookCrafters of Fredericksburg, Virginia.

The text was set in Weiss, a typeface inspired by
those of the Italian Rennaisance and designed in
1926 by the German designer Emil Rodolf Weiss.
Its special grace derives from vertical strokes that
are heavier at the top of letters than the bottom.

DATE DUE